A Teacher's Guide to
Using Technology in the Classroom

A Teacher's Guide to Using Technology in the Classroom

SECOND EDITION

Karen S. Ivers

LIBRARIES
UNLIMITED
A Member of the Greenwood Publishing Group

Westport, Connecticut • London

ISBN: 978-1-59158-556-5

First published in 2009

Libraries Unlimited, 88 Post Road West, Westport, CT 06881
A Member of the Greenwood Publishing Group, Inc.
www.lu.com

Printed in the United States of America

The paper used in this book complies with the
Permanent Paper Standard issued by the National
Information Standards Organization (Z39.48–1984).

10 9 8 7 6 5 4 3 2 1

Contents

Preface xi

Chapter 1: Teachers and Technology 1
   A Scenario 1
   Introduction 1
   Technology Standards for Teachers 2
      National Educational Technology Standards for Teachers 3
      State Technology Standards for Teachers 3
   Computers 101 4
      Computer Basics 4
         System Recommendations 4
         Secondary Storage Devices 5
         Printers and Other Peripherals 6
      Learning More About Computers 6
   Computer Support 7
      Getting to Know Your Technology Resource Teacher 7
         Roles and Responsibilities 7
         Resource Assistance 8
      Technology Tips and Tricks 8
         Accessing Special Characters 9
         Taking a Picture of the Computer Screen 11
         Other Tips and Tricks 13
      Professional Development Opportunities 14
   Summary 15
   Activities 15
   References 16
   Blackline Masters 17

Chapter 2: Teacher Tools 23
   A Scenario 23
   Introduction 23
   Productivity Tools 24
      Instructional and Creative Tasks 24
      Assessment 25
      Record Keeping 26
   Internet Resources for Teachers 28
      Productivity and Management Tasks 28
      Lesson Plans 28
      Digital Discussions 30
         E-mail 30
         Listservs 32
         Usenet Newsgroups 33
         Discussion Forums 34
         Blogs 35

Wiki 36
Chat. 36
Additional Resources 37
Summary. 38
Activities. 38
Blackline Master. 39

Chapter 3: Meeting the Needs of All Students. 41
A Scenario. 41
Introduction 41
Promoting Twenty-first-Century Learning Environments 42
Multiple Intelligences 44
Constructivism 44
Cooperative Learning 46
Technology and Special-Needs Students 46
English-Language Learners 46
Assistive Technologies. 48
Software. 49
Input Devices 51
Output Devices 55
Gifted Learners. 57
Summary. 58
Activities. 59
Resources 59
References. 61

Chapter 4: Prerequisites to Using Computers in the Classroom. 65
A Scenario. 65
Introduction 65
Technology Standards for Students 66
National Education Technology Standards (NETS) 66
State Technology Standards 67
Local Technology Standards. 68
Computer Policies and Issues 68
Acceptable Use Policies 68
Technology Use Plan 69
Gender and Equity Concerns. 70
Gender Issues 70
Equity Concerns 71
Ethics, Privacy, and Safety Issues 72
Ethics. 72
Privacy and Safety Issues 73
Summary. 74
Activities. 74
References. 75

Chapter 5: Evaluating Instructional Resources: Software 79
A Scenario 79
Introduction 80
Evaluating Software for Students 80
Software Categories 80
Applications 80
Tutorials 83
Drill and Practice 84
Simulations 86
Instructional Games 88
Problem Solving 89
Discovery, Reference, and Other Learning Tools 91
Evaluation Criteria 92
Instructional Objectives and Assessment 93
Appropriateness 93
Layout and Functionality 94
Management and Support Features 94
Evaluation Resources 95
Summary 95
Activities 96
Blackline Masters 97

Chapter 6: Evaluating Instructional Resources: The Internet 101
A Scenario 101
Introduction 101
Resources for Students 102
Web 2.0 Tools 102
Blogs 102
Wiki 103
Social Networking Sites 103
Social Bookmarking Sites 103
Photo and Video Sharing 104
Podcasts 104
Virtual Worlds 105
Interactive Programs 105
Online Experts 106
Web Sites for Children 106
Research Activities 108
Basic Research 108
WebQuests 108
Advanced Research 109
Search Engines 109
Search Strategies 110
Original Research 112
E-mail 112
Videoconferencing 113
Classroom Web Pages 113

Evaluation Criteria 115
   Intent. 115
      Domain Name. 115
      Reason 116
      Target Audience 116
      Layout 116
   Content 116
      Authority 116
      Currency 116
      Bias 116
      Verification of Information 117
Additional Tips. 117
   Issues to Consider 117
   Troubleshooting Tips for the Internet 118
Summary. 119
Activities. 119
Reference. 120
Blackline Masters 120

Chapter 7: Managing and Assessing Computer Use in the Classroom. 123
  A Scenario. 123
  Introduction 124
  When to Use Computers 124
   Objectives and Learner Outcomes 125
   Assessing Resources 125
      Computer Labs Versus Computers in the Classroom. 125
      Software and Peripherals 126
      Prerequisite Skills 127
      Monitoring and Assessing Students' Work 127
  Planning and Managing Computer-Based Lessons. 127
   Grouping Strategies. 128
      Cooperative Learning Techniques 129
      Group Size 130
   One-to-One Laptop Classrooms. 131
   Designing a Classroom Computer Schedule 132
   Lesson Ideas and Examples 136
      Planning and Managing Multimedia Projects. 136
      Additional Tips for Integrating Computers Throughout the Curriculum 138
  Monitoring and Assessing Students' Work. 139
   Ongoing Assessment 139
   Rubrics 141
  Summary 143
  Activities. 143
  Resources 143
  References. 144
  Blackline Masters 144

Chapter 8: Managing and Assessing Online Computing Environments. 151
A Scenario. 151
Introduction 151
Distance Education: Then and Now. 152
    Five Generations of Distance Learning. 152
    Standards for Delivering Instruction over the Internet. 153
Virtual Environments for Learning 154
    Course Management Systems 154
    Additional Support for Delivering Online Instruction 156
    Resources for Developing Course Content 156
Planning and Managing Online Learning 157
    Elements of Online Environments That Support Student Learning 157
        Layout and Design of an Online Learning Environment 157
        Organization, Structure, Delivery, and Sharing of Content. 157
        Skills of the Teacher 159
    Requirements, Expectations, and Recommendations. 161
        Prior Experience with Computers. 162
        Peer Interaction 163
        Teacher/Student Interaction. 163
        Institutional Support. 163
Monitoring and Assessing Students' Work in Online Learning Environments 164
    Rubrics for Online Participation 164
    Multiple Assessment Measures 164
    Helpful Tips and Tricks 165
Summary. 165
Activities. 166
References 166

Glossary 169
Index. 173

Preface

A Teacher's Guide to Using Technology in the Classroom, Second Edition is designed to assist new and practicing teachers with successfully implementing technology into the curriculum. It focuses on the pedagogical issues of technology: using technology as an instructional and management tool and to meet students' needs in a twenty-first-century learning environment. It emphasizes the importance of the teacher, detailing what a teacher should know before attempting to integrate technology into instruction.

The guide is divided into eight chapters and includes blackline masters to assist educators with using technology in their classrooms. Each chapter contains follow-up activities to encourage teachers to apply what they have learned. Throughout each chapter, teachers will find a wealth of recommended resources to support their use of technology.

Although there are many different types of technologies available for the classroom, this guide focuses on computer-based technologies, including the Internet, software applications, and peripherals. It begins with technologies for teachers. Chapter 1 examines technology standards for teachers, how to learn more about computers, and where to find technology support. Chapter 2 introduces teachers to a variety of productivity tools and resources designed to assist them with classroom management and creating instructional activities. It also provides teachers with information and links to a wealth of Internet resources, including lesson plans, online discussion groups, and professional organizations.

After examining how technology can assist teachers, Chapter 3 addresses how teachers can use technology to meet the needs of all students, including English-language learners (ELLs), gifted learners, students with physical challenges, and students with learning disabilities. Chapter 4 addresses technology standards for students, as well as important prerequisites to using technology in the classroom (for example, acceptable use policies, safety issues, and equity).

Chapters 5 and 6 provide teachers with the necessary information to effectively evaluate software and Internet resources. Chapter 5 helps teachers categorize the many different types of software, as well as make wise instructional choices. Teachers are provided with lists of effective and award-winning software titles, as well as software programs available on the Web. Chapter 6 provides a wealth of Internet resources and activities for students, as well as guidelines on how teachers can use these resources with their students.

Chapter 7 discusses strategies for effectively managing and assessing the use of technology in the classroom. It provides examples of ongoing and final assessment techniques, grouping strategies, one-to-one laptop tips, classroom computer schedules, and lesson ideas. As in the other chapters, teachers are provided with multiple resources to support their use of technology in the classroom.

A Teacher's Guide to Using Technology in the Classroom, Second Edition concludes with Chapter 8, a new chapter dedicated to managing and assessing online learning environments.

A Teacher's Guide to Using Technology in the Classroom, Second Edition addresses updated technologies and standards, emphasizes twenty-first-century learning outcomes, and provides preservice and inservice teachers with numerous resources, strategies, and guidelines for integrating technology into their classrooms. Its purpose is to help educators become aware of and use technology for themselves and use it effectively with their students.

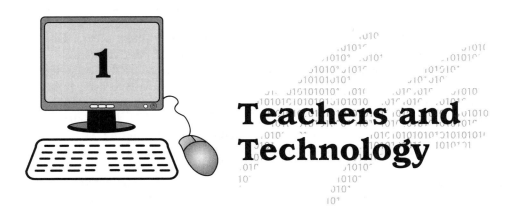

Teachers and Technology

A Scenario

Mrs. Martinez was in her eighteenth year of teaching and had many preservice teachers observe her and practice teaching in her classroom. She was highly regarded by her peers and the administration; she had won several teaching awards, plus Teacher of the Year in her school district. Mrs. Martinez was a firm believer that children learn best when they are active participants in meaningful learning. She strived to keep current with educational research and maintained regular communication with her students' parents through e-mail and her blog. In fact, parents could subscribe to her RSS feed and receive immediate updates via their computer or handheld mobile device. Mrs. Martinez was not a technology guru, but she did know the importance of being current and keeping parents involved in students' educational success. Fortunately, the school's media specialist was able to assist Mrs. Martinez with many of her technology requests.

Mrs. Martinez kept current with technology by attending workshops and through her preservice teachers. Her preservice teachers typically came into the classroom with little teaching experience but were avid users of current technologies. Unfortunately, one of her preservice teachers was dismissed because she repeatedly used her cell phone for outside, unrelated calls and text messaging during instruction. As with all technologies, there are appropriate and inappropriate uses.

To help support her preservice teachers in the effective and appropriate use of technology, Mrs. Martinez shared how she used technology to engage her students in active and meaningful learning. Her current preservice teacher, Sylvia, always felt comfortable using the latest technologies, but never thought about technology's use in the classroom. Mrs. Martinez introduced Sylvia to a variety of teacher tools and resources available on the Internet and reviewed current technology standards, ensuring Sylvia was informed of the technology expectations for teachers and students. In turn, Sylvia shared new "tips and tricks" of the current consumer technologies she had with her and together they brainstormed how these technologies could be used as learning tools. Together they attended workshops on the latest educational technologies: Mrs. Martinez sharing her wealth of pedagogical expertise and Sylvia thinking, "Why weren't these technologies in school when I was a kid?"

Introduction

Technology continues to evolve at a rapid pace. Looking back ten years and comparing it to today's technology can be mindboggling. Perhaps more mindboggling is trying to imagine what technology may exist ten years from now. This may excite some and frighten others. How do educators prepare students to work in environments where the technology does not yet exist?

Researchers and leading organizations note that the focus should not be on the technology itself, but on how teachers are using technology with their students to promote such skills as critical thinking, problem solving, communication, collaboration, innovation, and global literacy in an increasingly digital world (ISTE, Partnership for 21st Century Skills, and SETDA 2007; UNESCO 2008). They stress the importance of integrating the use of technology across the curriculum and not limiting the use of technology as a tool for developing students' Internet and computer skills. Technology must be used to empower students and to create a twenty-first-century learning environment where students learn core subjects, twenty-first-century themes (global awareness; financial, economic, business, and entrepreneurial literacy; civic literacy; and health literacy), and twenty-first-century skills (learning and innovation; information, media, and technology; and life and career) (Partnership for 21st Century Skills 2007).

In order for students to achieve twenty-first-century outcomes, teachers need to feel comfortable using technology, and they need to apply sound pedagogical practices to their use of technology in the classroom. Technology standards have been written for both teachers and students. Technology standards for teachers describe how educators should be using technology for instruction, assessment, and their own professional practice. Technology standards for students list grade level technology proficiency skills (see Chapter 4). This chapter examines technology standards for teachers and reviews basic computer terminology and resources. Topics include:

- Technology Standards for Teachers

  National Education Technology Standards for Teachers

  State Technology Standards for Teachers

- Computers 101

  Computer Basics

  Learning More About Computers

- Computer Support

  Getting to Know Your Technology Resource Teacher

  Technology Tips and Tricks

  Professional Development Opportunities

Technology Standards for Teachers

Before implementing student use of technology in the classroom, teachers should consider their own use and abilities. Research continues to show that teachers who view themselves as proficient users of technology are more likely to integrate technology into their instruction (Gado, Ferguson, and van't Hooft 2006; Littrell, Zagumny, and Zagumny 2005; Sahin 2007–08; Shaunessy 2007). To foster instructional technology use, research supports integrating the use of technology in preservice education courses, modeling by faculty, and using technology as a tool for enhancing critical thinking, communication, and research skills (Fleming, Motamedi, and May 2007; Franklin 2007; Littrell, Zagumny, and Zagumny 2005).

Technology is a tool to assist teachers to gather and learn new information, locate lesson plans, participate in collaborative projects, engage in peer discussions and teaching forums, manage student records, conduct assessments, and create instructional materials and presentations. It is a professional resource that teachers can use at home and school. Similarly, technology is a tool to assist students to gather and learn new information; participate in lessons and collaborative projects; engage in peer discussions and real-world learning experiences; manipulate, organize, and evaluate information; and create projects and presentations. It is a learning resource that some students may not have at home and often fail to benefit from in many classroom environments. How computers are used in the class-room dictates their effectiveness as an instructional tool.

Without standards and effective training, it is unlikely that the classroom computer will be used as a creativity and thinking tool to stimulate higher order thinking skills, cooperative learning, or to address the multimodalities of learning. Fortunately, both national and state standards have been established to help improve teachers' technological proficiencies.

National Educational Technology Standards for Teachers

The International Society for Technology in Education (ISTE) provides guidelines for integrating technology into teaching and learning. ISTE has written technology standards for students (see Chapter 4) as well as teachers. Many states and accreditation agencies have adopted ISTE's National Educational Technology Standards (NETS) for teachers.

NETS for teachers is comprised of five standards that reflect the needs of twenty-first-century learning. ISTE's standards (ISTE 2008) call for teachers to:

- Facilitate and Inspire Student Learning and Creativity (through virtual and face-to-face environments)

- Design and Develop Digital-Age Learning Experiences and Assessments (reflecting authentic learning experiences and current assessment tools)

- Model Digital-Age Work and Learning

- Promote and Model Digital Citizenship and Responsibility

- Engage in Professional Growth and Leadership (in educational technology research, digital tools, and resources)

Additional details regarding NETS for Teachers can be found on the ISTE Web site (http://www.iste.org) under NETS.

State Technology Standards for Teachers

Many state accreditation agencies require teacher education programs to integrate technology instruction into their preservice programs also. For example, the California Commission on Teacher Credentialing (CCTC) has defined technology standards for preservice teachers and practicing teachers applying for preliminary and professional clear credential status (CCTC 2007). The Colorado Department of Education defines performance-based standards for teachers, including knowledge of technology. This standard requires teachers to demonstrate a variety of technology skills. Alabama, Connecticut, Florida, and other states also have technology requirements for their teacher education programs. In fact, according to the Editorial Projects in Education (EPE) Research Center (Bausell 2008), forty-four states have technology standards for teachers; forty-eight states have technology standards for students. Fewer states (thirty-five) have technology standards for administrators.

Even though steps are being taken to help new teachers understand how to use technology in the classroom, veteran teachers remain at a disadvantage unless they have the support of their school and district administrators to further their own technology skills. Researchers assert that there is a clear connection between professional development in technology use, the integration of technology, and improved student outcomes (CDW-G 2006; ISTE, Partnership for 21st Century Skills, and SETDA 2007; UNESCO 2008). One-day seminars or after-school workshops without any follow-up or support are not enough; professional development in using technology needs to be ongoing (Watson 2006). Schrum (1999) notes that models of professional development with presentation of theory, clear demonstrations, practice with feedback, coaching, and ongoing follow-up are more likely to produce changes in how teachers use technology in their classrooms than traditional models of staff development. Researchers recommend that training be geared toward teachers' perceived needs and goals (Besnoy 2007; Brand 1998; Littrell, Zagumny, and Zagumny 2005).

Although the needs of beginning and experienced teachers differ, the focus of how to effectively use technology in the classroom remains the same. Some teachers may be more technology proficient than others, but the ability to use technology does not necessarily equate to the ability to effectively teach with technology. It is a start, however. The better prepared a teacher is to use technology, the more likely he or she will see the benefits of using technology with students.

Computers 101

Teachers cannot be expected to use technology if they are unfamiliar with it; however, educators do have a responsibility to better prepare themselves to meet the needs of their students. As noted in Chapter 4, teachers need to ensure their students meet national, state, or district technology standards. Although knowing how to effectively integrate technology throughout the curriculum requires more than knowing how to use a computer, having the ability to use a computer (or other technology device) is the first step.

Computer Basics

A computer, like a car, is a device that you should be familiar with before attempting to use it. Before driving a car, you become familiar with the steering wheel, gas and brake pedals, gearshift, mirrors, ignition, and so forth. After learning about the components, you learn how to use them to drive the car. A computer is not any different; users should be familiar with its basic components—CPU, monitor, keyboard, ports, and drives—and how to turn the computer on and off.

Analogous to driving, users learn how to use (drive) a specific program (for example, word processing) to create, save, and print documents. As users become more familiar with the computer (or car), they learn new things. Given the car example, some drivers may learn where to put gasoline, oil, washer fluid, and, perhaps, how to change a tire. Other drivers may have service attendants do everything for them. Given the computer example, some computer users may learn how to connect new devices to their system, install new software, troubleshoot software problems, or even install RAM. Others may have their school technology resource teacher perform these tasks for them.

In short, you can operate a car or computer knowing the basics and with practice. The more you learn and can do yourself, the less dependent you are upon others. You do not need to know how a computer works—logic gates, circuits, and so forth—in order to use it. How many drivers know how their car engine works?

Teaching how computers work is not the purpose of this book; however, resources for learning more about computers are provided later in this section (see Learning More About Computers). While the focus of this book remains on using technology for instructional purposes, it is important to discuss computer terms teachers may encounter when purchasing and using hardware and software. These are discussed under System Recommendations and Secondary Storage Devices.

System Recommendations

Technology changes at such a rapid pace it makes no sense to list "optimal system" recommendations in a book. In addition, computer designs continue to change: what were once big boxes are now small thin boxes or devices that can fit in the palm of your hand. Recommended memory (RAM—random-access memory) and hard drive space continually change, too. Bottom line: the more RAM and hard drive space, the better.

RAM is like the short-term memory of a computer, while the hard drive is like its long-term memory. When a computer is turned on, the operating system (the program that manages all of the other programs in the computer) loads itself into RAM, as do other programs when they are opened (see Figure 1.1).

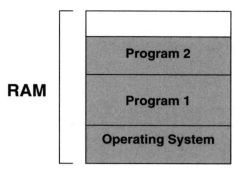

Figure 1.1. Example of how RAM is used.

Larger amounts of RAM allow more programs to be opened at one time and help to facilitate programs that need large amounts of RAM to operate efficiently.

Information can be read from and written to RAM much faster than the other kinds of storage in a computer (for example, hard drive, CD-ROM, or DVD). When the computer is turned off, the information in RAM is lost. RAM is considered temporary storage; that's why new and updated documents should be saved on the hard drive or other permanent storage area (for example, CD-RW or DVD-RW).

Another computer term teachers may come across is ROM—read-only memory. Unlike RAM, ROM retains information when the computer is turned off. ROM stores the programming that allows the operating system to load into RAM each time the computer is turned on.

Speed is another consideration educators may consider when purchasing a computer. The speed of the computer is dependent upon several things, including its microprocessor. There are various kinds of microprocessors, and these continue to evolve as well, including Intel processors for PCs and Apple Macintosh computers. Quicker processors generally cost more money.

When purchasing a laptop, other considerations are battery life, weight, and size. Tablet computers and other mobile devices are available as well; choose the technology that will best meet your needs. You can keep current with the latest technologies through a variety of online resources (see Learning More About Computers).

Secondary Storage Devices

Educators will face a plethora of secondary (backup) storage devices, also. These include flash drives, recordable compact discs (CD-R), recordable and rewriteable compact discs (CD-RW), recordable digital versatile discs (DVD-R), and recordable and rewriteable digital versatile discs (DVD-RW). Flash drives vary in storage capacity and use flash memory. Flash memory allows the user to electronically erase and program information. CDs and DVDs store information optically. Information is written to and read with a low-powered laser beam. How the information is stored, written, and read determines how much data can be stored on a particular medium. For example, a compact disc (CD) typically holds 650 megabytes of information; a standard digital versatile disc can store up to seventeen gigabytes (twenty-eight times as much as a CD).

A "byte" represents one character of data. Computers operate using a binary (base-2) number system. Eight binary digits (bits) represent one byte or character of information. Lots of bytes are represented with the following prefixes:

- Kilo: 1,000 bytes (kilobyte or KB)

- Mega: 1,000,000 (megabyte or MB)

- Giga: 1,000,000,000 (gigabyte or GB)

- Tera: 1,000,000,000,000 (terabyte or TB)

Higher numbers equal more storage. Newer storage devices continue to replace older methods of storage. New technologies are speeding up how data are stored and retrieved and are increasing the amount of data that can be stored on a single device.

Printers and Other Peripherals

Educators can choose from a vast assortment of peripherals to meet their own needs as well as the needs of their students. There are an abundance of assistive technologies (see Chapter 3) and other tools that take advantage of the computer's capabilities. Printers (ink jet and laser) are common in classrooms, as are large screen monitors and other forms of technology. Interactive whiteboards, such as those manufactured by SMART Technologies, Inc. (http://www.smarttech.com/) and Promethean (http://www.prometheanworld.com/us/) come bundled with software that allows educators and students to manipulate the projected computer screen on the whiteboard. The user's hand or a "pen" is used to manipulate programs, objects, and whatever else may be on the interactive whiteboard. Digital cameras enable educators to transfer pictures and video directly to their computer. Probeware can be used with computers to collect, display, and analyze real-time data. Because these devices are continually upgraded and reduced in price, it is best to check with current online magazines for existing products, prices, and reviews. You may be amazed at what is available!

Learning More About Computers

Because of its timeliness, the Internet is an excellent resource for learning more about current technologies and computer terms. Educators can increase their own basic knowledge as well as find activities to help students use and take care of the computer. Resources for educators include:

- WhatIs.com (http://whatis.techtarget.com/): an online dictionary of computer terms.

- How Stuff Works (http://www.howstuffworks.com/): a searchable archive of articles explaining how technologies (and other things) work.

- *An Educator's Guide to School Networks* (http://fcit.usf.edu/network/): an online book that discusses the different types and components of a network.

- *CNET* (http://www.cnet.com/), *MacWorld* (http://www.macworld.com/), and *PC World* (http://pcworld.com/): online magazines featuring technology reviews and more.

Ideas and activities for introducing students to the different parts of the computer can be found at:

- Kids Domain Computer Connections, http://parenting.kaboose.com/education-and-learning/learning-resources/brain-computer-lesson.html

- Goodwill Global Learning: Tutorial http://www.gcflearnfree.org/computer/

- Intel: The Journey Inside, http://educate.intel.com/en/thejourneyinside/

These resources may be used to refresh or expand educators' background with computers as well. Several "getting to know the computer" activity sheets are provided at the end of this chapter. Educators may wish to use these with their students. For example, using the "Getting to Know the Computer: Keyboard Activity" blackline master, teachers may ask students to complete the keyboard and color-code the keys (index finger keys are colored light blue, middle finger keys are colored yellow, and so forth). A dark line is drawn through the middle of the keyboard distinguishing the right-hand side from the left-hand side. After the keyboards are corrected, they can be laminated and kept at students' desks. Students can practice typing spelling words, their names, and sentences to reinforce their knowledge of the location of letters, numbers, and symbols on the keyboard.

In addition to the Internet, educators can find resources and training opportunities available through their school, district, and local colleges and universities. Many universities offer master's degrees or certificate programs in educational technology. Districts may offer inservices on specific software programs, troubleshooting tips, hardware devices, and so forth.

Computer Support

Besides insufficient training, educators frequently note that lack of computer support prohibits their use of technology. Educators should discuss their needs with the school principal. Grants, donations, and community support can help teachers gain hardware, software, and Internet access (see Equity Concerns in Chapter 4). Inservices, workshops, and courses can help teachers increase their technology skills.

Many schools and districts have technology resource teachers or media specialists to assist teachers with technology needs and questions. Typically, the role of a technology resource teacher is instructional, although technical and administrative responsibilities are expected also. It is important for teachers to introduce themselves to the technology resource teacher and learn how he or she can support their technology needs.

Getting to Know Your Technology Resource Teacher

Technology resource teachers should work closely with classroom teachers, assisting them with effectively integrating technology across the curriculum. Too often classroom teachers view technology resource teachers as substitutes, providing a break for the classroom teacher while the students are dropped off at a lab. This reinforces the notion that computers are not an integral part of or tool for learning, but rather a separate activity in isolation, outside of regular classroom instruction. It is important that the technology resource teacher and classroom teacher plan and work together to ensure the best learning opportunities for students.

Roles and Responsibilities

Technology resource teachers may be part time or full time. Some may hold teaching credentials; others may not. They may be asked to perform a variety of tasks. In addition to providing assistance in the school's computer lab or media center, technology resource teachers may be asked to:

- find curriculum resources for teachers;
- troubleshoot computers;
- develop and maintain Web sites;
- develop and update school technology plans;
- provide technology inservices for teachers and staff;
- maintain classroom computers, computer labs, laptop carts, and computer networks;
- prepare a technology budget;
- order, install, and inventory software and hardware;
- write technology grants;
- work with groups of students; and
- establish after-school computer programs.

Many districts have district-level technology coordinators as well. Their responsibilities may include the organization and purchase of district-wide technology equipment and materials, district technology workshops for teachers, consultation with curriculum committees to insure technology is being integrated throughout the curriculum, and submission of grant proposals and district technology use plans.

Resource Assistance

A school's technology resource teacher or media specialist can assist teachers with obtaining additional technology tools. For example, a school may have a policy whereby teachers can check out additional computers, scanners, digital cameras, video cameras, projection devices, overhead calculators, and DVD players from the school's media center (see "Technology Resources" blackline master). Teachers should check to see if there is a waiting list, how long in advance they need to request the items, how long they can keep them in their classroom, whether or not items can be taken off campus, if the batteries for cameras are charged, where they can obtain media for data storage, and how to get replacement cartridges (ink or toner) for their classroom printers. The technology resource teacher may be able to help teachers locate grants for additional funding for classroom computers, software, and other items also. If a school does not have a technology resource teacher or media specialist, educators should check with their principal or school secretary.

Knowing who to ask and what resources are available will help teachers as they begin to implement the use of technology in their classrooms. Technology, like any other instructional tool, requires planning. For example, when using a chalkboard, the teacher needs chalk and an eraser; when drawing on a whiteboard, the teacher needs the proper writing pens and eraser; when using an overhead projector, the teacher needs to ensure the bulb is not burnt out, the machine is in working order, the classroom screen and electrical outlets work, the proper writing pens and eraser are available, and overheads are prepared. It seems the more advanced the technology, the more complex things get. On the other hand, the more advanced the technology, the more opportunities for learning exist, allowing teachers to address the multiple needs and learning styles of their students.

Technology Tips and Tricks

The school technology resource teacher, media specialist, fellow computer-using educators, and the Internet are invaluable resources for learning more about computers. Still, it is handy to know some basic troubleshooting tips before seeking technical support. Table 1.1 presents some common troubleshooting tips.

Table 1.1. Troubleshooting Tips and Tricks

Concern	Possible Solution(s)
Computer won't turn on; monitor is dark	• Check cable connections to computer and outlet • Check cable connections to computer and monitor • Check cable connections to monitor and outlet • Make sure outlet works • Adjust brightness and contrast controls on monitor • Make sure both monitor and computer are turned on
Screen is frozen	• Check cable connection to computer and keyboard/mouse • Check the batteries of wireless keyboards and mice, as well as the cable of the receiver (if applicable) • Try a "force quit" (PC: press Ctrl, Alt, Delete keys; MAC: press Apple, Control, Esc keys) • If screen freezes during startup on a Macintosh, restart holding the Shift key down

Macintosh error code 11 (program won't run)	• Program needs additional memory allocated to it:
	   • Highlight program on your hard drive
	   • Go to File Menu, choose Get Info
	   • Increase memory

Software doesn't work	• If Mac, see error code 11 above • Read package documentation to see if the program is compatible with your operating system (that is, Windows 95/98/ME/XP/Vista, Mac OS 8.x, Mac OS 9.x, Mac OS 10.x, etc.) • Ask your tech if your computer has enough physical RAM and hard drive space to run the program
There isn't any sound	• Check the sound volume on your computer (see Control Panel) and speakers • Check cable connections between computer and speakers • Make sure speakers are plugged in and turned on • Make sure outlet works • If an older PC, ask tech if computer has a speaker card
Documents won't print	• Make sure the correct printer is selected in the print dialog box • Check cable connections between computer and printer • Make sure printer is plugged in and turned on • Make sure there is paper in the printer • Determine if the ink, toner, or ribbon cartridge needs to be replaced or adjusted

Additional troubleshooting tips for the Macintosh can be found at http://www.macfixit.com/ and at Apple's Web site (http://www.apple.com/) under Support. Windows users can find more troubleshooting tips at http://www.answersthatwork.com/ and http://support.microsoft.com/. Most computers and software programs come with troubleshooting guides. Ask your technology resource teacher for copies of these guides as well as any other tips he or she may have for keeping computers running smoothly.

In addition to troubleshooting, teachers may have questions regarding how to access special characters or how to capture a picture of the computer screen for instructional purposes. Answers to these questions, as well as additional tips, follow.

Accessing Special Characters

Accent marks and other symbols are often necessary when creating instructional documents or correspondences to parents. To insert special characters such as accented letters (é), symbols (®), or mathematical notations (½), most users can do this within their word processing and other software by choosing Symbol under the Insert menu. Otherwise, PC users can access the Character Map (see Figure 1.2) under System Tools in Accessories by the following sequence: Programs/Accessories/System Tools/Character Map.

Click and select the desired characters to copy, then paste them into a document. Note that keystrokes also can produce the desired characters (see the bottom right corner of Figure 1.2). For example, holding down the Alt key and pressing numbers 0, 2, 3, and 3 on the keypad will insert an accented "e" (é).

Macintosh users can access Key Caps under the Apple menu (Mac OS 9 or earlier) or from the Utilities folder within Applications (Mac OS 10.1 and 10.2) to view available characters (see Figure 1.3). Using the Control key, Option key, or Shift key changes the view of available characters (see Figure 1.4). Pressing the Option key with the Shift key produces another character set.

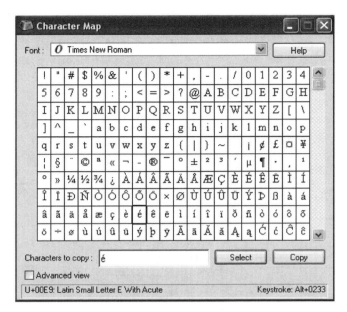

Figure 1.2. Character Map in Windows.

Figure 1.3. Key Caps keyboard available under the Apple menu.

Figure 1.4. Access different character options by pressing the Option key.

These keyboard shortcuts allow users to enter special characters directly into their documents. For example, to insert an "ñ" character, Macintosh users press the Option key, followed by the letter N. Some character options may change dependent upon the chosen font.

Taking a Picture of the Computer Screen

By taking screenshots, educators can create their own quick start or review guides for helping themselves or their students recall how to do certain tasks on the computer. Screenshots may be incorporated into other instructional documents or used in multimedia projects as well. Screenshots can be directly copied into a word processing, drawing, or other program, or they may be edited in a paint program before they are transferred. To create and edit a screenshot on a PC:

1. Press the Print Scr (print screen) key at the top of the keyboard. This takes a snapshot of the current screen and places it on the computer's clipboard.

2. Open the Paint program in the Program menu, under Accessories (Programs/Accessories/Paint).

3. Choose Paste under the Edit menu (see Figure 1.5).

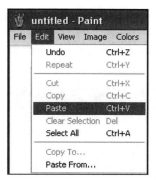

Figure 1.5. Choosing Paste under the Edit menu in Paint.

4. Use the Select tool (see Figure 1.6) to select the portion of the screen you would like to keep. Select Copy from the Edit menu.

Figure 1.6. Select tool in Paint.

5. Under the File menu, choose New. Select No when asked if you want to save changes to untitled (see Figures 1.7 and 1.8)

Figure 1.7. Select New under the File menu in Paint.

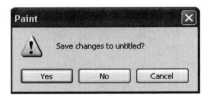

Figure 1.8. Select No at the prompt.

6. Once again, select Paste from the Edit menu and make any necessary changes to your picture using the paint tools. When you are finished, select your picture with the Select tool and select Copy from the Edit menu.

7. Open your word-processing program and choose Paste from the Edit menu. If using Microsoft Word, choose Paste Special from the Edit menu, and choose Picture as the format and click OK (see Figures 1.9 and 1.10). The picture format provides a higher-quality printed picture than the bitmap format.

PC users can take a picture of the active window by pressing the Alt key and the Print Screen (Print Scr) key together. This, too, places a copy of the picture on the computer's clipboard. Users can paste the document into a desired program (for example, word processing) or paste and edit it into the Paint program, as above.

It is possible to take a screenshot on a Macintosh by pressing the following keys simultaneously:

• [Open-Apple], Shift, 3 takes a snapshot of the screen and places the file on the hard drive as Picture 1, Picture 2, etc.

• [Open-Apple], Shift, 4 changes the cursor into a plus sign (+), allowing you to select the portion of the screen you want to copy. Drag the cursor across the area to copy and release the mouse button. This, too, leaves a copy of the selected picture on the hard drive.

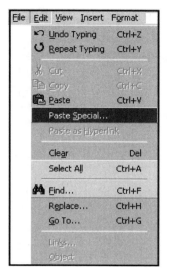

Figure 1.9. Select Paste Special under the Edit menu in Microsoft Word.

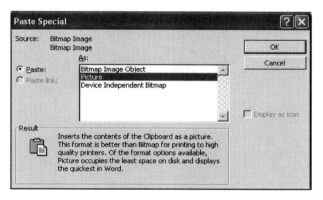

Figure 1.10. Choose Picture and click OK.

• [Open-Apple], Shift, Cap Lock, 4 takes a picture of a selected window. The cursor changes into a circle; click the circle in the window you want to copy. A copy of the picture is placed on the hard drive.

To copy a snapshot to the clipboard instead of saving it as a file to the hard drive, press the Control key as part of the above combinations. Pictures saved to the hard drive can be opened and copied from SimpleText (simply double-click on the Picture file to open the program). Pictures saved to the clipboard can be pasted into other programs (for example, word processing, drawing, etc.). Similar to the PC, a paint program is needed to make advanced edits to the picture.

Other Tips and Tricks

There are several other tips and tricks of interest to educators. These include keyboard shortcuts, selecting multiple items (icons) at once, and saving resources from the Internet. Keyboard shortcuts are handy for copying and pasting documents, using Undo, and saving and printing documents. PC users press the Ctrl (Control) key with a designated letter (for example, C for copy) and Macintosh users press the Open-Apple (Command) key with a designated letter (see Table 1.2)

To select multiple items or icons on a desktop, hold down the Ctrl key (PC) or the Shift key (Macintosh) while clicking on the items with the mouse. These items can be dragged as a group or

Table 1.2. Keyboard shortcuts

Command	PC Keyboard Shortcut	Macintosh Keyboard Shortcut
Copy	Ctrl+C	[Open-Apple]+C
Paste	Ctrl+V	[Open-Apple]+V
Undo	Ctrl+Z	[Open-Apple]+Z
Save	Ctrl+S	[Open-Apple]+S
Print	Ctrl+P	[Open-Apple]+P

opened and printed all at once. To save images or sound files from the Internet, ensure the files are not copyrighted and that you have permission to use them. To save an image or other file, PC users click on the file with the "right" mouse button and choose the desired command (for example, Save Target As …) from the pop-up menu (see Figure 1.11).

Open Link
Open Link in New Window
Save Target As...
Print Target

Show Picture
Save Picture As...
E-mail Picture...
Print Picture...
Go to My Pictures
Set as Background
Set as Desktop Item...

Cut
Copy
Copy Shortcut
Paste

Add to Favorites...

Properties

Figure 1.11. Pop-up menu.

The Macintosh mouse typically has one button; users need to hold the button over the image until the pop-up menu appears.

Special characters, screenshots, and free Internet resources can help educators design instructional resources for their students. Additional ideas of how teachers can use the computer as a productivity tool are presented in Chapter 2.

Professional Development Opportunities

Having mastered or at least become comfortable with basic computer skills, the ability to effectively integrate technology into the curriculum requires more than knowing how to operate a computer and piece of software. Everyone comes into teaching with his or her own unique set of skills, experiences, and level of technology expertise. To further their abilities, educators can pursue professional development opportunities through their school, district, and local colleges and universities. Many offer courses online. In addition to online classes that may be offered by their school, district, and local colleges and universities, teachers may opt to enroll in Web-based training opportunities such as Atomic Learning (http://movies.atomiclearning.com/k12/home), a "just-in-time" training approach that allows educators to choose topics that are specific to their own needs. Tutorials are platform-specific (Macintosh or Windows) and are available in English and Spanish.

Webinars, similar to seminars but on the Web, are another way for educators to learn more about technology (and other topics) and teaching. TechLEARNING (http://www.techlearning.com/techwebinar/index.php) offers ongoing webinars, as do other educational technology sites such as ISTE (http://www.ISTE.org/webinars).

Podcasts also are available for professional development. Podcasts, audio (often combined with video) broadcasts, are digital files that can be distributed over the Internet and played back on computers and portable media devices (for example, cell phones, MP3 players, and Apple's iTouch). A podcast can be syndicated, subscribed to, and downloaded automatically when new content is added via RSS feeds (see Chapter 2). Educators can access a variety of podcasts designed for professional development from the Teachers' Podcast (http://www.teacherspodcast.org/) and the Education Podcast Network (http://www.epnweb.org/). Podcasts are available from Podcast Alley (http://podcastalley.com/), the Podcast Directory (http://www.podcastdirectory.com/), and iTunes (http://www.apple.com/itunes/store/). Several universities participate in iTunes U, a dedicated area of the iTunes store featuring free access to course lectures, demonstrations, professional development, and so on. Specific sites include the University of South Florida (http://itunes.usf.edu/), Stanford University (http://itunes.stanford.edu/), the University of California, Berkeley (http://itunes.berkeley.edu/), and Texas A&M Univesity (http://itunes.tamu.edu/).

Summary

Even though national and state technology standards are being implemented to ensure that new teachers are prepared to teach with computers and other technologies, it is important that all educators are familiar with and appropriately use today's technologies. Educators need to realize the benefits of using technology for their own needs as well as for their students' needs. Technology can help all learners (educators and students alike) gather and learn new information; collaborate and learn from others; manipulate, organize, and evaluate information; and create products. Technology can empower teachers and pupils and is a necessity if teachers are to create twenty-first-century learning environments for their students.

Technology resource teachers can assist teachers with technology questions and finding additional resources. Knowing a few basic computer tricks and troubleshooting tips also can help educators with their own use of technology. Follow-up and support is necessary to ensure that teachers feel comfortable using technology for themselves and with their students. Teachers can learn more about the computer, different technologies, how to effectively integrate technology throughout the curriculum through the Internet (including digital discussions—see Chapter 2, webinars, podcasts, and online courses), as well as face-to-face workshops, university courses, and inservices.

Activities

1. List and describe your state's technology standards for teachers. Discuss how they compare to ISTE's technology standards for teachers.

2. Create a lesson that introduces students to the computer's basic operation, input and output devices, and the care and handling of equipment and software. For students who are already familiar with computer basics, design a lesson that encourages them to imagine what technology may exist and look like ten years from now.

3. Complete the "Getting to Know the Computer: Tech Terms" activity sheet at the end of this chapter. Use WhatIs.com (http://whatis.techtarget.com) or another resource for assistance. Share how being familiar with these terms may be of value to you.

4. Interview a technology resource teacher or other computer-using educator to learn more about their background, expertise, education, and tips for using technology in the classroom.

5. Complete the "Technology Resources" activity sheet at the end of this chapter.

6. Create a "how-to" guide or other activity that includes the use of screenshots.

7. Review and recommend (or not) podcasts designed to support teachers' ability to use technology.

References

Bausell, C. V. 2008. Tracking U.S. trends: States vary in classroom access to computers and in policies concerning school technology. *Education Week.* Available at http://www.edweek. org/ew/articles/2008/03/27/30trends.h27.html. (Accessed May 10, 2008).

Besnoy, K. 2007. Creating a personal technology plan for teachers of the gifted. *Gifted Child Today* 30 (4): 44–48.

Brand, G. A. 1998. What research says: Training teachers for using technology. *Journal of Staff Development* 19 (1): 10–13.

California Commission on Teacher Credentialing (CCTC). 2007. Multiple subject teaching credential: Requirements for teachers prepared in California. Available at http://www.ctc.ca. gov/credentials/leaflets/cl561c.pdf. (Accessed April 21, 2007).

CDW Government, Inc. (CDW-G). 2006. Teachers Talk Tech® reveals technology access and professional development are driving improved teacher and student performance. Available at http:// newsroom.cdwg.com/news-releases/news-release-06-26-06.html. (Accessed May 18, 2008).

Editorial Projects in Education (EPE) Research Center. 2007. Technology counts: A digital decade: Detailed state reports. Available at http://www.edweek.org/ew/articles/2007/03/29/ 30dsr.h26.html. (Accessed April 21, 2007).

Fleming, L., Motamedi, V., and May, L. 2007. Predicting preservice teacher competence in computer technology: Modeling and application in training environments. *Journal of Technology and Teacher Education* 15 (2): 207–231.

Franklin, C. 2007. Factors that influence elementary teachers use of computers. *Journal of Technology and Teacher Education* 15 (2): 267–293.

International Society for Technology in Education (ISTE). 2008. *National Educational Technology Standards for Teachers.* 2nd ed. Eugene, OR: ISTE.

International Society for Technology in Education (ISTE), Partnership for 21st Century Skills, and State Educational Technology Directors Association (SETDA). 2007. Maximizing the impact: The pivotal role of technology in a 21st century education system. Available at http://www.setda.org/web/guest/maximizingimpactreport. (Accessed April 3, 2008).

Littrell, A. B., M. J. Zagumny, and L. L. Zagumny. 2005. Contextual and psychological predictors of instructional technology use in rural classrooms. *Educational Research Quarterly* 29 (2): 37–47.

Partnership for 21st Century Skills. 2007. Framework for 21st century learning. Available at http://www.21stcenturyskills.org/documents/frameworkflyer_072307.pdf. (Accessed April 3, 2008).

Sahin, I. 2007–08. Faculty instructional computer use model: Differentiating instructional and mainstream computer uses. *Journal of Computing in Teacher Education* 24 (2): 57–64.

Shaunessy, E. 2007. Attitudes toward information technology of teachers of the gifted: Implications for gifted education. *Gifted Child Quarterly* 51 (2): 119–135.

United Nations Educational, Scientific and Cultural Organization (UNESCO). 2008. ICT competency standards for teachers: Policy framework. Available at http://unesdoc.unesco.org/images/0015/001562/156210E.pdf. (Accessed April 4, 2008).

U.S. Department of Education, Office of Postsecondary Education. *The Secretary's Fourth Annual Report on Teacher Quality: A Highly Qualified Teacher in Every Classroom.* Washington, D.C.: 2005.

Watson, G. 2006. Technology professional development: Long-term effects on teacher self-efficacy. *Journal of Technology and Teacher Education* 14 (1): 151–166.

Blackline Masters

• Getting to Know the Computer: Draw and Label

• Getting to Know the Computer: Keyboard Activity

• Getting to Know the Computer: Tech Terms

• Technology Resources

Getting to Know the Computer: Draw and Label

Draw your classroom computer and label the following: monitor, CPU, keyboard, mouse, disc drive, and other features of your computer. If you have a printer, scanner, or other device attached to your computer, draw and label those items, too.

List how you can help take care of your classroom computer.

Getting to Know the Computer: Keyboard Activity

Complete the keyboard and color code the keys. Color the index finger keys light blue, the middle finger keys yellow, the ring finger keys light green, and the pinkie finger keys pink.

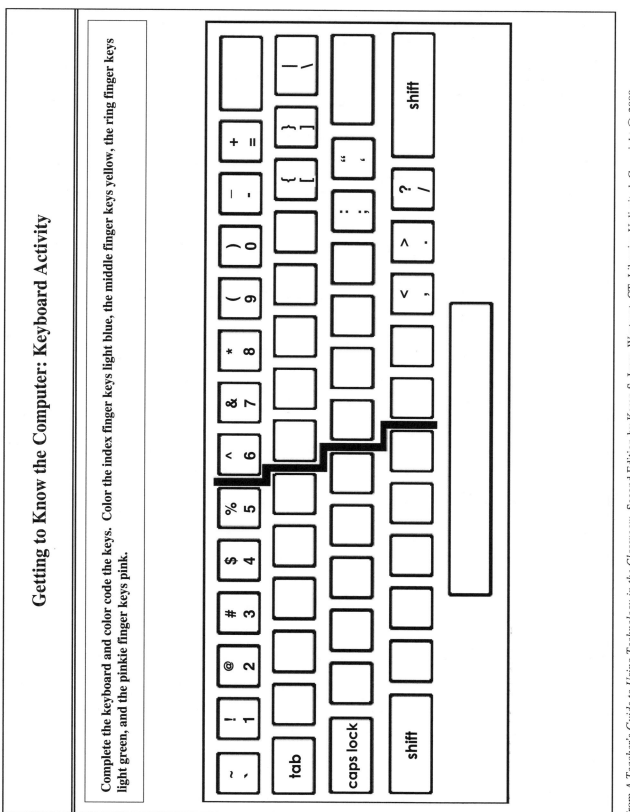

Getting to Know the Computer: Tech Terms

Use WhatIs.com (http://whatis.techtarget.com/) and other resources to define the following. Include where you found the information.

Word	Definition	Resource
ASCII		
Blue Tooth		
Dot pitch		
Dots per inch (re: printing)		
IEEE		
LAN		
MP3		
NIC		
Resolution		
Rich Text Format		
TCP/IP		
Find and define your own tech term.		

From *A Teacher's Guide to Using Technology in the Classroom*, Second Edition by Karen S. Ivers. Westport, CT: Libraries Unlimited. Copyright © 2009.

Technology Resources

Note the available resources at your school. In the comments section, list information regarding support materials for the device (such as obtaining storage media, DVDs, ink or toner cartridges, charged batteries, Internet, etc.)

Device	Number available for checkout or scheduled use	Number in your classroom	Comments
Computers (laptop, tablet, and/or desktop)			
Printers			
Scanners			
Digital cameras (note video and/or still)			
Large monitors for whole class viewing			
Interactive whiteboards			
Projection systems			
DVD players			
Probeware			
Other			

From *A Teacher's Guide to Using Technology in the Classroom*, Second Edition by Karen S. Ivers. Westport, CT: Libraries Unlimited. Copyright © 2009.

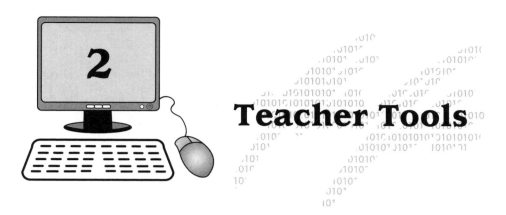

Teacher Tools

A Scenario

Mr. Abbott was just hired to teach in a one-to-one laptop school. He felt fortunate because his preservice training prepared him to use technology to engage students in higher-level thinking skills using project-based learning and other strategies that incorporated collaboration, innovation, and research. One of his preservice teaching assignments was in a one-to-one laptop classroom. His mentor teacher, Ms. Castello, not only modeled twenty-first-century teaching, she taught Mr. Abbott how to use technology to be more effective in the classroom. In addition to showing Mr. Abbott how to set up a digital lesson plan book, she demonstrated how the school used technology to track students' attendance, grades, and other information. She shared online resources, including those for standards-based lesson, record keeping, assessment, multimedia projects, professional development, and collaboration. Mr. Abbott was not new to technology, but seeing it through the needs of students and teachers made him realize how much he had to learn. He had been a consumer of technology; now he needed to be an educational leader of technology.

Introduction

As mentioned in Chapter 1, professional development in the effective use of technology must be ongoing if educators are to stay abreast of the latest educational technologies to support student learning. It is important for teachers to be familiar with and use the technologies themselves before they can be expected to effectively integrate technology into the curriculum. Knowing how technology can benefit teachers may help educators examine ways that it can better assist students. This chapter focuses on teachers' use of technology for instructional, assessment, and management purposes. Topics include:

- Productivity Tools

  Instructional and Creative Tasks

  Assessment and Record Keeping

- Internet Resources for Teachers

  Lesson Plans

  Digital Discussions

  Additional Resources

Productivity Tools

Numerous programs exist to assist teachers with creating instructional materials, presentations, lesson plans, flyers, newsletters, quizzes, puzzles, and more. Other programs are available for helping teachers manage classroom instruction. This section discusses and provides resources for various teacher productivity tools, software programs available to assist and expedite instructional and management tasks.

Instructional and Creative Tasks

Programs designed to help teachers with instructional and creative tasks have been around since the early 1980s, when Apple IIe computers first made their way into classrooms. Since then, these programs have become much more sophisticated and produce professional-looking products—thanks to advancements in computers and printer capabilities, including printers ("fabbers") designed to print in 3-D (see http://fabathome.org for more information). There are a variety of commercial programs designed to help teachers perform specific tasks: create certificates, make newsletters, design cards and posters, create puzzles and quizzes, and so forth. Many contain templates, clip art, or fonts specifically designed for use in the classroom. Table 2.1 provides a description of some of these programs.

Table 2.1. Commercial Productivity Programs

Name	Company and Product Description
The Print Shop	Broderbund http://www.broderbund.com/ • Make greeting cards, banners, calendars, signs, labels, Web pages, skins for iPods, and more • Thousands of graphics and layouts • Photo-editing options • Various versions available to meet individual needs
PageMaker	Adobe http://www.adobe.com/ • Make fliers, newsletters, brochures, booklets, reports, and more • Thousands of graphics and hundreds of templates • Option to export documents to PDF (Adobe Portable Document Format) • Adobe's InDesign is another option
Teachers' Power Pack	Centron Software, Inc. http://www.centronsoftware.com/ • Includes Test Creator and Puzzle Power • Create multiple choice, true/false, essay, and fill-in-the-blanks questions • Import text and graphics into questions • Make a variety of puzzles—crossword, word search, Sudoku, and more

Teachers' Tool Kit	TeacherTools.com
	http://www.teachertools.com/
	• Make word searches and word scrambles
	• Create a database of true/false, multiple choice, and short essay questions for customizable quizzes
	• Rated "Exemplary" by the National Education Association
Worksheet Magic Plus	Gameco Educational Software
	http://www.gameco.com/
	• Create crossword puzzles, scrambled words, word searches, multiple choice, mix and match, secret code, review sheets, and more
	• Use database to store word lists
SmartDraw	SmartDraw.com
	http://www.smartdraw.com/specials/award-gift-certificates.asp
	• Create certificates, awards, newsletters, and more
	• Thousands of graphics and border templates
	• Free trial version available
Rubric Software	New Measure, Inc.
	http://www.rubrics.com/
	• Make rubrics
	• Includes customizable database of content standards
Teacher Font Bundle	Visions Technology in Education
	http://www.teamvistech.com/
	• Includes School Fonts, Arithmefonts, and Festive Fonts
	• Font packages also may be ordered separately

In addition to specialized programs, teachers will find "teacher-friendly" templates in several application programs. For example, Pages (part of Apple's iWork suite, which also includes Keynote—presentation software—and Numbers—a spreadsheet application) is a word-processing program that includes templates for stationary, newsletters, resumes, brochures, reports, proposals, and business cards. Educator-created templates for Pages can be downloaded from http://www.apple.com/education/digitalauthoring/pages.html. Microsoft provides various templates within Microsoft Works and Microsoft Office, also. In addition, numerous templates can be downloaded for Microsoft Office from http://office.microsoft.com/en-us/templates/default.aspx. Users may search for specific templates as well. Additional templates for Microsoft Works are available at http://www.microsoft.com/products/works/templates.mspx. More programs designed to help teachers with instructional and creative tasks can be found in Internet Resources for Teachers.

Assessment

There are a variety of technology tools that can assist teachers with formative assessment. Personal or audience-response systems ("clickers") enable students to respond to teacher-created multiple choice and other questions projected on a large screen or monitor. Results appear in chart or graph formats, allowing the teacher to immediately check students' understanding. Each student receives a handheld device that can be "coded" to identify the user. The devices are wireless and can include text options in addition to single letter or number inputs. For more information, go to TurningPoint Technologies at http://www.turningtechnologies.com/ or iRespond at http://www.irespond.com/.

Online quizzes via an online learning-management system (for example, Blackboard) are another way teachers can assess students' learning. Educators can also use Web-based survey programs like Zoomerang (http://www.zoomerang.com/) to answer short questions about what they learned about a particular topic, what they'd still like to learn, and what questions they may have. ProProfs (http://www.proprofs.com/) provides a variety of free Web resources for teachers, including flash cards and online quizzes.

Turnitin (http://turnitin.com/) provides a Digital Assessment Suite that includes Plagiarism Protection, Peer Review, GradeMark, and Gradebook. Plagiarism Protection helps students and teachers identify papers containing unoriginal material; this can help pupils assess their own writing and need for their own words and creativity. Peer Review facilitates students' ability to read, evaluate, and learn from the work of their classmates. GradeMark provides teachers with the resources to edit and grade students' papers online. This program allows teachers to associate comments with personalized rubrics that make it possible to identify and assess students' writing problems. Assessment also can be viewed over time, helping educators track and address students' difficulties. GradeBook is a customizable, online gradebook.

Teachers can also use spreadsheets and digital logs (information about students' progress recorded into a personal digital assistant [PDA], laptop, or other digital device) to help inform them how students are progressing. While data collection is important, it is just as vital to do something with the data! What do the data tell you? Formative assessment should be used to guide teachers' instruction.

Record Keeping

Keeping records and tracking students' progress are daily tasks performed by teachers. Technology can help streamline these activities. Spreadsheet programs can be used to track students' grades, classroom expenses, student book orders, fund-raising events, and more. Databases can be used to maintain student records (such as guardians, addresses, phone numbers, emergency contacts, and allergies), classroom library books and software, lesson plans, parent volunteers, field trips, and so on. Seating charts, computer schedules, and checklists can be made using tables in a word processor or tools in a drawing program. As mentioned previously, many application programs provide templates to help structure and create various documents. Gradebook templates, classroom databases, progress reports, and other items can be downloaded from Microsoft's and Apple's Web sites.

Teachers have the choice of purchasing programs specifically designed for tracking student grades, creating seating charts, and other record-keeping tasks. Many of these programs support the use of handheld computer technologies, often referred to as PDAs, and the Internet. PDAs allow teachers to track students' progress during instruction; Internet features enable teachers to post password-protected information to the Internet and to e-mail parents student reports. Example programs are listed in Table 2.2.

Gradebook and other programs also are available through shareware sites. Shareware are programs distributed on a "buy it if you like it" basis. Users may need to pay for the software to access the full features of the program or to continue using the program after a certain number of days. Teachers will find shareware gradebook programs at CNET Shareware.com (http://shareware.cnet.com/) by entering "gradebook" in the search option. Before purchasing a digital gradebook, check with your school to see if one is available or planned for use within the school or district. Many more schools are moving record keeping and other tasks online via learning-management systems.

When selecting a gradebook program, teachers may want to consider the following criteria:

• Security features

  Is the program password protected?

Table 2.2. Record-Keeping Programs

Name	Company and Product Description
GradeQuick	Edline http://www.edline.com/ • Provides customized reports and report cards, classroom attendance options, seating charts with student photos, and flexible grading options • Includes PDA and Internet options • Full-feature demo available
Learner Profile	Learner Profile http://www.learnerprofile.com/ • Combines instructional goals, observations, grading, attendance, and reports into one system • Includes PDA and Internet options • Demo available
Easy Grade Pro	Orbis Software http://www.orbissoft.com/ • Provides multiple grading, attendance, report, and seating chart options • Includes PDA and Internet options • Demo available
Teacher Information Manager Deluxe	Visions Technology in Education http://www.teamvistech.com/ • Includes gradebook program, scheduler, attendance and seating chart features, and lesson plan maker
ThinkWave Educator	ThinkWave http://www.thinkwave.com/ • Allows teachers to manage grades, create lesson plans and assessments, track attendance, and design seating charts • Includes Internet options • Free basic program
Making the Grade	Jay Klein Productions http://www.gradebusters.com/ • Provides customizable letter grades, grading scales, and comments • Includes attendance records and seating charts, PDA and Web options, and free lifetime upgrades • Trial version available

• Flexibility

Is there a limited number of students, classes, or assignments that can be entered into the program?
Are sorting and find features available?

• Grading options

Does the program allow for letter, number, check, and weighted scores?
Does the program allow the teacher to designate ranges (that is, 90 to 100) for letter and other grades?
Can the lowest scores be dropped from final calculations?

• Graphs

Are bar, pie, line, and other graphs available to display classroom and individual data?

• Reports

Is it possible to generate reports by group, individual, assignment, and other categories?

Can the reports be customized?

• Ease of use

Is it easy to add, edit, and delete student information, classes, and assignments?

Is the interface and design appealing and intuitive?

• Other features

Does the program include options for tracking attendance, creating seating charts, or managing other aspects of instruction?

Does the program allow teachers to make notes about students (such as documenting that a student's low score may have been the result of the student not feeling well that day)?

Does the program allow teachers to import and export data?

Is it possible to securely post assignments, grades, attendance, and other information to the Internet?

Are e-mail features built in?

Are PDA features available?

Is the program able to translate information into different languages?

Teachers' needs vary depending on their grade level, number of students, and other factors. In addition to discussing gradebook programs with other teachers, it is recommended that educators download and try demonstration copies of various gradebook programs. Teachers should consider their individual needs and the criteria listed earlier. When using a gradebook program, it is recommended that educators maintain a backup copy of their gradebook files, as well as a printout of their most recent class report.

Internet Resources for Teachers

There are many Internet tools available to assist educators. These include resources for productivity and management tasks, lesson plans, and electronic discussions. This section examines a variety of Internet resources for teachers; additional resources are mentioned throughout this book, dependent upon the chapter topic.

Productivity and Management Tasks

Teachers can find many productivity and management programs on the Internet (see Table 2.3). Most are free of charge and allow teachers to create greeting cards, certificates, puzzles, rubrics, and worksheets directly on the Internet.

Lesson Plans

Numerous lesson plans exist on the Internet. Lesson plans may be posted by individual teachers or by educational, commercial, and other organizations. Sometimes, lesson plans are critiqued or evaluated by other educators before they are posted; other times, they are not. Educators need to assess the validity of online lesson plans, considering the stated objectives, methods, evaluation

Table 2.3. Programs on the Internet

Name	Company and Product Description
Certificate Creator	CertificateCreator.com http://www.certificatecreator.com/ • Create and print certificates off the Internet
Ivy's Greeting Cards	Ivy's Domain http://www.ivyjoy.com/printcards/index.html • Print customized greeting cards • Also see Ivy's Printable Activity Sites at http://www.ivyjoy.com/printcards/printablelinks.html
My Teacher Tools	My Teacher Tools http://www.myteachertools.com/ • Numerous links to teacher resources and tools: maps, worksheet generators, puzzle and certificate makers, and much more
Teach-nology Web Tools	Teach-nology http://www.teach-nology.com/web_tools/ • Numerous online generators: create puzzles, rubrics, graphic organizers, WebQuests, and much more
Teaching Tools	Discovery Education http://school.discovery.com/teachingtools/teachingtools.html • Create worksheets, quizzes, lesson plans, and more • Sign up for free Custom Classroom to save your work and access additional teacher tools
t-source: Tools for Teachers	American Federation of Teachers http://www.aft.org/tools4teachers/index.htm • Access tips for managing your classroom • Explore a variety of instructional material, including teaching tips • Investigate funding opportunities and more
RubiStar	High Plains Regional Technology in Education Consortium http://rubistar.4teachers.org/ • Create customized rubric or choose from a library of premade rubrics

procedures, and other factors. Just because it exists on the Internet does not mean it is "good" information. In some cases, a lesson plan or activity will be acceptable as is; other times, teachers may disregard it or modify it to meet the needs of their students. Teachers will find lesson plans that are designed to help them integrate technology across the curriculum, conduct science experiments, teach mathematics concepts, teach reading for meaning, and much more. Lesson plans can be found at the following locations:

- The Educator's Reference Desk
  http://askeric.org/Virtual/Lessons/

- Discovery Education Lesson Plan Library
  http://school.discovery.com/lessonplans/

- HotChalk's Lesson Plans Page
  http://www.lessonplanspage.com/

- Lesson Plan Search
  http://www.lessonplansearch.com/

- Teachnet.com
  http://www.teachnet.com/lesson/

- The Lesson Bank
  http://www.teachers.net/lessons/

Several state-sponsored organizations maintain Web sites designed to provide teachers with instructional resources. For example, the California Learning Resource Network (CLRN) provides reviews of electronic resources and identifies how each connects to specific California academic content standards (see http://www.clrn.org/). In addition to learning resources for several different subject areas, teachers can learn about different assessment tools, access recommended Web sites, and subscribe to RSS feeds for recent updates. RSS feeds are usually indicated by an orange button with a dot and two curved lines (see Figure 2.1) or the letters "XML" or "RSS." To receive RSS content, users must have an "RSS Reader" or "aggregator." To receive updates to a Web site, users need to enter the URL address of the Web site they wish to subscribe to into the RSS reader. In most cases, users can click on the RSS icon within the Web page to initiate the process. Current Web browsers have built-in RSS readers. Look for the RSS icon on your browser's tool bar. For updates, check your browser's Web site. Free RSS readers can be reviewed and downloaded from CNET Download.com and other shareware/freeware sites.

Figure 2.1. RSS icon.

The Federal Resources for Educational Excellence (FREE) provides links to teaching and learning resources (http://www.free.ed.gov/). Business-sponsored resource sites also are available. For example, AT&T Education sponsors Blue Web'n (http://www.kn.pacbell.com/wired/bluewebn/), a Web site that includes lessons, WebQuests, and other information for teachers and librarians. Internet sites that are judged "outstanding" are categorized by subjects, grade levels, and formats (lessons, resources, tutorials, references, tools, and so on). The site is searchable. Educators can subscribe to the site to receive updates, too. Teachers will want to check with their district, county department of education office, and state department of education to see what resources may be available.

Digital Discussions

The Internet allows educators to stay connected with their peers and engage in professional development through e-mail, Listservs, discussion forums, blogs, wikis, and chat rooms (chatboards). With the exception of chat rooms, educators can correspond with each other at different times; there is no need to be on the computer at the same time. Educators have the opportunity to communicate and exchange ideas with educators from all over the world. This section provides resources for e-mail, Listservs, newsgroups, discussion forums, blogs, wikis, and chat rooms.

E-mail

E-mail may be one of the most common uses of the Internet. It allows users to communicate worldwide without the expense or time restrictions of using a telephone or traditional mail. To send e-mail, you need an Internet Service Provider (ISP), an e-mail address, and a software program to access the e-mail system. Most ISPs provide users with an e-mail account and e-mail address. They usually provide users with e-mail software, too.

E-mail accounts can be obtained for free through certain Web sites. For example, Yahoo (http://www.yahoo.com/) offers Yahoo! Mail, Microsoft Network (http://www.msn.com/) distributes Hotmail, and Google offers Gmail (http://www.google.com/). Users will need an Internet connection or their own ISP and a browser (for example, Internet Explorer, Safari, or Firefox) to access these sites.

E-mail addresses begin with the user's account name (for example, kivers), followed by the "at" sign (@), and the location and domain of the account. For example, looking at kivers@fullerton.edu, "kivers" is the username (account name), "fullerton" is the institution where the account is located, and "edu" is the type of organization—education (see Chapter 6 for more information about Internet addresses).

Users create, send, and receive e-mail using e-mail software. Figure 2.2 shows a blank e-mail form for sending e-mail in Microsoft Outlook.

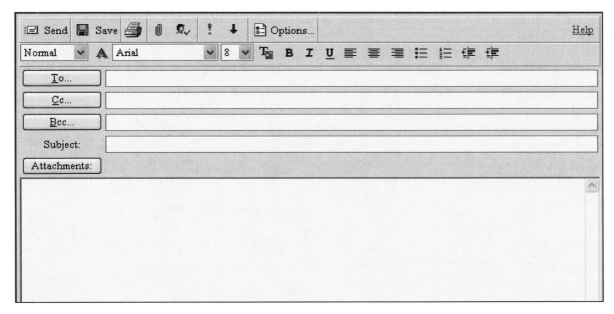

Figure 2.2. Blank e-mail form in Microsoft Outlook.

The sender places the e-mail address of the person(s) he/she wants to send the message to in the "To" field. Note that carbon copies (Cc) and blind carbon copies (Bcc) also can be sent. In the "Subject" field, senders should include a brief title or description of what the message is about. The message is entered in the bottom box. Messages can be typed directly into the field or cut and pasted from a word-processed document.

It is possible to send attachments with e-mail messages, too. It is always a good idea to let the receiver know which program you used to create the attachment (for example, Microsoft Word, Excel, etc.). If the recipient does not have the program in which you created the document, he may not be able to open the attachment. Some programs allow you to save documents in a different format. For example, Microsoft Excel lets you save Excel documents in various formats, allowing the data to be accessed by other database or spreadsheet programs. Many word-processing programs allow users to save documents as ASCII (text) or RTF (rich text format) files, making it easy for different word-processing programs to open the documents. It is also possible to save documents in PDF (Portable Document Format). This creates an image of the document that can be viewed using Adobe's free Acrobat Reader (see http://www.adobe.com/). If your software does not have PDF as a save or print option, programs such as CutePDF (http://www.cutepdf.com/) can be downloaded for free and used to print (save) files to PDF.

When receiving attachments, be wary of who sent it. When in doubt, do not open the attachment. Many viruses are sent as attachments, causing great havoc when they are opened. Avoid opening attachments that end in ".exe" or ".vbs," as well as those that you are not expecting. It is possible for a virus to spread itself by using an infected computer's address book to send itself to others. In this case, it appears as though the e-mail is coming from someone you know.

E-mail messages can be saved, printed, or filed for archive purposes. E-mail is an easy way to keep in touch with other educators and to conduct classroom exchanges (see Chapter 6). It is one of the many ways technology can be used to increase collaborative learning opportunities for teachers and students.

Listservs

A Listserv distributes e-mail messages to everyone (subscribers) on a mailing list. When someone sends an e-mail to the Listserv, everyone on the mailing list will receive the message (see Figure 2.3).

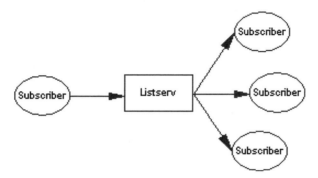

Figure 2.3. Sending an e-mail to a Listserv.

Users can subscribe to or unsubscribe from a Listserv. Joining a Listserv may result in numerous e-mail messages to the subscriber's mailbox.

Topica (http://lists.topica.com/) hosts free Listservs on a variety of topics, including education. Listservs for educators include:

- Teaching Multimedia (TeachMedia)
  Teachers share ideas and questions about using multimedia in the classroom.
  To subscribe, send an e-mail to teachmedia-subscribe@topica.com.

- Teaching Mathematics in the Middle School (math-teach)
  Teachers share middle school mathematics strategies.
  To subscribe, send an e-mail to math_teach-subscribe@topica.com.

- Bright Eyed Primary Teachers (Bright Eyed K-6)
  K-6 teachers share advice, swap lesson ideas and activities, and share humorous moments.
  To subscribe, send an e-mail to Bright.Eyed-subscribe@topica.com.

Educators can create their own Listserv as well. Other Listservs include:

- The Reading Teacher Listserv (RTEACHER)
  This is one of several Listservs on the International Reading Association Web site.
  RTEACHER is designed for literacy teachers working with students up to age twelve. Teachers share their reading ideas, questions, concerns, and successes.
  To subscribe, send an e-mail to listserv@bookmark.reading.org.
  In the message window, type: SUBSCRIBE RTEACHER full name (such as, SUBSCRIBE RTEACHER Joe Smith). Make sure the message is left blank; disable your "signature" option if you have one. Additional Listservs include Critical Literacy, History of Reading, Teaching as a Researching Profession, and Readability (see http://www.reading.org/resources/community/discussions.html).

• National Council for Social Studies
The National Council for Social Studies supports several Listservs for exchanging information about social studies. Go to http://www.socialstudies.org/lists for more information.

• Global SchoolNet Mailing Lists
The Global Schoolhouse offers several Listservs, also, including HILITES (K-12 collaborative projects list), Online Expeditions (announcement of online expeditions and virtual field trips), and WWWEDU (the World Wide Web in education discussion list). Go to http://www.gsn.org/gsh/lists/ for more information.

Listservs provide educators with the advantage of receiving information and feedback from numerous educators. Listservs exist for all grade levels and subject areas. Many educational organizations provide Listserv options for their members. Additional Listservs can be found through Google and other search engines.

Usenet Newsgroups

Usenet, a contraction of "USEr's NETwork," is a collection of ongoing discussions called newsgroups. Unlike Listservs, newsgroups do not send messages or replies out to their members. Instead, members post their messages on a bulletin board where other members can read and respond to the messages at their leisure. Usenets, one of the oldest computer network communications, may be considered the precursor to Web-based discussion forums. Users access newsgroups by using newsgroup reader software, included in most browsers. Internet Explorer users can find this software under Tools. Choose Mail and News, then Read News (see Figure 2.4).

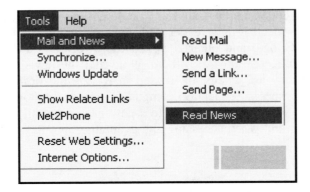

Figure 2.4. Accessing newsgroups in Internet Explorer.

The user's ISP controls newsgroup access. An ISP may provide limited or full access to available newsgroups on the Internet. Contact your ISP if you have difficulty accessing newsgroups through your browser. Once connected, you may see a window similar to Figure 2.5.

To access a newsgroup, click on it, and then click Subscribe. This will give you access to the newsgroup's discussion area where you can read, reply to, and post messages. You can unsubscribe at any time.

There are thousands of newsgroups, organized into categories. Common categories are:

• alt: alternative discussions

• biz: business and commercial topics

• comp: computers

• misc: topics that do not fit in any other category

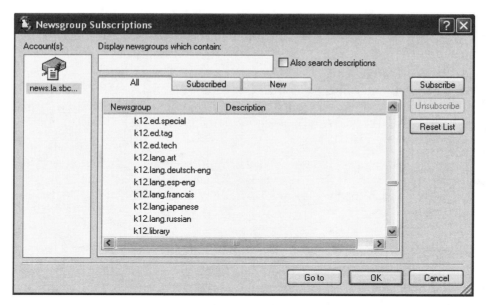

Figure 2.5. Newsgroup window.

• k12: kindergarten through grade 12 discussions

• rec: recreation

• soc: social issues

A list of archived newsgroups can be found at Google Groups (http://groups.google.com/). Using Google Groups, you will not need a newsreader and you can search the archive the same way you would search on the Web. Google and other sites provide directories and search options for newsgroups and help you register to participate in them. Note that the newsgroups visible in Figure 2.5 begin with k12, indicating they are discussions based in K-12 education. Specific topics within the k12 newsgroup list include special education, language arts, technology, foreign languages, and others. Also note that anyone can create and post to a newsgroup; not all newsgroups are moderated. Educators must keep this in mind when accessing and evaluating newsgroup information.

Discussion Forums

Discussion forums, or discussion boards, are similar to newsgroups except they are accessed only through Web sites. Like newsgroups, users can read, reply to, and post messages on various topics. Messages are often "threaded," meaning they are indented to show which response goes to which message. For example, in Figure 2.6 "Using computers in the classroom" is a message or thread started by Karen Ivers (1). Diane and John (2) replied to Karen's message; Karen and Connie (3) replied to John's response. John (4) replied to Connie's response.

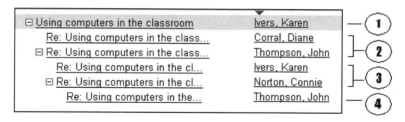

Figure 2.6. Example of a threaded discussion.

Unthreaded responses are listed in the order they are received. In some cases, users will need a username and password to access a discussion forum. Examples of Web sites with discussion forums for teachers include:

- Mrs. Glosser's Math Goodies
  http://www.mathgoodies.com/

- Dave's ESL Cafe
  http://www.eslcafe.com/

- Education World
  http://forums.educationworld.com/

- Teachers.Net
  http://teachers.net/

- The Teacher's Corner
  http://www.theteacherscorner.net/

Several of these sites include chat options, also (see Chat), as well as other resources for teachers.

Discussion forums, like newsgroups, are an excellent way for teachers to exchange ideas and elicit help from other educators. They can participate in discussions to share thoughts with teachers from all over the world, collaborate with other educators, and post, read, and reply to messages at their leisure.

Blogs

A blog, or Web log, is an online journal or communication tool that is updated frequently and intended for a specific group or the general public. Entries are posted to a single page, usually in reverse-chronological order. Bloggers, authors of blogs, may post text, pictures, audio, video, and links to outside Web sites, as well as allow readers to post comments. Anyone can create and host a blog. Free blog creation sites include Blogger (https://www.blogger.com/), WordPress.com (http://WordPress.com), and LiveJournal (http://www.livejournal.com/).

There are several Web sites that support teacher communities and include blogs to support teacher interaction, collaboration, and reflection. These include:

- ProTeacher Blogs
  http://blogs.proteacher.net/

- Teacher Magazine
  http://www.teachermagazine.org/tm/index.html

- TeacherLingo
  http://teacherlingo.com/

Other sites provide blog service to support teachers with hosting and managing blogs for students:

- 21classes
  http://www.21classes.com/

- ClassPress
  http://www.classpress.com/

- Gaggle.Net
  http://www.gaggle.net/

- Class Blogmeister
  http://classblogmeister.com/

In many cases, users can subscribe to blogs via an RSS feed. Educators can find blogs on specific topics by using Google's Blog Search (http://blogsearch.google.com/).

Wiki

A "wiki" is a server program that allows users to collaboratively create and edit the content of a Web site using a regular Web browser. Perhaps the most commonly known wiki is Wikipedia—an online encyclopedia created by users from all over the world (see http://en.wikipedia.org/). Wikis can be public or private and are a great collaboration tool. Teachers can create their own wiki or wikis for their classrooms at:

- pbwiki
  http://pbwiki.com/education.wiki

- Wetpaint
  http://www.wetpaint.com/

- Wikispaces
  http://www.wikispaces.com/

Wikis designed to support collaboration and the sharing of resources among teachers include:

- Model Schools Wiki
  http://wiki.monroe.edu/

- TeacherLibrarianWiki
  http://teacherlibrarianwiki.pbwiki.com/

- Wiki-Teacher
  http://www.wiki-teacher.com/index.php

There are numerous wikis available on the Web. Like other Web resources, teachers (and students) must evaluate the information posted and verify its accuracy by comparing the information with other sources.

Chat

Unlike other forms of communication (such as e-mail, newsgroups, discussion forums, blogs, and wikis), chat is synchronous—meaning "real time." This means users must be logged into a specified chat room at the same time. Users' statements, questions, and replies are displayed in the chat room. Conversations are typed rather than spoken (see Figure 2.7).

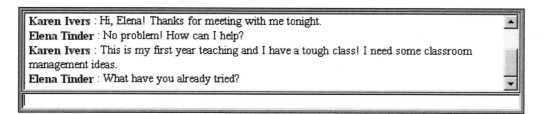

Figure 2.7. Chat room discussion.

Chat rooms enable users to communicate instantly with another or many other users. If too many users are involved, conversations may become confusing as users try to read, reply, and keep up with current questions and replies.

Several Web sites offer chat rooms for educators. These include:

• Schoolhouse Door
http://schoolhousedoor.com/teacher.htm

• Teachers.Net
http://teachers.net/

Note that Teachers.Net also hosts state and other specific sites. For example:

• California.Teachers.Net
http://california.teachers.net/

• Florida Teachers Chatboard
http://teachers.net/states/fl/posts.html

You can access different state chatboards by going to http://teachers.net/ and selecting States from the Chatboards menu. Note that there are specific chatboards for a variety of different topics as well. These can be accessed by clicking on Chatboards.

Chat is not necessarily limited to text. Today's tools allow users to share audio, video, pictures, Web sites, and more in real time. Mobile devices (for example, cell phones) make it possible to send and receive text, audio, video, pictures, etc. from almost anywhere. Texting (text messaging) continues to be a popular form of communication among users of cell phones and other handheld devices. Instant messaging (IM) is another form of real-time communication. By connecting through a specific service (for example, AOL, MSN Messenger, Yahoo! Messenger, and Apple's iChat), users are able to exchange information "instantly" with others who are connected to the same service, are currently online, and are on the user's "buddy" or selection list. Again, users are not limited to text; voice messaging, file sharing, and live video can be sent as well.

There are a variety of tools to support distant communication (and teaching) in real time. Many programs use VoIP (Voice over Internet Protocol) to send voice over the Internet. Skype is one example. Using a proprietary Internet telephony (VoIP) network, users of Skype can make phone calls over the Internet to other users of Skype free of charge. There is a charge to connect to landlines and cell phones. Videoconferencing is possible with Skype as well. For more information, go to http://skype.com/. Gizmo (http://gizmo5.com/) is a similar product. Both Skype and Gizmo are available for mobile devices.

Additional Resources

There is a plethora of information available on the Internet to assist educators. Many Web sites offer multiple tools for teachers—lesson plans, collaboration tools, instructional and management resources, and more. Examples include:

• Epals
http://www.epals.com/

• ProTeacher
http://www.proteacher.com/

• Scholastic: Teachers
http://www2.scholastic.com/browse/teach.jsp

• Teacher Focus
http://www.teacherfocus.com/

• Teachers.net
http://teachers.net/

• Shareology
  http://www.shareology.org/

Podcasts (discussed in Chapter 1) are available to support instruction, also. For example, The Education Podcast Network (http://www.epnweb.org/) provides subject-specific podcasts, student and class podcasts, and podcasts for professional development. National Geographic (http://www.national geographic.com/podcasts/) and the Smithsonian (http://www.si.edu/podcasts/) are additional sources for educational podcasts. ESL Teacher Talk (http://www.eslteachertalk.com/) provides podcasts featuring interviews with ESL experts, discussions of classroom activities, and insights of ESL teachers. Teachers (and students) may choose to create their own podcasts using free Web resources such as PodOmatic (http://www.podomatic.com/), PodBean (http://www.podbean.com/), Gcast (http://www.gcast.com/), and MyPodcast (http://www.mypodcast.com/). Macintosh computers come with software to help users create audio and video podcasts (for example, GarageBand and iMovie). Apple's QuickTime Pro (available for Macintosh and Windows) can help users create audio and video podcasts. Additional resources for teachers include United Streaming, the IRIS Center, and TeacherTube. United Streaming from Discovery Education (http://streaming.discoveryeducation.com/) is another great resource for teachers. It provides online, educational videos that are aligned to state standards. A free thirty-day trial is available. The IRIS Center (http://iris.peabody.vanderbilt.edu/) is a free site for learning more about educating students with disabilities. Material is available in Spanish, too. TeacherTube (http://www.teachertube.com/) is an online community for sharing instructional videos. Additional resources for teachers can be found in the "Internet Resources for Teachers" blackline master at the end of this chapter. The Internet can be overwhelming, so start with a few recommended sites and explore what each has to offer. Internet searches (see Chapter 6) can help you locate additional information.

Summary

There are many ways technology can assist teachers with instructional and management tasks. Computer programs and templates are available to assist teachers with record keeping and creating instructional material; the Internet provides teachers with opportunities to locate lesson plans, instructional resources, professional education groups, teacher networks, and more. Technology provides opportunities for teachers to expedite mundane tasks, create professional-looking documents, collaborate with other teachers, share information, and conduct research. It provides educators (and students) with benefits and opportunities that they might not otherwise have.

Activities

1. Use a template designed for Microsoft Word, Microsoft Works, or iWorks to create a homework sheet, newsletter, certificate, or other document you would use in a school setting.

2. Download and compare two different gradebook programs (see Table 2.3). Use the criteria presented on pages 26–28.

3. Review and create materials from three different Web sites that allow teachers to create and print instructional resources (see Table 2.3).

4. Locate and evaluate three lesson plans on the Internet. Make sure they address the same topic (for example, introduction to fractions) and grade level. Identify the objectives, methods, and evaluation procedures. Discuss the strengths and weaknesses of each lesson and how they might be improved.

5. E-mail your favorite lesson plan or activity as a PDF attachment to a fellow teacher or your instructor.

6. Participate in a discussion forum for teachers (see page 35). Summarize what was discussed, what you learned, and whether or not the forum is of value to you.

7. Select one of the IRIS modules or a video from United Streaming and share how the material or information provided can be used to enhance instruction.

Blackline Master

• Internet Resources for Teachers

Internet Resources for Teachers

Professional Education Groups

American Association of School Librarians
http://www.ala.org/aasl/

International Reading Association
http://www.reading.org/

International Society for Technology in Education
http://www.iste.org/

National Council for the Social Studies
http://www.socialstudies.org/

National Council of Teachers of Mathematics
http://www.nctm.org/

National Education Association
http://www.nea.org/

National Science Teachers Association
http://www.nsta.org/

Multimedia Resources

Audacity Free Sound Editor
http://audacity.sourceforge.net/

Awesome Clipart for Educators
http://www.awesomeclipartforeducators.com/

Barry's Clipart
http://www.barrysclipart.com/

Bellsnwhistles.com
http://www.bellsnwhistles.com/

Clipart for Students and Teachers
http://www.stemnet.nf.ca/CITE/clipart.htm

Clipart Gallery
http://www.clipartgallery.com/

Multimedia Resources for Educators and Students
http://www.uen.org/curriculum/multimedia_resources.shtml

SoundAmerica
http://www.soundamerica.com/

Teacher Networks and Resources

A to Z Teacher Stuff
http://www.atozteacherstuff.com/

Awesome Library
http://www.awesomelibrary.org/

The Best on the Web for Teachers
http://teachers.teach-nology.com/index.html

The Educators' Network
http://theeducatorsnetwork.com/

PBS Teachers
http://www.pbs.org/teachers/

ProQuest K-12
http://www.proquestk12.com/

ProTeacher
http://www.proteacher.com/

Sites for Teachers
http://www.sitesforteachers.com/

Teacher Tap
http://eduscapes.com/tap/index.htm

Teachers' Domain
http://www.teachersdomain.org/

4Teachers
http://www.4teachers.org/

Miscellaneous Sites

Education Week
http://www.edweek.org/

Education World
http://www.education-world.com/

Teacher Freebies
http://www.sassysue.com/teacher.htm

Turn It In—Plagiarism Prevention Site
http://www.turnitin.com/

U.S. Department of Education
http://www.ed.gov/

From *A Teacher's Guide to Using Technology in the Classroom*, Second Edition by Karen S. Ivers. Westport, CT: Libraries Unlimited. Copyright © 2009.

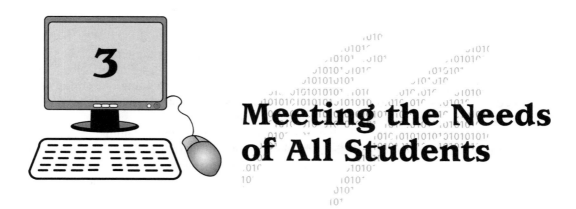

Meeting the Needs of All Students

A Scenario

Mr. Hernandez was part of a new one-to-one laptop program at his school. He attended the professional development workshops on one-to-one laptop computing offered by his district. He felt it was important for all students to have a computer of their own. His was the first school in the district to provide laptops to all of their students. One of his colleagues, Mr. Williams, had transferred to another school because he refused to be part of the program. They met at a district grade-level meeting.

"My students play enough video games at home. The last thing I'm going to do is provide every kid with a video game at their desk! School is a place to learn, not play some mindless dumb box and ignore the rest of the world," touted Mr. Williams.

"You've got to be kidding!" laughed Mr. Hernandez. "First of all, the computer provides much more than 'video games,' and research shows that gaming actually increases students problem-solving and critical-thinking skills. But, as I mentioned, the computer is not all about playing games. My students are totally engaged in learning and supporting each other through research, multimedia production, collaborative projects with students in other countries, and more. I've never had a class so willing and anxious to share what they've learned. Even my low kids are making great progress. It's as though I've found a way to meet their individual learning needs. Manuel, my gifted student, is accelerating like never before, and my English language learners—Rosie and Xu—are active participants and contributors. Students are working together to solve problems, ask questions, find innovative and creative solutions—everything we were taught at our one-to-one laptop professional development workshops. My students are empowered, and I feel great that they are learning twenty-first-century skills."

"Some of my students are not ready for the twenty-first century. They don't get their work done on time," grinned Mr. Williams. "I do allow computer time for students who get their work done. It is a privilege and something I can easily control with two computers. I have two games and the students have to figure them out themselves. Not everyone deserves computer time and, frankly, I think the computer is too advanced for some of my students."

Mr. Hernandez cringed, realizing that Mr. Williams wasn't joking. Mr. William's ignorance of technology was a detriment to his students. Worse yet, Mr. Williams was at a school where the majority of students came from low-income families and were not likely to have computers of their own.

Introduction

Not knowing how technology can benefit themselves or their students can cause some educators to misuse or ignore the potential of technology. They settle themselves in a comfort zone of familiarity, unaware of, unwilling, or afraid to explore new instructional methods and uses of technology. While traditional tools can be used with some success, they do not prepare our students for the challenges of today's (or tomorrow's) society. Restricting technology tools to fulfill traditional roles (for example, note taking) is also limited, although when it becomes a means to do something one could not do before (as with someone who has a related disability or as a tool to support language acquisition), it is miraculous. Limiting technology use to a select few is inexcusable (see Chapter 4).

Technology can benefit all learners: low ability, high ability, English-language learners, and students with learning and physical disabilities. It is important that learner needs and outcomes drive the use of technology, not vice versa. As you become more familiar with software applications and hardware devices, you will find times when the computer is the most effective tool, and other times when it is not. Much will depend on the computer's capabilities, available peripherals, Internet access, available computers and software, your students' prerequisite skills, and so on. In any case, technology should be used as a learning tool, not as a means to an end, but as a means to a means, promoting critical thinking and supporting innovation, creativity, collaboration, and communication.

Knowing when to use technology is closely linked to "why use technology." This chapter examines research related to the benefits of technology, its role in instruction, and meeting students' needs. Topics include:

- Promoting Twenty-First-Century Learning Environments

  Multiple Intelligences

  Constructivism

  Cooperative Learning

- Technology and Special-Needs Students

  English-Language Learners

  Assistive Technologies

  Gifted Students

Promoting Twenty-first-Century Learning Environments

There are many research studies supporting the use of technology in the classroom. The effectiveness of technology depends upon the technology selected and how it is implemented into the teaching and learning environment. It is no longer a question of whether or not technology can increase student achievement, motivation, communication, and self-confidence; it is a question of how educators can best use technology to support twenty-first-century student outcomes (ISTE, Partnership for 21st Century Skills, and SETDA 2007; UNESCO 2008).

At one time, the teacher's role was to impart knowledge in teacher-centered instructional environments that encouraged independent work in what many refer to as passive or traditional learning environments. Students sat while instructors lectured. Over the years, teachers' roles and responsibilities have changed. Schools moved from "traditional" learning environments to "new" learning environments. New learning environments included student-centered learning, collaborative learning, information exchange, and active/exploratory/inquiry-based learning in an authentic, real-world context. Teachers were no longer the dispensers of all knowledge but facilitators of learning. New learning environments promoted active learning, higher-level thinking skills, collaboration, and multisensory learning.

New learning environments have evolved into what is now called twenty-first-century learning environments. Twenty-first-century learning environments emphasize much of what is defined in new learning environments but requires "... broad and intensive use of technology and a strong technology infrastructure" (p. 3, ISTE, Partnership for 21st Century Skills, and SETDA 2007). In addition, twenty-first-century learning environments emphasize mastery of core subjects and twenty-first century themes: Global Awareness; Financial, Economic, Business, and Entrepreneurial Literacy; Civic Literacy; and Health Literacy. Skills include Learning and Innovation; Information, Media, and Technology; and Life and Career.

So how does this affect the role of the teacher? It means promoting creativity and innovation; critical thinking and problem solving; communication and collaboration; information, media, and communication literacy; flexibility and adaptability; initiative and self-direction; social and cross-cultural skills; productivity and accountability; and leadership and responsibility—a far cry from standing in front of a classroom and giving a lecture.

In his book, *A Whole New Mind: Why Right-Brainers Will Rule the Future*, Daniel Pink (2006) describes how society evolved from an Agriculture Age (farmers) to the Industrial Age (factory workers), from the Industrial Age to the Information Age (knowledge workers), and now, how society is evolving from the Information Age into a Conceptual Age—"... a society of creators and empathizers, of pattern recognizers and meaning makers" (p. 50). According to Pink, affluence, technological progress, and globalization drive our evolution. He states, "Mere survival today depends on being able to do something that overseas knowledge workers can't do cheaper, that powerful computers can't do faster, and that satisfies one of the nonmaterial, transcendent desires of an abundant age" (p. 51).

Technology continues to be a defining force in our society. Saettler (1990) documents this, noting how proponents of new educational technologies seemed to promise their technology would suddenly make kids want to come to school, solve all of our educational woes, and replace teachers. These promises have been unfulfilled for more than 100 years. Still, it strikes fear in many teachers that they may one day be replaced by computers or other technology. It is not the teacher who is being replaced; it is the instructional environment that is being replaced, and unless teachers are able and willing to work in these new instructional environments, the teacher—no matter how learned—will become obsolete.

Educators need to be in touch, aware, and prepared to work with students submersed in a multi-sensory, digital world of, perhaps, overstimulation. This means understanding and becoming a part of their students' world because their world is the future. Their world is about creativity and innovation, critical thinking and problem solving, communication and collaboration, and globalization. It means staying abreast of the latest educational technologies and delivery systems, engaging in professional development to become competent with new technology tools, and focusing on the outcomes of twenty-first-century learning skills rather than on a particular technology or software program. Technology will continue to evolve, as will software. Educators must focus on technology as a learning tool rather than a tool within itself. Educators need to move "... beyond narrowly focused 'computer courses' to deploying technology more broadly, improving student performance and revitalizing the classroom experience" (p. 3, CDW-G 2006). Technology should be an integral component of all coursework, implemented to support twenty-first-century learning skills.

Educators, like their students, need to embrace technology as a tool for learning, sharing, creating, problem solving, and communicating. In order to do this, educators need the tools and the support (for example, professional development, release time, funding, etc.) to enable them to create technology-rich environments (online or face-to-face) to support twenty-first-century learning outcomes. Even with the tools and support, however, educators must be willing to take on the challenges of stepping into a new learning and instructional environment. If the educator is unwilling to move forward and step into the twenty-first-century learning and teaching environment, the loss to students is great—especially to those who may be coming from disadvantaged backgrounds.

Twenty-first century learning environments promote active learning, higher-level thinking skills, conceptual understanding, inquiry and investigation, apprenticing with experts, differentiated instruction, collaboration, and multisensory stimulation. Understanding multiple intelligences can help educators address differentiated instruction and multisensory stimulation; creating constructive learning environments can help educators engage their students in active learning, higher-level thinking skills, conceptual understanding, and inquiry and investigation; and placing students in cooperative learning situations can promote collaboration and apprenticing with experts.

Multiple Intelligences

Technology can help students learn by addressing their intellectual profiles. Gardner (1999) and others (Samples 1992; Sternberg 1994) have developed theories suggesting that students possess several different intelligences or ways of knowing. Of these theories, Gardner's (1983, 1999, and 2006) is the most recognized. He suggests students have at least eight different intelligences:

1. Linguistic intelligence—the ability to use words effectively, whether orally or in writing.

2. Logical-mathematical intelligence—the capacity to use numbers effectively and to reason well.

3. Spatial intelligence—the ability to perceive the visual-spatial world accurately and to perform transformations based upon those perceptions.

4. Bodily-kinesthetic intelligence—expertise in using one's body to express ideas and feelings and facility in using one's hands to produce or transform things.

5. Musical intelligence—the ability to perceive, discriminate, transform, and express musical forms.

6. Interpersonal intelligence—the ability to perceive and make distinctions in the moods, intentions, motivations, and feelings of other people.

7. Intrapersonal intelligence—self-knowledge and the ability to act on the basis of that knowledge.

8. Naturalist intelligence—expertise in the recognition and classification of living and non-living forms within one's environment.

Advancements in technology and software design now make it easier for educators to find software that addresses multimodal and multimedia approaches to learning. Well-designed applications present content in a variety of media formats—providing sound, text, graphics, and video—and allow students to use their own individual learning styles. Students no longer are limited to reading about a famous event or person; now they can see, hear, and often interact with the topic of study. Computers enable students to receive immediate and corrective feedback, review what they have learned as often as they wish, and receive individualized instruction.

Technology has opened up students to a world of learning opportunities—literally. The Internet and cell phone technologies are common, everyday communication tools in today's society. They provide learning experiences and opportunities that are unavailable in the traditional classroom, enhancing linguistic and other intelligences.

Multimedia production tools (for example, HyperStudio by Roger Wagner, Kid Pix by The Learning Company, Microworlds by LCSI, and iMovie by Apple) can be used to address different intelligences. In their book, *Multimedia Projects in the Education: Designing, Producing, and Assessing* (3rd ed.), Ivers and Barron (2006) discuss how students are placed into design teams and describe the role of multiple intelligences in the creation of multimedia projects (see Table 3.1).

Ivers and Barron (2006) note that, "one of the many benefits of developing multimedia projects is that it allows students to construct and communicate knowledge in various ways" (p. 6). Although multimedia applications can effectively teach content, student-created multimedia projects and other forms of student-led projects allow students to gain skills beyond content-area knowledge. Publishing their work via podcasts enables students (and teachers) to share their work globally. Kid Pix, iMovie, HyperStudio, and many other programs support exporting projects to iPod video format.

Constructivism

Technology can help students learn by allowing them to construct knowledge. Constructivist principals emphasize inquiry, decision making, problem solving, critical thinking, creativity, and

Table 3.1 Roles of Multiple Intelligence in the Creation of Multimedia Projects

Intelligence	Observed Student Behaviors	Leadership Roles in Multimedia Projects
Linguistic	Loves to read books, write, and tell stories; good memory for names, dates, and trivia; communicates well	Gather and develop text for project; provide narration; keep journal of group progress
Logical-mathematical	Excels in math; has strong problem-solving skills; enjoys playing strategy games and working on logic puzzles	Design flowchart; write scripting and programming code; develop navigation routes
Spatial	Needs a mental or physical picture to best understand things; draws figures that are advanced for age; doodles a lot	Create graphics, animation, and other visual media for project; design layout
Body-kinesthetic	Excels in one or more sports; good fine motor skills; tendency to move around, touch things, and gesture	Keyboard information; manipulate objects with mouse; operate multimedia equipment
Musical	Remembers melodies; recognizes when music is off-key; has a good singing voice; plays an instrument; hums a lot	Identify works for content integration; create musical score for project; input audio/sound effects
Interpersonal	Enjoys socializing with peers; has leadership skills; has good sense of empathy and concern for others	Coordinate group efforts; help set group goals; help solve group disputes
Intrapersonal	Has strong sense of self; is confident; prefers working alone; has high self-esteem; displays independence	Conduct independent research to share with teammates; pilot test multimedia projects; lead multimedia presentations
Naturalist	Enjoys the outdoors, plants, and animals; easily recognizes and classifies things within his/her environment	Collect or video outside elements for incorporation into projects; organize project work

reflection. Several computer-based applications support these approaches to learning: simulation software (for example, Choices, Choices and Decisions, Decisions by Tom Snyder Productions, Hot Dog Stand by Sunburst), problem-solving software (for example, The Factory by Sunburst, Thinkin' Things by Riverdeep), and instructional games (for example, the Carmen Sandiego series by The Learning Company). According to Devaney (2008), "Online gaming can help students develop many of the skills they'll be required to use upon leaving school, such as critical thinking, problem solving, and creativity" (p. 1). She also notes, "Studies of the brain have pointed to data suggesting that repeated exposure to video games reinforces the ability to create mental maps, inductive discovery such as formulating hypotheses, and the ability to focus on several things at once and respond faster to unexpected stimuli" (p. 1).

Multimedia production tools support knowledge construction as well. Multimedia production tools enable students to construct knowledge that is meaningful, applicable, and memorable (Ivers and Barron 2006). Studies show that students who are engaged in learning that involves multimodal design typically outperform students who learn using traditional approaches with single modes (Metiri Group 2008).

Cooperative Learning

Technology can help students learn by encouraging the use of cooperative groups and pairs. Working together encourages collaborative help-seeking and help-giving, peer teaching, the accommodation of individual differences, increases use of metacognitive and elaboration strategies, self-reflection, increased motivation and performance, and positive attitudes toward learning (Adams and Hamm 2008; Stansbury 2008; and Tan and Cheung 2008). [Several] computer programs are specifically designed for cooperative group learning—[many] by Tom Snyder Productions—while others encourage the use of cooperative groups (for example, The Oregon Trail by the Learning Company, Crosscountry USA by Ingenuity Works, and the Carmen Sandiego series by The Learning Company). Ivers and Barron (2006) recommend placing students in cooperative groups when designing multimedia projects, noting benefits related to learning, student interactions, time, resources, and classroom management. Blogs, wikis, discussion forums, and other online communication tools also support cooperative and collaborative learning.

Technology and Special-Needs Students

Understanding the benefits of technology and how technology can help students learn can assist educators in supporting all learners, especially those with special needs. Special-needs students include those with limited English proficiency, physical challenges, learning disabilities, and gifted talents. This section examines technology resources for English-language learners and assistive technologies for physically challenged and learning-disabled students. It addresses how technology can support gifted learners, also.

English-Language Learners

Students with limited English proficiency, or English-language learners (ELL), can benefit from technology in multiple ways. Multimedia software and production tools provide ELL students with a richer linguistic environment—one that accommodates their needs by providing animations, video, and graphics to demonstrate difficult concepts, as well as clear audio to model correct pronunciation and to repeat sounds and words (Waters 2007). Burns (1996) notes that "integrating technology throughout the instructional program not only pays off in terms of language proficiency, it also creates students who feel comfortable with and enjoy using twenty-first-century technology" (p. 51). Knox and Anderson-Inman (2001) describe how ELL students use wireless laptops to communicate with note-taking/mentoring partners. Note takers and students use a collaborative word-processing and graphics program on wireless, networked computers. Students can read the note taker's translation of key words and what the teacher says. According to Knox and Anderson-Inman (2001, p. 20), "the note taker writes about what the teacher says in a combination of English and Spanish, which challenges the students to learn the content-area vocabulary of the class while supporting their understanding of what is expected of them." Results of the program include ELL students earning higher grades, developing written and spoken English skills, improving their computer skills, and enhancing their self-confidence. Online language-learning communities, games, and other interactive tools are available to assist ELL students as well.

Programs specifically designed for ELL students are referred to as Computer Assisted Language Learning (CALL) applications. These programs are designed to assist English-language instruction, helping students develop key language skills. Table 3.2 provides information about several CALL programs.

Table 3.2. CALL Programs

Name of Program	Grade Levels	Platform	Product Information
The Rosetta Stone	K-12	Mac/PC	Rosetta Stone http://www.rosettastone.com/ • All level learners
ESL ReadingSmart	4-12	Online	ESL ReadingSmart http://www.eslreadingsmart.com/ • All level learners • Web-based
I Speak English	K-12	PC	Intechnica International http://www.intechnica.com/ • All level learners
Tell Me More	9-12	PC, mobile devices	Tell Me More http://www.tellmemorestore.com/ • All level learners • Free demo available
Let's Go English Language Learning	K-5	Mac/PC	DynEd International, Inc. http://www.dyned.com/products/lg/ • Beginning or early intermediate level learners • Other ELL programs available
Longman English Interactive	9-12	Online	Pearson Education, Inc. http://www.longmanenglishinteractive.com/ • Beginning to intermediate level learners • Free thirty-day trial for instructors
English Language Learning Instruction System (ELLIS)	K-12	Mac/PC	Pearson Education, Inc. http://www.pearsonschool.com/ • Beginning to intermediate level learners
Core Reading & Vocabulary Development	6-12	Mac/PC	ESL.net http://www.esl.net/core_reading.html • Beginning level learners
Focus on Grammar	9-12	PC	Exceller Software Corporation http://www.exceller.com/ • All levels

Good CALL software simulates the natural language learning process, focusing on listening comprehension, reading comprehension, speaking, and writing. CALL software often provides real-life images, written text, and voices of native speakers; an interactive learning process; key language skills; self-pacing; assessment tools for the student and teacher; a management system allowing teachers to customize the program for each student; and written materials that reinforce and expand the students' learning.

Bilingual and translation programs are available, too. Bilingual and translation programs can be used to assist ELL learners with assignments. Translation programs also may be used to communicate with parents. Note that mechanical translations may not always be correct, so it is a good idea to have someone who knows the language review the results of the translation program. Commercial translation programs include Instant Spanish by Bilingual Software, Easy Translator by Transparent Language, and Systran Language Translator by Systran. AltaVista provides a free online translation program called Babel Fish at http://babelfish.altavista.com/. Google also provides free language translation tools (http://www.google.com/language_tools). Companies that produce bilingual software include The Learning Company, Optimum Resources, and Tom Snyder Productions.

Other resources for teachers working with ELL students and parents include products that offer multilanguage features, allowing users to change the language of the user interface and Help, as well as use proofing tools (for example, spell checkers and grammar checkers) for editing different languages. Microsoft Office offers these features. Many companies develop their software for international markets (for example, Microsoft, Apple, Corel, and Lotus). These companies have other language versions of their products—you just have to ask for them. Keyboard overlays to support various languages are available, too. One resource is DataCal (http://www.datacal.com/).

There are multiple computer-based resources to assist ELL students: multimedia software and production tools, CALL applications, bilingual software, and computerized text translators. There are numerous Internet resources related to ELL instruction, too. These include:

- The National Association for Bilingual Education
  http://www.nabe.org/

- Activities for ESL Students
  http://a4esl.org/

- Interesting Things for ESL Students
  http://www.manythings.org/

- The Internet TESL Journal
  http://iteslj.org/

- The National Clearinghouse for English Language Acquisition and Language Instruction Education
  http://www.ncela.gwu.edu/

Additional resources for locating and learning more about different resources for ELL and other special-needs students are available at the end of this chapter.

Assistive Technologies

The Education of All Handicapped Children Act, the Americans with Disabilities Act, Individuals with Disabilities Education Act (IDEA), and other federal laws have been written to protect people with disabilities. These laws help to ensure students equal access to educational opportunities, services, facilities, and employment. For example, Section 508 of the Rehabilitation Act requires federal agencies to make their electronic and other information technologies accessible to people with disabilities. States that received federal funding through specific technology grants also must meet these requirements. This has impacted Web page design. For example, in order for a Web page to be 508 compliant, it must be accessible to those who are hearing or visually impaired. Among other things, this means audio must have captions (for those who are hearing impaired) and pictures must have written descriptions (for Braille or voice-based systems for those who are visually impaired). For more information about Section 508 of the Rehabilitation Act, see http://www.section508.gov/. The Adaptive Technology Resource Center provides a Web accessibility checker at http://checker.atrc.utoronto.ca/.

IDEA requires educators to consider assistive technologies when planning an individualized education program (IEP) for students with disabilities (U.S. Department of Education, 2006). Fortunately, there are numerous technologies available to assist students with physical, learning, and other challenges. Assistive technologies for the computer include specially designed software, input devices, and output devices.

Software

Speech recognition, speech output, word prediction, and display software offer assistance to students with vision-related problems. Speech or voice recognition software allows students to verbalize a command, for example, "Save File," as well as dictate, edit, and revise documents. Products are available to help users "verbally" navigate the Internet, control mobile devices, interact with their cars, provide game commands, control household appliances, and much more. Several speech recognition products are listed in Table 3.3.

Table 3.3. Speech Recognition Software

Product	Company
Dragon NaturallySpeaking®	Nuance http://www.nuance.com/
Embedded ViaVoice	IBM http://www-306.ibm.com/software/pervasive/embedded_viavoice/
Voice and Speech Recognition	e-Speaking.com http://www.e-speaking.com/
Say2Play	One Voice Technologies http://www.onevoicetech.com/
MacSpeech Dictate	MacSpeech http://www.macspeech.com/index.php?cPath=85

Speech output software is available for students with learning, cognitive, or vision problems. Most use text-to-speech synthesizers—the computer-generated simulation of human speech. Several are designed to provide output to Braille devices. "Screen readers" can read system icons, menu bars, operating information, and text generated through applications. Some programs are limited to reading back text; others can convert written text into audio files such as MP3 or WAV for CD players or MP3 players (for example, iPod) also. Table 3.4 lists screen readers and other text-to-speech products.

Table 3.4. Text-to-Speech Products

Product	Company
JAWS	Freedom Scientific http://www.freedomscientific.com/ Outputs to Braille devices, too
ReadPlease	ReadPlease http://www.readplease.com/ Free version available
NaturalReader	NaturalSoftware http://www.naturalreaders.com/ Can convert files to MP3 and WAV formats, also
Hal™ Screen Reader	Dolphin Computer Access http://www.yourdolphin.com/products.asp Outputs to Braille devices, too
TextAloud	NextUp Technologies http://www.nextup.com/ Can convert files to MP3 and WAV formats, too

Product	Company
Aurora Echo	Aurora Systems, Inc. http://www.aurora-systems.com/ Thirty-day free trial
Window-Eyes	GW Micro http://www.gwmicro.com/ Outputs to Braille devices, also
Penfriend XL	Penfriend http://www.penfriend.biz/ Includes word prediction and onscreen keyboard for many languages

When purchasing text-to-speech software, you will want to consider the quality of the simulated speech (for example, does it sound human or is it too robotic?) and its ability to correctly translate homographs and other words. For example, can the software distinguish between *live* (verb) and *live* (adjective) in the following sentences: *I live in town. The show is live.* Like other software, text-to-speech software is available in multiple languages.

The Macintosh operating system includes basic speech recognition capabilities, as well as a built-in text-to-speech synthesizer. The speech recognition system allows users to use pre-existing "speakable commands," as well as teach the computer to perform new commands. Microsoft's latest operating system (Vista) has text-to-speech and voice recognition built in as well.

Text-to-speech options are available in many educational software packages, too, including HyperStudio by Roger Wagner, Kid Pix by The Learning Company, EasyBook Deluxe and Kids Media Magic by Sunburst, and the Kid Works Deluxe by Knowledge Adventure. Other options include tools such as OPENBook by Freedom Scientific that allow teachers to scan documents into their computer so blind and vision-impaired students can have access to printed materials. OPENBook converts the material into a format that can be read by a synthesizer and displayed on the screen.

Word-prediction software is designed to help students with language deficits. The program provides a list of words while the student is typing, basing its prediction or list on the context of the text. Many word-prediction programs include other features as well, including text-to-speech, spell checkers, and so on. Table 3.5 lists several word-prediction software packages.

Table 3.5. Word-Prediction Programs

Product	Company
Co:Writer	Don Johnston http://www.donjohnston.com/
Read & Write	TextHelp http://www.texthelp.com/
Aurora Prediction	Aurora Systems, Inc. http://www.aurora-systems.com/
EZ Keys	Words+ http://www.words-plus.com/
Gus! Word Prediction	Gus Communications, Inc. http://www.gusinc.com/wordprediction.html
WordQ	Quillsoft Ltd. http://www.wordq.com/

Display or magnification software is available to assist vision-impaired students. Products include InLARGE by Alva, MAGic by Freedom Scientific, and ZoomText Xtra by Ai Squared. Onscreen keyboards are available, also, including Click-N-Type Virtual Keyboard by Lake Software, and My-T-Soft by Innovation Management Group, Inc. Bookshare.org provides free access to more than 38,000 books and 150 periodicals to qualifying U.S. students with print disabilities. Text is converted to large print, Braille, or into a digital format for text-to-speech audio. Visit http://www. bookshare.org/ for more information.

Both Macintosh and Windows operating systems have built-in accessibility options to assist vision-impaired users, as well as other features to help users with special needs. For example, Windows Vista features an onscreen keyboard, speech recognition, screen magnifier, visual notifications, and more. Features for each system can be found at (Macintosh) http://www.apple.com/accessibility/ and (Windows) http://www.microsoft.com/enable/products/.

Many other software programs are available to assist students with special needs. Laureate Learning Systems designs software for students with language-learning disabilities, developmental disabilities, physical impairments, attention deficits, hearing impairments, vision impairments, and autism; Sign Enhancers provides CDs, DVDs, and books for the hearing impaired and instructors; and Riverdeep provides multiple software titles for students with special needs.

Input Devices

Alternative input devices help users with physical limitations to communicate with the computer. Alternative keyboards, touch screens, trackballs, joysticks, switches, and pointers are some of the options available.

ALTERNATE KEYBOARDS. Alternate keyboards come in different sizes and layouts to assist the needs of various learners. KeyTime provides overlays and software to redefine standard (QWERTY) keyboards to Dvorak and Chubon layouts. Dvorak layouts reduce the amount of motion required to type common English words. Three Dvorak layouts are available: one for two-handed users, one for one-handed typing using the right hand, and one for one-handed typing using the left hand. The two-handed Dvorak layout provides the most common consonants on the right side of the middle (home) row and the vowels on the left side (see Figure 3.1).

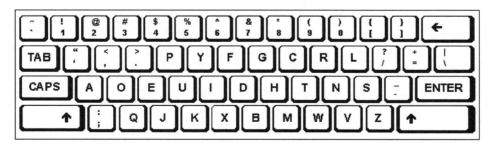

Figure 3.1. Two-handed Dvorak layout.

Proponents of the two-handed Dvorak layout note that the layout helps to increase typing speed, is more comfortable, and requires less effort than the standard QWERTY keyboard layout. Note that Dvorak layouts differ for one-handed typists (see Figures 3.2 and 3.3). Each keyboard places the most commonly used letters near the center and index finger of each hand.

Both Macintosh and Windows operating systems allow users to modify their computers to work with Dvorak keyboards.

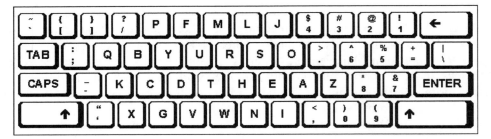

Figure 3.2. One-handed Dvorak layout, left hand.

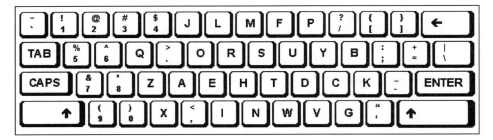

Figure 3.3. One-handed Dvorak layout, right hand.

The Chubon layout is designed for students with a limited range of motion. The layout is helpful for those who type with one finger, a headwand, or a mouthstick. The most commonly used keys are placed around the space bar in the center of the keyboard. The less commonly used keys are placed around the perimeter (see Figure 3.4).

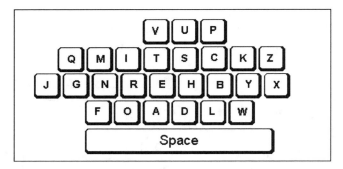

Figure 3.4. Chubon layout.

ABC layouts are available also. ABC keyboards make it easier for students to find letters; letters are arranged according to the alphabet (see Figure 3.5).

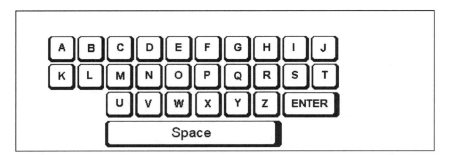

Figure 3.5. ABC layout.

ABC layouts are often used with younger students and those who are easily confused with standard layouts.

Programmable keyboards, such as IntelliKeys by IntelliTools, offer a wide range of keyboard options and allow students with cognitive, visual, or physical disabilities to easily type, enter numbers, navigate onscreen displays, and perform menu commands. The keyboard displays are changed by inserting new overlays into the keyboard. Overlays feature well-spaced keys in high-contrast colors. Different overlays are available to facilitate physical and cognitive access. Educators can customize and create their own overlays using Overlay Maker by Intellitools. Customized, programmable keyboards are available from a variety of companies, including DataCal and Electronic Keyboards, Inc.

In addition to various layouts, alternative keyboards range in size and shape. BigKeys by Greystone Digital, Inc., is a keyboard with keys four times larger than the standard keyboard (see Figure 3.6). Available in QWERTY and ABC layouts, BigKeys provides keys that are easy to read, one-inch square, and brightly colored. Another large keyboard is Clevy Keyboard by AbleNet. AbleNet also manufactures mini keyboards.

Figure 3.6. BigKeys keyboard by Greystone Digital, Inc.

Mini keyboards are compressed or miniature keyboards to assist students using a headstick or mouthstick to type. Keys are closely spaced and allow users to keyboard and make mouse movements. In Touch Systems makes the Magic Wand mini keyboard.

Chording keyboards are small keyboards with fewer keys, usually for each finger and the thumbs (see Figure 3.7). Keys are pressed simultaneously, like a chord on a piano, for each character typed. The Bat Personal Keyboard by Infogrip is a chording keyboard designed for one hand.

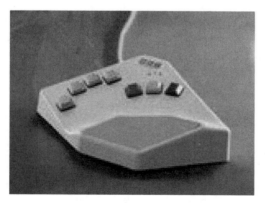

Figure 3.7. Chording keyboard: Bat Personal Keyboard.

Ergonomic keyboards are designed to minimize the effect of keyboard use. Many are "split" into separate pieces, allowing users to adjust them to their individual needs. Makers of ergonomic keyboards include Kinesis Corporation and KeyOvation. Ergonomic keyboards, as well as specialized key sets, custom keyboards, programmable keyboards, and more are also available from Fentek Industries, Inc.

Self-contained keyboards, such as AlphaSmart's Neo 2, are portable writing tools designed for word processing. In addition to a keyboard, these portable writing tools typically provide a small LCD display where users can view their work, a line or more of text at a time. Most can be connected to a printer. Several of these devices can be connected to a computer for transferring documents. Many provide wireless options and a variety of supporting applications. For example, Co:Writer is a word-prediction program specifically designed for the Neo. Accelerated Reader is available for the Neo also.

Self-contained keyboards are available to assist visually impaired students, too. These are commonly called "Braille note takers." Several have e-mail and other capabilities. BrailleNote by Humanware provides a refreshable Braille display, Braille keyboard, speech, and e-mail options. Bluetooth and Wi-Fi are also standard. Users can connect BrailleNote to a computer or Braille embosser (see Output Devices).

TOUCH SCREENS. Touch screens enable users to use their finger or an adaptive pointer to make selections, issue system commands, move and draw objects on the screen, move the cursor, and so on. Touch screens may be built in or attached. Touch Screens, Inc., Keytec, Inc., and Troll Touch offer a variety of touch screens, including built-in and attached screens for CRT monitors, laptops, and plasma televisions.

SMART board by SMART Technologies and Activboard by Promethean provide students with opportunities to manipulate, draw, and interact with information projected to a specially designed whiteboard. The touch-sensitive surface allows students to use their hand or "ActivePen" as a mouse, accessing and controlling any computer application projected on the whiteboard. Specially designed pens enable students to draw, write, or highlight information that can be printed as documents. SMART Technologies and Promethean also offer response systems, wireless slates, and other tools that support interactivity with their specially designed whiteboard. Each company's software supports multiple languages and is compatible with Windows and Macintosh platforms.

TRACKBALLS, JOYSTICKS, AND TOUCH PADS. Trackballs, joysticks, and touch pads are alternatives to using the standard mouse. Trackballs have a ball on the top side of a fixed base. The ball is rotated to move the cursor on the screen. Trackballs vary in size and programmable features. For example, BIGTrack by Infogrip is a large, durable, three-inch yellow trackball designed to help students' hand dexterity. Left and right buttons work like a standard mouse and are behind the trackball to avoid unintentional clicks. Mini trackballs, such as MicroTRAC by Clearly Superior Technologies are available, also, allowing users to hold the trackball in their hand. Other trackballs are designed for specific users. Roller II Trackball by Traxsys is especially designed for users with moderate to severe motor-skill difficulties. It features a removable finger guard to support and guide the hand.

Traxsys produces joysticks for special needs users as well. Cursor movement is achieved by moving a joystick rather than rolling a trackball. Certain users may find this easier, especially those with more severe motor impairments. Any joystick can be made to function like a mouse with Joystick-to-Mouse by Innovation Management Group, Inc. Some joysticks come with their own software that allows users to use it like a mouse. Specialized joysticks such as the Mouth Joystick Controller by Broadened Horizons are operated with the user's mouth. Commands are made with the sip, puff, and lip switches built into the mouthpiece (see switches).

A touchpad is a small, smooth surface that allows users to use one finger to manipulate the cursor. They are often found on laptop computers, but these assistive devices can be purchased and connected to most computers. Touchpads do not require arm movement and some activate mouse clicks by tapping on the surface. Cirque Corporation makes a variety of touchpad products, including the Smart Cat Touchpad with one-touch, customizable buttons at the fingertips.

SWITCHES. Switches are input tools that allow users to control devices with almost any part of their body. Switches include oversized button mechanisms activated by pressing anywhere on the top surface; head-mounted sip and puff switches activated by the user's breath; "no touch" switches controlled by movement detected by sensors; and switches that are activated by the slightest skin contact. Some switches are activated by voice, light, or small muscle contractions also. A variety of switches are available from AbilityHub, Words+, and Assistive Technologies.

POINTING DEVICES. Pointing devices include wands or sticks held in the mouth, worn on the head, or strapped to the hand to help students manipulate keyboards, activate touch screens, or touch switches. Devices such as HeadMouse Extreme by Origin Instruments and Eyegaze Communication System by LC Technologies, Inc., are more complex pointing devices. HeadMouse Extreme is a small, wireless unit that can be placed on the desktop monitor or laptop computer to track the user's head movement.

Head movements are used to manipulate a cursor on the computer screen, in place of a mouse. The Eyegaze system is controlled by the user's eyes.

Output Devices

In addition to sound cards and speakers, there are many hardware devices available to assist visually impaired, communicably disabled, and other learners. These include augmentative and alternative communication (AAC) devices, screen magnifiers, specialized monitors, Braille embossers (printers), and refreshable Braille displays.

AAC DEVICES. Numerous augmentative and alternative communication (AAC) devices are available to assist people who are unable to speak, have a severe speech disability, or may not speak for other reasons. Prentke Romich Company specializes in AAC devices, offering a variety of speech output devices. For example, the company's SpringBoard Lite (see Figure 3.8) is a portable pictorial keyboard device designed for children and other entry-level AAC communicators. Its communication capacity can grow with the user's capabilities. It has built-in and customized vocabulary features, choice of male or female voices, and much more.

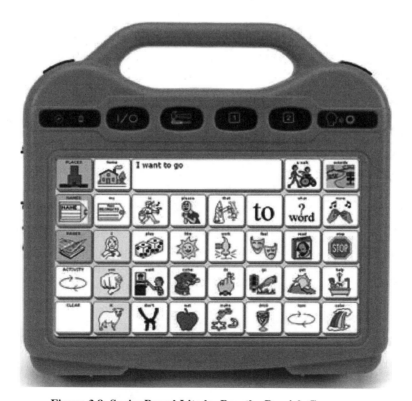

Figure 3.8. SpringBoard Lite by Prentke Romich Company.

The ECO-14 (see Figure 3.9) is a much more sophisticated device, combining advanced AAC features with robust computing. More information can be found at the company's Web site (http://www.prentrom.com/).

Figure 3.9. ECO-14 by Prentke Romich Company.

Zygo, GUS Communications, Words+, and rehabtool.com also specialize in AAC devices. These devices include those especially designed for cell phone and e-mail use, Pocket PCs, and other mobile technologies.

SCREEN MAGNIFIERS AND SPECIALIZED MONITORS. Screen magnifiers attach to an existing computer screen and are designed to enlarge the character display, enhance contrast, and reduce glare. Screen magnifiers are available from Freedom Scientific, Less Gauss, Inc., Kantek, Inc., and other companies. Humanware offers a variety of specialized monitors to assist visually impaired computer users. Their SmartView monitors offer a variety of magnification settings, are ergonomically designed, and provide large control knobs on the front panel. Pocket-sized viewers are also available. Both Windows and Macintosh operating systems include magnifications options.

BRAILLE EMBOSSERS. Braille embossers are output devices used to produce raised Braille dots on paper. Speeds vary among machines, as does the ability to emboss six-or eight-dot Braille. Some embossers are capable of embossing graphics, embossing on both sides of the paper, and embossing in a variety of sizes. Audible command and error messages are available on some machines.

Computer documents must be translated into Braille before they can be printed on an embosser. Several software programs are available to convert text documents into Braille, including Duxbury Braille Translator by Duxbury Systems and those mentioned in Table 3.4. Braille embossers are available from Enabling Technologies, NanoPac Inc., and Freedom Scientific.

REFRESHABLE BRAILLE DISPLAYS. Refreshable Braille displays are output devices that are used to read text from a computer or Braille note takers. The tactile peripheral enables users to read one line at a time, then "refresh" the display to read the next line. The display, which can sit under a keyboard, consists of changing Braille cells as the user scrolls through an electronic document (see Figure 3.10).

Cells are made up of small pins (six or eight), allowing users to read six-or eight-dot computer Braille. A row of eighty cells provides the user with one line of information from the computer screen—equivalent to the number of characters across the width of a word-processed document. Shorter rows or displays (for example, forty and sixty-five cells) provide partial lines, providing the information in more stages. These are usually less expensive than eighty-cell displays. Refreshable Braille displays are available from Freedom Scientific, Enabling Technologies, Assistive Technologies, Humanware, and other assistive-technology vendors.

Numerous technologies exist to assist students with physical, learning, and other challenges (see AbilityHub at http://abilityhub.com/). Technology helps equalize students' opportunities to communicate,

Figure 3.10. Refreshable Braille display.

participate, and engage in the learning process. It is important for educators to be aware of how technology can assist all students.

Gifted Learners

The definition of gifted students continues to evolve. The current federal definition of "gifted and talented" students is as follows:

> The term gifted and talented, when used with respect to students, children, or youth, means students, children, or youth who give evidence of high achievement capability in areas such as intellectual, creative, artistic, or leadership capacity, or in specific academic fields, and who need services or activities not ordinarily provided by the school in order to fully develop those capabilities. (U.S. Department of Education 2002, p. 535)

Karnes and Stephens (2000) report that most states use some form of the federal definition; other states use the definition from the U.S. Department of Education report, *National Excellence: A Case for Developing America's Talent*, or some form of the Marland definition (see Table 3.6). They note that some states have yet to define gifted or talented students, leaving it up to local school districts.

Each of the definitions states the need to provide gifted students with "activities beyond the regular school program." Technology can be used to meet the needs of these children, supporting interests and abilities beyond the scope of the standard curriculum. Technology provides gifted students with opportunities to explore more complex, in-depth, and varied topics; fosters accelerated and advanced learning; stimulates creativity and risk taking; and helps to extend the students' higher-level thinking skills (Duwell and Bennett 2000; Nugeni 2001; Rotigel and Bosse 2007; Wallace 2005).

A variety of software may be used to assist gifted learners. Tutorials may be used to teach gifted students new information, providing self-paced, accelerated learning opportunities on advanced topics. Simulations provide a discovery approach to learning and call upon the students' critical thinking and problem-solving skills. Multimedia and authoring tools allow gifted students to apply and extend their creativity, problem-solving skills, and other talents. Ebooks extend gifted learners' access to material, as does the Internet.

The Internet provides numerous sites that focus on gifted learners. These include:

- National Association for Gifted Children
  http://www.nagc.org/

- Hoagies' Gifted Education Page
  http://www.hoagiesgifted.org/

- Gifted Children Monthly
  http://www.gifted-children.com/

Table 3.6. Definitions of a Gifted Student

Author	Definition of Gifted/Talented Student
Marland (1972)	Gifted and talented children are those identified by professionally qualified persons, who by virtue of outstanding abilities are capable of high performance. These are children who require differentiated educational programs and/or services beyond those normally provided by the regular school program in order to realize their contribution to self and society. Children capable of high performance include those with demonstrated achievement and/or potential ability in any of the following areas singly or in combination. 1. General Intellectual Ability 2. Specific Academic Aptitude 3. Creative or Productive Thinking 4. Leadership Ability 5. Visual and Performing Arts 6. Psychomotor Ability
U.S. Department of Education (1993)	Children and youth with outstanding talent perform or show the potential for performing at remarkably high levels of accomplishment when compared with others of their age, experience, or environment. These children and youth exhibit high performance capability in intellectual, creative, and/or artistic areas, possess an unusual leadership capacity, or excel in specific academic fields. They require services or activities not ordinarily provided by the schools. Outstanding talents are present in children and youth from all cultural groups, across all economic strata, and in all areas of human endeavor.

• Supporting Emotional Needs of the Gifted (SENG)
   http://www.sengifted.org/

• American Association for Gifted Children
   http://www.aagc.org/

These and other technology resources can help teachers meet the needs of their gifted students.

Summary

Technology can benefit all learners: low ability, high ability, English-language learners, and students with learning and physical disabilities. Technology can help teachers address students' multiple intelligences, support constructivist learning environments, and facilitate cooperative learning. Numerous resources are available to assist English-language learners and students who are physically, mentally, or emotionally challenged. Although there are a variety of hardware and software products available to assist students with special needs, teachers' choices and implementation of these products determine the effectiveness of the technology. Teachers need to use technology as a learning tool, not as a means to an end, but as a means to a means, promoting critical thinking and supporting innovation, creativity, collaboration, and communication as well as other twenty-first-century learning skills.

Activities

1. Consider your own preference of style of learning. According to Gardner's Theory of Intelligence, list your intellectual strengths and weaknesses. Discuss how this might affect your instructional approach. Describe how you can address a variety of modalities during instruction. Create a lesson to demonstrate this.

2. Discuss and compare the free translations programs available at http://babelfish.yahoo.com/ and http://www.google.com/language_tools). Work with a partner who is proficient in another language so you can assess the accuracy of each program.

3. Describe the current technologies and other resources that are available in your school and district to assist students with physical challenges.

4. Explore and describe the accessibility features for the Macintosh or Windows operating system.

5. Discuss how your school or district defines gifted learners. Describe the programs and resources that are available in your school or district to assist gifted learners.

6. Visit and write a brief summary describing two of the sites that focus on gifted learners on pages 57–58.

7. Visit and write a brief summary of at least five of the resources in the Resources section at the end of this chapter.

Resources

AbilityHub
http://www.abilityhub.com/

Ai Squared
http://www.aisquared.com/

AlphaSmart, Inc.
http://www.alphasmart.com/

Alva
http://www.aagi.com/

Assistive Technologies
http://www.assistivetechnologies.com/

Bilingual Software
http://www.bilingualsoftware.com/

Broadened Horizons
http://www.broadenedhorizons.com/

Cirque Corporation
http://www.cirque.com/

Clearly Superior Technologies
http://clearlysuperiortech.com/

DataCal
http://www.datacal.com/

Don Johnston
http://www.donjohnston.com/

Duxbury Systems, Inc.
http://www.duxburysystems.com/

Enabling Technologies
http://www.brailler.com/index.htm

Fentek Industries, Inc.
http://www.fentek-ind.com/

Freedom Scientific
http://www.freedomscientific.com/

Greystone Digital, Inc.
http://www.bigkeys.com/

GUS Communications Devices, Inc.
http://www.gusinc.com/

Humanware
http://www.humanware.com/

In Touch Systems
http://www.magicwandkeyboard.com/

Infogrip, Inc.
http://www.infogrip.com/default.asp

Ingenuity Works
http://www.ingenuityworks.com/

Innovation Management Group, Inc.
http://www.imgpresents.com/joy2mse/j2m.htm

IntelliTools
http://www.intellitools.com/

Kantek, Inc.
http://www.kantek.com/

KeyOvation
http://www.keyovation.com/

Keytec, Inc.
http://www.magictouch.com/

KeyTime, Inc.
http://www.keytime.com/

Kinesis Corporation
http://www.kinesis-ergo.com/

Knowledge Adventure
http://www.knowledgeadventure.com/

Lake Software
http://www.lakefolks.org/

Laureate Learning Systems
http://www.laureatelearning.net/

LC Technologies, Inc.
http://www.eyegaze.com/

LCSI
http://www.microworlds.com/

The Learning Company
http://www.learningcompany.com/

Less Gauss, Inc.
http://www.lessgauss.com/

NanoPac Inc.
http://www.nanopac.com/

Optimum Resources
http://www.stickybear.com/

Origin Instruments
http://orin.com/index.htm

Prentke Romich Company
http://www.prentrom.com/

Promethean
http://www.prometheanworld.com/

Riverdeep
http://web.riverdeep.net/portal/page?_pageid=813,1&_dad=portal&_schema=PORTAL

Rehabtool.com
http://www.rehabtool.com/

Sign Enhancers
http://www.signenhancers.com/

SMART Technologies
http://www.smarttech.com/

Sunburst
http://www.sunburst.com/

Systran
http://www.systransoft.com/

Tom Snyder Productions
http://www.teachtsp.com/

Touch Screens, Inc.
http://www.touchwindow.com/

Transparent Language
http://www.transparent.com/

Traxsys
http://assistive.traxsys.com/

Troll Touch
http://www.trolltouch.com/

Words+
http://www.words-plus.com/

Zygo Industries, Inc.
http://www.zygo-usa.com/

References

Adams, D., and M. Hamm. 2008. *Helping Students who Struggle with Math and Science: A Collaborative Approach for Elementary and Middle Schools.* Blue Ridge Summit, PA: Rowman & Littlefield Education.

Burns, D. 1996. Technology in the ESL classroom. *Technology and Learning* 16 (6): 50–52.

CDW Government, Inc. (CDW-G). 2006. Teachers Talk Tech® reveals technology access and professional development are driving improved teacher and student performance. Available at http://newsroom.cdwg.com/news-releases/news-release-06-26-06.html. (Accessed April 23, 2008).

Devaney, L. 2008. Gaming helps students hone twenty-first-century skills. *eSchool News*. Available at http://www.eschoolnews.com/news/top-news/index.cfm?i=53586;_hbguid=937dd4fd-2413-42f6-981a-2511115010f6. (Accessed April 29, 2008).

Duwell, M. J. and E. Bennett. 2000. Weaving technology into gifted curriculum. *Understanding Our Gifted* 12 (3): 9–13.

Gardner, H. 2006. *Multiple Intelligences: New Horizons in Theory and Practice.* New York: Basic Books.

Gardner, H. 1999. *Intelligence Reframed: Multiple Intelligences for the Twenty-first Century.* New York: Basic Books.

Gardner, H. 1983. *Frames of Mind: The theory of Multiple Intelligences.* New York: Basic Books.

International Society for Technology in Education (ISTE), Partnership for Twenty-first Century Skills, and State Educational Technology Directors Association (SETDA). 2007. Maximizing the Impact: The Pivotal Role of Technology in a Twenty-first Century Education System. Available at http://www.setda.org/web/guest/maximizingimpactreport. (Accessed April 23, 2008).

Ivers, K. S. and A. E. Barron. 2006. *Multimedia Projects in Education: Designing, Producing, and Assessing.* 3rd ed. Englewood, CO: Libraries Unlimited.

Karnes, F. A. and K. R. Stephens. 2000. State definitions for the gifted and talented revisited. *Exceptional Children* 66 (2): 219–38.

Knox, C. and L. Anderson-Inman. 2001. Migrant ESL high school students succeed using networked laptops. *Learning and Leading with Technology* 28 (5): 18–21, 52–53.

Marland, S. P. 1972. Education of the gifted and talented (Vol. 1). Report to U.S. Congress by the Commissioner of Education. Office of Education (DHEW). Washington, D.C.: (ERIC Document Reproduction Service No. ED 056 243).

Metiri Group. 2008. Multimodal Learning Through Media: What the Research Says. Available at http://www.cisco.com/web/strategy/docs/education/Multimodal-Learning-Through-Media.pdf. (Accessed April 29, 2008).

Nugeni, S. A. 2001. Technology and the gifted: Focus, facets, and the future. *Gifted Child Today* 24 (4): 38–45.

Pink, D. 2006. *A Whole New Mind: Why Right-brainers will Rule the Future.* New York: Penguin Group.

Rotigel, J. V. and M. J. Bosse. 2007. Mathematically talented children: How can parents help? *Gifted Child Today* 30 (1): 17–23.

Saettler, P. 1990. *The Evolution of American Educational Technology.* Westport, CT: Libraries Unlimited.

Samples, B. 1992. Using learning modalities to celebrate intelligence. *Educational Leadership* 50 (2): 62–66.

Stansbury, M. 2008. Tech encourages students' social skills. Available at http://www.eschoolnews.com/news/top-news/index.cfm?i=53593;_hbguid=a6aa6ee2-9494-429a-ab78-0a4f991e2477. (Accessed April 29, 2008).

Sternberg, R. J. 1994. Diversifying instruction and assessment. *Educational Forum* 59 (1): 47–52.

Tan, T. S. and W. S. Cheung. 2008. Effects of computer collaborative group work on peer acceptance of a junior pupil with attention deficit hyperactivity disorder (ADHD). *Computers & Education* 50 (3): 725–741.

U.S. Department of Education. 2006. Building the Legacy: IDEA 2004. Available at http://idea.ed.gov/explore/home. (Accessed May 2, 2008).

U.S. Department of Education. 1993. National Excellence: A Case for Developing America's Talent. Available at http://www.ed.gov/pubs/DevTalent/toc.html. (Accessed May 3, 2008).

U.S. Department of Education. 2002. No Child Left Behind (Public Law 107-110). Available at http://www.ed.gov/policy/elsec/leg/esea02/107-110.pdf. (Accessed May 3, 2008).

Wallace, P. 2005. Distance education for gifted students: Leveraging technology to expand academic options. *High Ability Studies* 16 (1): 77–86.

Waters, J. K. 2007. ESL technologies: The universal language. *T.H.E. Journal* 34 (1): 34–40.

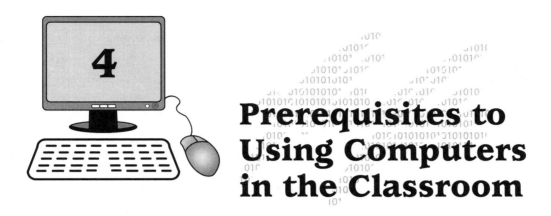

Prerequisites to Using Computers in the Classroom

A Scenario

Penelope was in her first semester of a teaching credential program and felt frustrated because much of what she was learning at the university did not take place in the classroom. She complained to her friend, Clyde, sharing that she was learning some great reading strategies at the university, but had to "read a script" from a teacher's manual when she went to student teach. Her mentor teacher felt frustrated, too, but it was the district's policy.

"And technology," Penelope went on to say, "is a joke. Why is the university wasting my time with integrating technology into the curriculum when our surrounding schools have outdated or no technology resources? Can you believe my instructor wants me to create a one-to-one laptop or shared computer activity and management plan? Our instructors really need to get out in the schools and get a reality check."

Clyde gave Penelope a puzzled look. "Penelope," he said, "if the only tools these students had were a piece of coal and a shovel, you think the university should be teaching us with coals and shovels? Our instructors are teaching us to be change agents, to address inequities, and to teach according to what research says about how kids learn. If we are not aware of the possibilities, how can we initiate change?"

Penelope reflected for a moment and sighed, "You're right. I guess I'm frustrated that some of our classmates get to teach in technology-rich schools and have more opportunities to teach outside of a script! I shouldn't be frustrated with them; perhaps I'm really frustrated with the fact that the kids in my school have nothing and no one there seems to care that these kids are falling further behind. All this talk about twenty-first-century learning skills; how can these students succeed if they don't have the tools at school or home?"

"That's the point," said Clyde. "Hopefully you got into this profession to make a difference. It isn't always easy."

"Well, I can start by talking to my instructor and mentor teacher with some ideas," shared Penelope. "My mentor teacher is very open, but she's not that comfortable with technology. She has a school laptop for taking attendance; maybe I can use that, along with my own laptop, to get started. Maybe I can check out a projection system from the district office or the university."

"It's a start," said Clyde, "and you're on your way to giving these kids a chance."

Introduction

Inequity among schools still exists, especially when it comes to technology and how it is used. Many people may take technology for granted and assume that students are provided with the tools and skills necessary in school for success in the twenty-first century. According to ISTE, Partnership for 21st Century Skills, and SETDA (2007, p. 3):

> The assumption that education already is using technology widely is unfounded. Despite federal, state, and local investment in technology and Internet connectivity, most schools still use technology sparingly, rather than as a critical component of all educational operations.

The researchers also note that schools may teach kids how to be technology proficient, but that proficiency is only the point of entry to the digital world. They state that technology is a very powerful, enabling tool for necessary knowledge and skills.

Schools may be the only place many kids have access to technology. How educators make use of the technology is important. If computers go unused, are nonexistent, or are marginalized, students are at a tremendous disadvantage.

Anyone who has successfully integrated the use of computers in the classrooms will agree that it is much more than knowing how to use a specific program. Knowing how to use a particular program with students is important, but teaching skills are key. Instructors decide what to teach based upon state or district standards, students' background and ability levels, and available resources. Educators continually plan, manage, and assess instruction. They review material before teaching with it, use various grouping strategies, teach proper methods for conducting research, and adhere to school and district policies. It is not any different when integrating technology into the classroom.

As noted in the preface, this book is designed to assist new and practicing teachers with successfully implementing technology into their curriculum to support twenty-first-century learning skills. Before diving into the use of technology with students, however, it is important to examine some fundamental topics related to using technology in the classroom. These topics include:

- Technology Standards for Students

  National Education Technology Standards (NETS)

  State Technology Standards

  Local Technology Standards

- Computer Policies and Issues

  Acceptable Use Policies

  Technology Use Plan

  Gender and Equity Concerns

  Ethics, Privacy, and Safety Issues

Technology Standards for Students

Chapter 1 discussed technology standards and performance indicators for teachers. This chapter addresses technology standards for students. Hence, just as there are grade-level standards for mathematics, language arts, social studies, and other subjects, there are grade-level standards for technology. This section investigates three levels of technology standards for students—national, state, and district.

National Education Technology Standards (NETS)

NETS for students was initiated by the International Society for Technology in Education (ISTE) and funded by the U.S. Department of Education, the National Aeronautics and Space Administration (NASA), the Milken Exchange on Education Technology, and Apple Computer, Inc. Project partners included the National Education Association (NEA), the Association for Supervision and Curriculum and Development (ASCD), the American Federation of Teachers (AFT), the Council for Exceptional Children (CEC), national associations of elementary and secondary school principals, and other educational organizations. In 2006, ISTE began revising the standards, focusing more on skills and expertise and less on tools. The current standards (ISTE 2007) are divided into six categories, reflecting twenty-first century learning skills: Creativity and Innovation, Communication and Collaboration, Research and Information Fluency, Critical Thinking, Problem Solving, and Decision Making, Digital Citizenship, and Technology Operations and Concepts. Standard descriptions and additional details regarding NETS for Students can be found on the ISTE Web site (http://www.iste.org) under NETS.

The NETS profiles describe indicators of achievement at specific stages during a student's progression through school. Grade levels are divided into the following four categories: pre-K through second grade (ages four to eight), grades three through five (ages eight to eleven), grades six through eight (ages eleven to fourteen), and grades nine through twelve (ages fourteen to eighteen). For example, ISTE (2007, p. 12) provides an example of learning experiences that may be experienced by pre-K through second-grade students:

1. Illustrate and communicate original ideas and stories using digital tools and media-rich resources. (1, 2)

2. Identify, research, and collect data on an environmental issue using digital resources and propose a developmentally appropriate solution. (1, 3, 4)

3. Engage in learning activities with learners from multiple cultures through e-mail and other electronic means. (2, 6)

4. In a collaborative work group, use a variety of technologies to produce a digital presentation or product in a curriculum area. (1, 2, 6)

5. Find and evaluate information related to a current or historical person or event using digital resources. (3)

6. Use simulations and graphical organizers to explore and depict patterns of growth such as the life cycles of plants and animals. (1, 3, 4)

7. Demonstrate the safe and cooperative use of technology. (5)

8. Independently apply digital tools and resources to address a variety of tasks and problems. (4, 6)

9. Communicate about technology using developmentally appropriate and accurate terminology. (6)

10. Demonstrate the ability to navigate in virtual environments such as electronic books, simulation software, and Web sites. (6)

The numbers in parentheses following each statement refer to one of the six broad categories. Additional profiles for other grade levels can be found on ISTE's Web site (http://www.iste.org) under NETS.

State Technology Standards

As of 2008, forty-eight states have technology standards for students (Bausell 2008). Some states (AR, DE, MA, SD, TN, and WV) have stand-alone standards as well as technology standards embedded into subject areas such as English, mathematics, science, and history; other states (CA, CO, FL, GA, HI, IL, IN, KS, ME, MN, MO, NM, PA, RI, SC, and WY) have embedded or stand-alone (AL, AK, AZ, CT, ID, KY, LA, MD, MI, MT, NE, NV, NH, NJ, NY, NC, ND, OH, OK, OR, TX, UT, VT, VA, WA, and WI) standards only. Bausell (2008) reports that only five states (AZ, GA, NC, PA, and UT) assess students' competence on state technology standards through a required, state-administered test. State reports that discuss and compare computer access, use, capacity, and overall grades among states are available at http://www.edweek.org/ew/articles/2008/03/27/30dsr.h27.html.

Local Technology Standards

In some cases, districts may be required to adopt state technology standards. If state technology standards are optional, districts may choose to adopt them or create their own standards. For example, Kent School District in Kent, Washington, aligns its standards with state standards and national organizations (ISTE and Partnership for 21st Century Skills) and includes local enhancements. Overall outcomes for Kent School District students are categorized by the following topics (Kent School District 2008):

1.   The student as information navigator.

2.   The student as critical thinker and analyzer using technology.

3.   The student as creator of knowledge using technology, media, and telecommunications.

4.   The student as effective communicator through a variety of appropriate technologies/media.

5.   The student as a discriminating selector of appropriate technology for specific purposes.

6.   The student as a technician.

7.   The student as a responsible citizen, worker, learner, community member, and family member in a technology age.

Additional details about each of these outcomes can be found on the Kent School District Web site (see http://www.kent.k12.wa.us/ksd/it/inst_tech/Standards/student_chart.html), including the grade level at which these outcomes should be introduced, developed, and utilized. The district posts technology standards for teachers as well.

West Bloomfield School District in West Bloomfield, Michigan, categorizes student standards for technology into seven broad areas: Basic Operations and Concepts; Social, Ethical, and Human Issues; Research and Learning Tools; Analysis and Problem Solving Tools; Collaboration and Communication Tools; Creativity Tools; and Management Tools. Benchmarks for each area are provided for pre-kindergarten through the second grade, third through fifth grades, sixth through eighth grades, and grades nine through twelve (see http://www.westbloomfield.k12.mi.us/technology/bench.html).

Not all districts may have technology standards. If not, school committees may create their own school technology standards. Educators need to ensure students' technology experiences develop throughout all grade levels. Standards should reflect recommendations made by state and national agencies.

Computer Policies and Issues

In addition to addressing grade-level technology standards, educators must be aware of their district and school policies regarding the use of computers. This includes acceptable use policies, technology use plans, safety, and other issues.

Acceptable Use Policies

Acceptable use policies (AUPs) define and address the responsibilities associated with using a school's computers and network. Most AUPs include the following components (Barron, Orwig, Ivers, Lilavois 2006):

• a description of the instructional philosophies and strategies to be supported by Internet access in schools

- a list of the responsibilities of educators, parents, and students for using the Internet, including a code of conduct for behavior on the Internet

- a description of what constitutes acceptable and unacceptable use of the Internet

- a description of the consequences of violating the AUP

- a disclaimer removing the school division, under specific circumstances, from responsibility

- a statement reminding users that Internet access and the use of the school's computer network is a privilege

- a signature form for teachers, parents, and students indicating their intent to abide by the AUP

AUPs may be developed by school board members, principals, or a work group of teachers, parents, students, administrators, and staff. By involving everyone concerned, chances are greater that the policy will be enforced and followed. After the AUP is finalized, it is important that everyone using the school network read, understand, and adhere to it. Sample AUPs can be found at the following sites:

- Kent School District
  http://www.kent.k12.wa.us/KSD/PS/forms/IT-001-05.pdf

- Los Angeles Unified School District
  http://notebook.lausd.net/portal/page?_pageid=33,136640&_dad=ptl&_schema=PTL_EP

- South Orange and Maplewood Public Schools
  http://www.somsd.k12.nj.us/media-technology/aup

- Ceres Unified School District
  http://www.ceres.k12.ca.us/cusdweb/information/accptable-use-policy.htm.

- Virginia Department of Education
  http://www.pen.k12.va.us/go/VDOE/Technology/AUP/home.shtml

Educators need to be aware of their school's policies regarding computer use. Although AUPs may emphasize the use of the Internet, AUPs should also consider policies and legal issues regarding privacy, the use and copying of software, spreading viruses, and accessing confidential computer files.

Technology Use Plan

A technology use plan (TUP) is written by a school or district committee to assess the technology needs and vision of a school or district. A two- to three-year plan is developed to address these needs, including an overall vision for the schools' use of technology, outcomes for students and staff, a timeline of events and anticipated outcomes, and a budget that will support the plan. Some states may require districts to submit technology plans before giving them money for school technology.

TUPs address what students, staff, and administrators should be able to do with technology; hence, TUPs are a good place to examine school or district standards for using technology, as well as AUPs. TUPs should address and follow the school's vision for learning and meet the needs of all students. Requested hardware and software needs to strengthen existing curricula and support meaningful learning. Plans should include support for teacher training, a schedule for revising and keeping the plan up-to-date, and ongoing technical support. The following Web sites provide examples of and guidelines for TUPs:

- Central School District
  http://www.csd.k12.ca.us/ed_tech/Technology_Use_Plan/technology_use_plan.html

- Rolling Hills Elementary
  http://www.powayusd.com/pusdrhes/techno/plan.htm

- Fullerton School District
  http://www.fsd.k12.ca.us/FSDTechPlan2008_2011.pdf

- Visalia Unified School District
  http://visalia.k12.ca.us/technology/tup/

- Technology Use Plans in Idaho Schools: Best Practices
  http://edtech.boisestate.edu/bschroeder/TUPS_Report/study.htm

To measure a TUP's effectiveness, periodic assessments must be taken to ensure that outcomes and benchmarks are being met, that is, that faculty is receiving training, technical support is in place, technology is being integrated in the classroom, and so forth.

Gender and Equity Concerns

Even after standards, policies, and procedures are in place, educators must continually examine how their use and portrayal of technology affects students. This includes how technology is perceived and used by different groups of pupils, as well as how educators ensure equal learning opportunities for all students.

Gender Issues

Researchers contend that the difference between girls' and boys' interest in computers is a result of subtle prejudices and unintentional cues displayed by both male and female teachers, as well as parents (Bhargava, Kirova-Petrova, and McNair 1999; Cooper 2006; Holzberg 1997; Plumm 2008). Biases also are present in software, advertising, and juvenile computer books (Bhargava, Kirova-Petrova, and McNair 1999; Bishop and Bishop 2000; Cooper 2006; Gannon 2007; Knupfer 1998). Boys are more likely than girls to participate in school computer clubs, attend advanced computer courses, and play computer games (Bhargava, Kirova-Petrova, and McNair 1999; Butler 2000; Cooper 2006; Mumtaz 2001; Willoughby 2008). There is a lack of female role models, too (Plumm 2008; Sacco 2008).

Gender differences become more prevalent as students progress through school (Christensen, Knezek, and Overall 2005; Fiore 1999; Holzberg 1997; Voyles, Fossum, and Haller 2008). Females are typically less confident than males about computer use, and males are more likely to perceive the computer as a "male dominated" tool (Plumm 2008; Young 2000). Females often form the following perceptions about computers (Bhargava, Kirova-Petrova, and McNair 1999; Bulter 2000; Plumm 2008):

- Computers are meant to be used by boys; therefore, mostly boys use them.

- Computers are like math, a field girls identify with boys.

- Computers are machines, something else associated with boys.

Researchers suggest that the predominant use of computers in the classroom is based on boys' interests (Bhargava, Kirova-Petrova, and McNair 1999; Butler 2000; Fiore 1999; Voyles, Fossum, and Haller 2008). They note that boys are goal-driven and see the computer as a recreational toy, an object of study, and a competitive game machine. Whereas boys see the computer as a simulated friend, girls tend to be more social, process-oriented, collaborative, and see the computer as a tool (Dickey 2006; Fiore 1999). Experts claim girls prefer computer activities that feature real-world problem solving, interesting characters, a sense of purpose, interaction, and writing (Dickey 2006; Mumtaz 2001; Passig and Levin 1999; Wood 2000).

It is important for girls to be introduced to computers at an early age before gender stereotypes steer them away from using computers. In addition to providing early and equal access to school computers, educators must help children challenge all stereotypes and sexist behaviors—as well as confront and remedy their own biased behaviors. Educators can help girls get more involved with technology in the following ways:

- Provide computer-learning opportunities that support girls' interests and learning styles. Choose activities that involve social interaction, are noncompetitive, and focus on process learning.

- Seek opportunities to bring in or discuss female role models involved with computers. Discuss technological careers. Emphasize the importance of computer skills. Promote girls as experts.

- Incorporate the use of the computer across all subject areas.

- Present the computer as a tool to access and create knowledge, a communication tool, and a creativity tool.

- Select software and other materials that are nonbiased. Consider nonviolent adventure and problem-solving software, multimedia tools, application tools, and simulations.

- Beware of software labeled "just for girls" which may reinforce stereotypes. More and more companies are addressing the need to create software geared toward girls. Many of the programs lack content, continue to promote women in stereotypical roles, and characterize girls as interested only in boys, clothes, and being popular. Look for programs that are content rich, break gender stereotypes, place women in leadership positions, and focus on problem solving (see Chapter 5).

- Start a computer club for girls.

- Educate parents about software and opportunities to promote girls' interest in and access to technology.

- Group girls together for computer activities. Research demonstrates that girls experience greater confidence, cooperation, and learning experiences when placed in same-gender groups or pairs during computer activities (Cooper 2006; Crombie and Armstrong 1999; Fitzpatrick and Hardman 2000; Logan 2007; Nicholson, Gelpi, Sulzby, and Young 1998; Rommes, Faulkner, and Van Slooten 2005; Underwood, Underwood, and Wood 2000; Voyles, Fossum, and Haller 2008).

It is important that educators communicate to students (and parents) that boys and girls are equally capable of using computers. If using mixed-gender groups in shared computer environments, assign rotating roles so that each student has a chance of using the keyboard, leading the group, and so on. Underwood, Underwood, and Wood (2000) note that boys have a tendency to "bully" girls away from the computer and dominate the group. The researchers suggest this is not necessarily true of all cultures, however, noting studies involving Hispanic American and Caribbean students wherein mixed-gender groups had positive outcomes. There also are differences in how males and females interact online. Boys tend to take an authoritative stance, disagree, and are more likely to "cyberbully" than girls (Guiller and Durndell 2006; Li 2006; Prinsen, Volman, and Terwel 2007). Educators need to ensure that boys and girls see themselves as equals, practice good "netiquette," and be prepared to succeed in a twenty-first-century society. Teachers need to take a proactive role to make sure every student receives the benefits technology has to offer.

Equity Concerns

Gender is not the only disparity when it comes to computer access. Income, race, location, and education are factors, too. This gap or difference separating the "haves" from the "have nots" is commonly referred to as the "digital divide." It is defined as "a gap in access to technology and information between groups by any of the following: income, race, gender, location, or education" (ISTE 2001, p. 6).

Although Internet access is available in most instructional classrooms (including school libraries, media centers, and computer labs) and student/computer ratios are less than four to one, reports reveal that only 37 percent of public school teachers integrate technology into instruction on a daily basis

(U.S. Department of Education 2007; CDW-G 2006). Teachers continue to report access as the number one obstacle to technology integration. In addition to teacher technology competence, access to computers determines the degree to which technology is integrated into the curriculum (CDW-G 2006).

Home access to computers and the Internet differs among students, with low-income, minority students having the least access (Carvin 2006; Kalyanpur and Kirmani 2005; Revenaugh 2000). Furthermore, studies show that students in high minority or low socioeconomic schools generally use computers for remediation and skill review, while pupils in higher socioeconomic schools use computers for written expression, presentations, and analyzing data (Becker 2000; DeWitt 2007; Volman, van Eck, Heemskerk, and Kuiper 2005).

In addition to providing all students with opportunities to use the computer as a higher-level thinking tool, educators can help narrow the digital divide by ensuring that students have access to technology resources at school and at home. Several options are available:

- Team up with businesses and other organizations to obtain usable, donated computers. Visit Share the Technology (http://www.sharetechnology.org) to locate equipment for donation or to post your own request or Computers for Learning (http://computersforlearning.gov/) to learn how to receive excess federal computer equipment.

- Visit One Laptop Per Child (http://www.laptop.org/) to learn more about low-cost computer options.

- Explore opportunities for financial support. Grant resources are available at Technology Grant News (http://www.technologygrantnews.com/), the U.S. Department of Education (http://www.ed.gov/), and TechLearning (http://www.techlearning.com/).

- Locate and learn more about organizations working toward eliminating the digital divide. These include the Digital Divide Network (http://www.digitaldividenetwork.org/) and the Community Technology Centers' Network (http://www.ctcnet.org/).

While closing the digital divide may not be an easy task, it is something that cannot be ignored. Teachers must make use of the tools and resources available to them, as well as look for resources and opportunities outside of their classroom walls. Educators must insist on providing educational environments that give students equal access and equal opportunities for using technology to support twenty-first-century skills.

Ethics, Privacy, and Safety Issues

Computer ethics, privacy, and safety issues are often included in a school's AUP. This includes references to copyright, student anonymity, filtering software, and other issues. This section takes a broader look at these issues.

Ethics

In addition to copyright issues, computer ethics involves computer fraud and theft, hacking, and viruses. It is important for educators to discuss these issues with their students and to model appropriate behavior. Students should be aware that copyright violations, computer fraud, theft, hacking, and intentionally spreading computer viruses are all considered crimes and are punishable by fines, jail time, or both.

Digital material raises new concerns and issues regarding copyright. New laws have been implemented to help protect creators of digital material, but illegal duplication of work continues. Educators need to discuss the purpose of copyright laws: to protect individuals' work and to provide fair compensation for their talent, time, and creativity, as well as to enable the industry to continue to produce new software. Penalties for copying software without the publisher's authorization include fines of up to $150,000, jail time, and a possible civil suit (SIIA 2008). For multiple copies of software, ask publishers about lab packs (usually five copies), site licenses, and network options, all usually available at a reduced price.

Educators and students also face copyright and fair-use issues when using the Internet. In addition to obtaining permission to use copyrighted materials, students must be aware of the consequences of plagiarism and the need to credit items taken from the Internet. Information on copyright and fair use can be found at:

- United States Copyright Office
  http://www.copyright.gov/

- Software & Information Industry Association: Anti-Piracy
  http://www.siia.net/piracy/default.asp

- Stanford University Libraries Copyright and Fair Use
  http://fairuse.stanford.edu/

- The Educator's Guide to Copyright and Fair Use
  http://www.education-world.com/a_curr/curr280.shtml

Computer fraud and theft include illegal transfer, deletion, or altering of funds or data from a computer system. This can involve hacking, the illegal access to computers. The unauthorized removal of software, computers, and other computer-related items is also theft. Students should understand school policies and consequences regarding the misuse and theft of computers.

By engaging in computer crimes, abusers are often removed from the people they hurt. This is true of those who make and purposely spread computer viruses. A computer virus is a program specifically written to cause damage or mischief to computer systems. It can be spread through e-mail, shared files, and downloads from the Internet. It is highly recommended that computers have antivirus programs installed. These programs can prevent, detect, and remove computer viruses. Products include:

- Norton AntiVirus by Symantec
  http://www.symantec.com/

- VirusScan by McAfee.com Corporation
  http://www.mcafee.com/

- Panda Antivirus by Panda Security
  http://www.pandasecurity.com/

Privacy and Safety Issues

Advancements in technology have created new windows to the world: windows that allow us to look at new possibilities and windows that enable others to look in upon us, creating new issues of personal privacy and safety. Educators need to ensure that students understand the importance of not giving away personal information over the Internet, including where they live, their phone number, and pictures of themselves. Students should understand the danger of sharing such information, as well as why they should not arrange to meet anyone they have met over the Internet without parental supervision. Students need to understand the dangers of chat rooms, social networking sites (such as MySpace and Facebook), and unsolicited e-mail. On the Internet, people can pretend to be anyone they want. Unfortunately, there are many in the world who victimize children.

Educators must take precautions when posting student work on the Internet. These include:

- Never attach names to photographs.

- Use students' initials in bylines rather than their name (for example, The Orange Cat by D.C.).

- Provide information about the class as a whole, not by individual students.

Educators may take additional steps to support Internet safety. They can install filtering software to prohibit students from accessing Web sites with undesirable content and sites that may be considered unsafe. Many schools do this at the district level. Although most software is not foolproof, it does allow a school some control over accessible sites. Many products monitor students' use of the Internet, as well, including the following:

- CYBERsitter by Solid Oak Software Inc.
  http://www.cybersitter.com/

- CyberPatrol by SurfControl, Inc.
  http://www.cyberpatrol.com/

- Net Nanny Home Suite by Net Nanny
  http://www.netnanny.com/

Products such as WebWhacker by Blue Squirrel (http://www.bluesquirrel.com/) provide alternatives to accessing the Web in real time. WebWhacker allows teachers to archive Web sites on flash drives, CD-R, DVD-R, or hard drives so the sites may be viewed later without an Internet connection. Educators have precise control over what their students can view. In addition, the teacher can make multiple copies of the downloaded sites so they can be displayed on multiple computers, even those without Internet access.

The Federal Trade Commission (FTC) is involved in protecting children. In 1998, the Children's Online Privacy Protection Act (COPPA) was passed. This law requires operators of commercial Web sites to get parental consent before collecting any personal information from kids under the age of thirteen (see http://www.ftc.gov/os/2006/03/P054505COPPARuleRetention.pdf). In some instances, teachers may provide consent (FTC 2000).

Ethics, privacy, and safety issues reinforce the need for schools to establish and enforce AUPs. Educators, parents, and students must understand the need for precautions and rules for using the Internet, as well as model ethical behavior.

Summary

Before educators begin using technology with their students, teachers need to review their schools' AUPs and other policies. They should be aware of their grade-level technology standards, issues related to gender and equity concerns, and how to advise students on privacy and safety issues related to computer use. Teachers are role models for their students and need to ensure they portray and teach ethical use of computers. These "prerequisites" will help teachers as they plan to integrate technology throughout the curriculum and prepare students to engage in twenty-first-century learner outcomes.

Activities

1. Go to the ISTE Web site (http://www.iste.org) and locate the National Educational Technology Standards 2007 under NETS. Print the NETS for Students 2007 standards and describe a specific activity that is appropriate for your pupils for each standard.

2. Go to the ISTE Web site (http://www.iste.org) and access the NETS Student Profiles under NETS. Choose the grade category of your students and use one of the sample activities to create a lesson that integrates into your curriculum.

3. List your school (or district) technology standards for students at your grade level. Compare and contrast these to ISTE's standards.

4. Compare your school's AUP with AUPs from two other schools. Summarize their similarities and differences. Discuss how your school AUP may be improved.

5. Compare your school or district TUP with TUPs from two other schools or districts. Summarize their similarities and differences. Discuss how your school or district TUP may be improved.

6. Create a plan to provide equitable and unbiased use of technology in your classroom. Include how you will assess the success of your plan.

7. Create a lesson that teaches students about computer ethics, privacy, and safety issues.

References

Barron, A. E., K. S. Ivers, N. Lilavois, and J. A. Wells. 2006. *Technologies for Education: A Practical Guide.* 5th ed. Westport, CT: Libraries Unlimited.

Bausell, C. V. 2008. Tracking U.S. Trends: States vary in classroom access to computers and in policies concerning school technology. *Education Week.* Available at http://www.edweek. org/ew/articles/2008/03/27/30trends.h27.html. (Accessed May 10, 2008).

Becker, H. J. 2000. Who's wired and who's not: Children's access to and use of technology. *The Future of Children: Children and Computer Technology* 10 (2): 44–75.

Bhargava, A., A. Kirova-Petrova, and S. McNair. 1999. Computers, gender bias, and young children. *Information Technology in Childhood Education Annual 1999*: 263–274.

Bishop, K. and J. Bishop. 2000. Gender and racial bias in juvenile computer books. *Knowledge Quest* 28 (3): 18–23.

Butler, D. 2000. Gender, girls, and computer technology: What's the status now? *Clearing House* 73 (4): 225–229.

Carvin, A. 2006. The gap: Once a hot topic, the digital divide seems all but forgotten, while the poor, mainly black and Hispanic, are still being left behind. *School Library Journal* 52 (3): 70.

CDW Government, Inc. (CDW-G). 2006. Teachers Talk Tech® Reveals Technology Access and Professional Development are Driving Improved Teacher and Student Performance. Available at http://newsroom.cdwg.com/news-releases/news-release-06-26-06.html. (Accessed May 18, 2008).

Christensen, R., G. Knezek, and T. Overall. 2005. Transition points for the gender gap in computer enjoyment. *Journal of Research on Technology in Education* 38 (1): 23–37.

Cooper, J. 2006. The Digital Divide: The special case of gender. *Journal of Computer Assisted Learning* 22 (5): 320–334.

Crombie, G. and P. I. Armstrong. 1999. Effects of classroom gender composition on adolescents' computer-related attitudes and future intentions. *Journal of Educational Computing Research* 20 (4): 317–327.

DeWitt, S. W. 2007. Dividing the digital divide: Instructional use of computers in social studies. *Theory and Research in Social Education* 35 (2): 277–304.

Dickey, M. D. 2006. Girl Gamers: The controversy of girl games and the relevance of female-oriented game design for instructional design. *British Journal of Educational Technology* 37 (5): 785–793.

Federal Trade Commission (FTC). 2000. How to protect kids' privacy online: A guide for teachers. Available at http://www.ftc.gov/bcp/edu/pubs/consumer/tech/tec10.shtm. (Accessed November 27, 2008).

Fiore, C. 1999. Awakening the tech bug in girls. *Learning and Leading with Technology* 26 (5): 10–17.

Fitzpatrick, H. and M. Hardman. 2000. Mediated activity in the primary classroom: Girls, boys, and computers. *Learning and Instruction* 10 (5): 431–436.

Gannon, S. 2007. Laptops and lipsticks: Feminising technology. *Learning, Media and Technology* 32 (1): 53–67.

Guiller, J. and A. Durndell. 2006. "I totally agree with you": Gender interactions in educational online discussion groups. *Journal of Computer Assisted Learning* 22 (5): 368–381.

Holzberg, C. S. 1997. Computer technology—it's a girl thing. *Technology and Learning* 17 (8): 42–48.

International Society for Technology in Education (ISTE), Partnership for 21st Century Skills, and State Educational Technology Directors Association (SETDA). 2007. Maximizing the Impact: "The Pivotal Role of Technology in a 21st Century Education System." Available at: http://www.setda.org/web/guest/maximizingimpactreport. (Accessed April 3, 2008).

International Society for Technology in Education (ISTE). 2007. *National Educational Technology Standards for Students.* 2nd ed. Eugene, OR: ISTE.

International Society of Technology in Education (ISTE). 2001. Feature introduction: Closing the digital divide. *Leading and Learning with Technology* 28 (5): 6–7.

Kalyanpur, M. and M. H. Kirmani. 2005. Diversity and technology: Classroom implications of the digital divide. *Journal of Special Education Technology* 20 (4): 9–18.

Kent School District. 2008. Kent School District Student Technology Chart. Available at http://www.kent.k12.wa.us/ksd/it/inst_tech/Standards/student_chart.html. (Accessed May 10, 2008).

Knupfer, N. N. 1998. Gender divisions across technology advertisements and the WWW: Implications for educational equity. *Theory into Practice* 37 (1): 54–63.

Li, Q. 2006. Cyberbullying in schools: A research of gender differences. *School Psychology International* 27 (2): 157–170.

Logan, K. 2007. Should computing be taught in single-sex environments? An analysis of the computing learning environment of upper secondary students. *Educational Studies* 33 (2): 233–248.

Mumtaz, S. 2001. Children's enjoyment and perception of computer use in the home and the school. *Computers & Education* 36 (4): 347–362.

Nicholson, J., A. Gelpi, E. Sulzby, and S. Young. 1998. Influences of gender and open-ended software on first graders' collaborative composing activities on computers. *Journal of Computing in Childhood Education* 9 (1): 3–42.

Passig, D. and H. Levin. 1999. Gender interest differences with multimedia learning interfaces. *Computers in Human Behavior* 15 (2): 173–183.

Plumm, K. M. 2008. Technology in the classroom: Burning the bridges to the gaps in gender-biased education? *Computers & Education* 50 (3): 1,052–1,068.

Prinsen, F. R., M. L. L. Volman, and J. Terwel. 2007. Gender-related differences in computer-mediated communication and computer-supported collaborative learning. *Journal of Computer Assisted Learning* 23 (5): 393–409.

Revenaugh, M. 2000. Beyond the digital divide: Pathways to equity. *Technology and Learning* 20 (10): 38–40, 44–50.

Rommes, E., W. Faulkner, and I. Van Slooten. 2005. Changing lives: The case for women-only vocational technology training revisited. *Journal of Vocational Education and Training* 57 (3): 293–317.

Sacco. A. 2008. Young Girls Not Interested in IT Careers Due to Lack of Female Role Models, RIM Study Finds. *CIO*. Available at http://www.cio.com/article/354763/. (Accessed May 18, 2008).

Software & Information Industry Association (SIIA). 2008. Anti-Piracy FAQ. Available at http://www.siia.net/piracy/faq.asp. (Accessed May 18, 2008).

Underwood, J., G. Underwood, and D. Wood. 2000. When does gender matter? Interactions during computer-based problem solving. *Learning and Instruction* 10 (5): 447–462.

U.S. Department of Education, Institute of Education Sciences National Center for Education Statistics. 2007. *Digest of Education Statistics: 2007*. Available at http://nces.ed.gov/programs/digest/d07/. (Accessed May 18, 2008).

Volman, M., E. van Eck, I. Heemskerk, and E. Kuiper. 2005. New technologies, new differences. Gender and ethnic differences in pupils' use of ICT in primary and secondary education. *Computers and Education* 45 (1): 35–55.

Voyles, M. M., T. Fossum, and S. Haller. 2008. Teachers respond functionally to student gender differences in a technology course. *Journal of Research in Science Teaching* 45(3): 322–345.

Willoughby, T. 2008. A short-term longitudinal study of Internet and computer game use by adolescent boys and girls: Prevalence, frequency of use, and psychosocial predictors. *Developmental Psychology* 44 (1): 195–204.

Wood, J. M. 2000. The girls have it! *Instructor* 109 (6): 31–35.

Young, B. 2000. Gender differences in student attitudes. *Journal of Research on Computing in Education* 33 (2): 204–216.

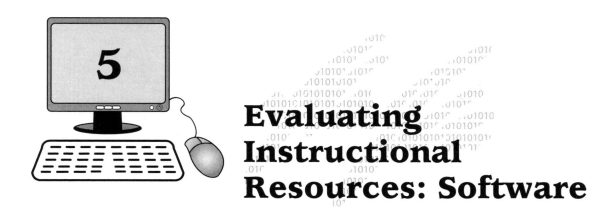

Evaluating Instructional Resources: Software

A Scenario

Ms. Gotham understood why her principal provided her with a poor evaluation of her lesson. The focus of the lesson was on differentiated instruction. She had a variety of learning centers set up while she worked with struggling readers. One of the centers was a technology center; students who finished their assignments early got to work on the classroom computers. Ms. Gotham picked up several new software programs at the local toy store that looked entertaining and encouraged problem solving. They were on sale, and the clerk said the kids would have fun. Ms. Gotham installed the software on the computers in advance of her lesson. The onscreen directions looked easy enough for her students to understand.

As her pupils completed their work, they went to one of the three computer stations. Ms. Monty, the principal, observed several things: one program was beyond the instructional level of the students; another encouraged girls to be popular by going to the mall and wearing lipstick and high heels; and the third program kept freezing on the computer. Among other things, this created all kinds of havoc that distracted Ms. Gotham from her struggling readers. The lesson was a disaster, and Ms. Gotham blamed the computers.

After conferencing with her principal, Ms. Gotham realized the problem was not with the computers but how she thought about computers in the classroom. Her principal went over the importance of not using computers as a reward but as a means to support the instruction taking place. The principal also pointed out the importance of reviewing and evaluating software programs before using them. Ms. Gotham realized she would never provide students with worksheets, books, or exams she hadn't reviewed; why would she think software would be any different? She concluded that she had always thought of the computer as a "game box," something self-contained that kept kids busy and got them used to working with technology. There was so much talk about the need to "close the digital divide" and supporting twenty-first-century learning skills. Ms. Gotham thought she was doing her kids a favor by letting them use the computer in class in case they didn't have one at home.

Ms. Gotham learned a lot from the conference with her principal and, later that week, enrolled in an online class at the local university that helped teachers learn more about integrating technology in the classroom.

Introduction

Just as a teacher takes time to evaluate textbooks, literature, science kits, and other instructional materials, it is important that educators take time to evaluate the software and the Web sites (see Chapter 6) they plan to use with their students. The use of technology should not be considered a reward, fill-in, or sponge activity; the decision to use technology should be driven by the benefits it has to offer students in regard to twenty-first-century learning outcomes in meaningful and applied settings. Simply providing students with computer time and declaring they are being prepared for twenty-first-century learning is missing the point. The key is how the technology is being used, not just that technology is being used. Decisions regarding the use of technology should be based on desired learner outcomes, appropriateness, and other instructional issues. This chapter examines what to consider when choosing software. Topics include:

- Evaluating Software for Students

    Software Categories

    Evaluation Criteria

    Evaluation Resources

Evaluating Software for Students

Educators need to take advantage of the features technology has to offer by taking the time to review different Web sites (see Chapter 6) and software programs. Reviews are available in educational journals and online. Educators may want to talk to their colleagues about certain software titles and online programs. Better yet, they can review the software and programs themselves. Many companies provide free demonstration copies (software with limited working features), trial versions (the program expires after so many uses or so many days), or review periods where the reviewer is charged for the software if it is not returned within the specified time (for example, thirty days). More and more programs are becoming Web-based, meaning they are accessible via the Web and are not platform specific.

Software Categories

There are several categories of programs, including applications, tutorials, drill and practice, simulations, instructional games, problem solving, discovery, and reference. Each has its own instructional purpose.

Applications

Application programs are considered tools—they allow users to create things. For example, a word processor allows users to create text documents, labels, newsletters, and so forth. Digital spreadsheets and databases are applications that empower users to manipulate, sort, and analyze data much more efficiently and quickly than paper-based methods. Several software programs are integrated, meaning they provide users with a choice of using a word processor, spreadsheet, database, and other application programs (for example, drawing and painting tools) within one menu. Microsoft Works by Microsoft is as an example of an integrated or "works" program. It includes a word processor, database, and spreadsheet, as well as many templates and wizards to help users create newsletters, certificates, calendars, cards, and so forth. Integrated programs make it very easy to share data between programs. For example, a teacher may create a student database that includes the students' guardian(s), address, telephone number, birthday, allergies, and other pertinent information and merge this information into letters and labels created in the word processor. Other programs designed to make it easy to share data are called "suites." Microsoft Office is a very popular software suite. The standard suite includes Microsoft Word, PowerPoint, Excel, and Outlook. iWork by Apple is designed for the Macintosh and includes a word processor (Pages), a presentation program (Keynote), and a spreadsheet application (Numbers). Suites differ from integrated programs in that each program in a suite is a separate program; they are not all integrated into one program such as Microsoft Works. Programs in suites may be purchased individually, too, and are usually more powerful than applications in integrated programs.

Multimedia production tools allow users to create interactive programs, presentations, digital videos, Web pages, and more. Multimedia production tools include PowerPoint and MovieMaker by Microsoft, HyperStudio by Roger Wagner, Kidpix by the Learning Company, and Camtasia by Tech-Smith. iLife by Apple is a suite of multimedia production tools including GarageBand, iMovie, iWeb, iPhoto, and iDVD. Adobe markets a suite of multimedia production tools (Creative Suite) that includes Flash, Dreamweaver, PhotoShop, and other multimedia programs, dependent upon the suite purchased: standard, master, premium, etc. Adobe also offers PhotoShop Express, a free Web-based photo-editing tool (see https://www.photoshop.com/express/).

There are many application programs for young children, including word processing, story, graphing, spreadsheet, database, mapping, painting, and other programs. Examples are presented in Table 5.1.

Table 5.1. Application Programs for Young Children

Name	Grade Level	Platform	Company and Product Description
Scholastic Keys	K-5	PC	Scholastic: Tom Snyder Productions http://www.tomsnyder.com/ • Kid-friendly interface for Microsoft Word, Excel, and PowerPoint
Tool Factory Workshop	K-12	Mac/PC	Tool Factory http://www.toolfactory.com/ • Program suite (word processor, database, spreadsheet, paint, and more) • Can be configured for elementary, middle, and high school students • Bilingual option • Also see Tool Factory Podcasting
Kid Works Deluxe	Pre K-4	Mac/PC	Knowledge Adventure http://www.knowledgeadventure.com/ • Word processor and painting program • Create books, stories, letters, invitations • Text-to-speech options
Kids Media Magic	Pre K-4	Mac/PC	Sunburst http://store.sunburst.com/ • Multimedia word processor • Rebus Bar and Text Anticipator • Text-to-speech options

Name	Grade Level	Platform	Company and Product Description
Kidspiration	K-5	Mac/PC	Inspiration Software http://www.inspiration.com/ • Students represent their ideas through symbols/text, simple maps, webs, and other visual learning diagrams • Inspiration, for grades 6-12, is also available • Free thirty-day trial
MaxData	2-6	PC	Tom Snyder Productions http://www.tomsnyder.com/ • Database interface for Excel • Includes ready-made data sets • Three functionality levels for differentiated instruction
Graph Club	K-4	Mac/PC	Tom Snyder Productions http://www.tomsnyder.com/ • Easy to use graphing tool that represents data five different ways • English and Spanish • Free forty-five-day review
Timeliner	K-12	Mac/PC	Tom Snyder Productions http://www.tomsnyder.com/ • Create, illustrate, and print time lines • Internet and multimedia features • English and Spanish • Free demo
Neighborhood MapMachine	1-5	Mac/PC	Tom Snyder Productions http://www.tomsnyder.com/ • Create and navigate maps • Internet and multimedia features
JumpStart Artist	K-4	PC	Knowledge Adventure http://www.knowledgeadventure.com/ • Introduction to art fundamentals • Paint, draw, and animation features
The Cruncher 2.0	3-12	PC	Knowledge Adventure http://www.knowledgeadventure.com/ • Animated spreadsheet program • Includes tutorials and learning projects • Can import other spreadsheet files

Application programs for young children differ from those designed for adults in their simplicity and design. For example, word processors designed for young learners typically have a very simple screen with large letters, icon commands, an uncluttered appearance, and text-to-speech. Some include multimedia tools. Options are limited to avoid confusion. Some programs offer various levels of complexity, dependent upon the ability of the learner. Among other things, application programs support twenty-first-century learning skills in that they can support creativity and innovation.

Google provides many free Web-based applications. Google Docs allows users to create documents, spreadsheets, and presentations. Users can also import existing documents, spreadsheets, and presentations into Google Docs. Google Docs can be used offline as well. Visit http://www.google.com/intl/en/options/ for additional options from Google. Other free Web-based application programs include Zoho Writer (http://writer.zoho.com/) and Num Sum (http://numsum.com/). Zoho Writer is a word-processing application that allows users to create, share, and collaborate on documents. Users can create and share spreadsheets with Num Sum. These applications are also free.

Tutorials

Tutorials are programs that teach students new concepts or skills. After the program provides instruction, it generally checks students' understanding by asking questions or providing practice before moving onto the next level. Unlike drill and practice programs, tutorials teach before they test. Like drill and practice programs, tutorials can help students master core subject areas.

Many programs contain tutorials to teach users how to use a particular feature of the program. For example, a drill and practice program may reward a user with a game at the end of a drill and use a tutorial to teach the user how to play the game. The tutorial is not designed to teach the instructional objectives of the program, so the program does not fall into the tutorial category. Instead, the program remains categorized as a drill and practice program. Some programs do offer a combination of teaching strategies designed to teach its instructional objectives, however. For example, a phonics program may include tutorial, drill and practice, and discovery sections to teach users about phonics.

Mavis Beacon Teaches Typing by Broderbund is a popular tutorial for teaching students keyboarding skills. It provides an introduction to keyboarding and presents keyboarding drills that gradually become more difficult as the student advances. The program tracks students' progress and provides remediation when necessary.

Another example of a tutorial is Math Concepts Step-by-Step by Gamco. The program provides interactive tutorials to help students understand key math concepts. It is designed for students ready to move on to more advanced concepts or for students who need remediation. Practice and test options assess students' understanding as they move through the program. Teachers are able to track students' progress through the program, too.

Tutorials are popular for teaching different languages, procedural skills, and new concepts. Examples of different tutorials are presented in Table 5.2.

Table 5.2. Tutorial Programs

Name	Grade Level	Platform	Company and Product Description
Mavis Beacon Teaches Typing	3-12	Mac/PC	Broderbund http://www.broderbund.com/ • Teaches keyboarding skills • Available in Spanish and English • One handed typing available, also • Provides lesson ideas/activities on Web site
Math Concepts Step-by-Step	7-9	Mac/PC	Gamco http://www.gamco.com/ • Teaches math concepts • Multiple titles available—algebra, geometry, percents, and more • Includes math journal • Tutorials are also available in other subjects

Name	Grade Level	Platform	Company and Product Description
Spanish Before You Know It	7-12	Mac/PC	Transparent Language http://www.transparent.com/ • Customized learning • MP3 audio available for iPod and other mobile devices • Many other language titles also available
Phraze Maze: Grammar through Phrases	7-12	Mac/PC	Word Associates, Inc. http://www.wordassociates.com/ • Teaches grammar • Tutorials are available in other subjects, also
My Reading Coach	K-12	PC	MindPlay http://www.mindplay.com/ • Teaches sounds, phonemic rules, decoding strategies, and more • Free reading aptitude test at http://www.test4free.com/
Fractions with Professor Von Strudel	2-6	Mac/PC	Micrograms Software http://www.micrograms.com/ • Animated professor teaches about fractions and guides students' instruction • Work is monitored, supported, and tracked • Teacher can individualize instruction

Web resources include Atomic Learning (http://movies.atomiclearning.com/) and Net Frog (http://frog.edschool.virginia.edu/). Atomic Learning provides simple tutorials or "how to's" for a variety of applications. Net Frog provides online tutorial/simulations for dissecting a frog. Many publishers provide supplemental, online material and tutorials to accompany their textbooks. For example, Holt, Rinehart and Winston (http://www.hrw.com/) provide "Lesson Tutorial Videos" to complement their mathematics textbooks for middle and high school students. There are numerous "tutorials" on the Web; however, not all conform to the standard definition of a tutorial. In some cases, you may find a "tutorial" that is a text paragraph of information without any follow-up. A "true" tutorial will check for understanding following modules or "chunks" of instruction.

Drill and Practice

Drill and practice programs are designed to reinforce concepts and skills that have already been taught. They test before they teach. For example, in Reading Who? Reading You! by Sunburst, students receive groups of words in small increments to help them with letter and word knowledge. Students receive positive reinforcement for correct answers and opportunities to try again for incorrect answers. Students build upon their skills as they advance through the program.

Most drill and practice are highly motivating. Several come in game formats or offer games as a reward for students' work. For example, Ultimate Math Invaders by The Learning Company is based on the old arcade game Space Invaders. Students shoot correct answers within a 3-D animated space environment. The Math Blaster series by Knowledge Adventure has a variety of Math Blaster titles for different age groups, each with its own Math Blaster theme and set of activities and games. Gamco also produces several arcade style games to help students learn basic skills.

Programs vary in sophistication. Several allow teachers to customize activities or enter content. Many track students' progress and provide different levels of difficulty. Some programs provide easier or more difficult problems based on the students' performance. Immediate feedback helps students assess their performance, and printable records help teachers evaluate students' progress.

Like any software, the decision to use drill and practice software should be based on the students' needs. Many students enjoy the game play of drill and practice programs. Unfortunately, in many classrooms, students end up playing games on the computer even though they have previously mastered the content or skills contained in the program. This results in poor instructional use of the computer and reinforces the misconception that computers are just for playing games.

Many drill and practice programs are available across all grade levels and subject areas. Examples are presented in Table 5.3.

Table 5.3. Drill and Practice Programs

Name	Grade Level	Platform	Company and Product Description
Reading Who? Reading You!	K-2	Mac/PC	Sunburst http://www.sunburst.com/ • Builds students' basic phonics skills through games and puzzles • Monitors students' progress
Math Blaster Series	All	Mac/PC	Knowledge Adventure http://shop.knowledgeadventure.com/ • Students practice basic addition, subtraction, multiplication, division facts, and other math skills • Correlated to state and national standards • Several titles available
Ultimate Math Invaders	K-10	Mac/PC	The Learning Company http://www.learningcompany.com/ • 3-D, Space Invaders format • Customizable content • Individual record keeping and tracking • Correlated with the National Council of Teachers of Mathematics Principles and Standards
Math Shop Deluxe	3-7	Mac/PC	Scholastic http://www.scholastic.com/ • Covers eight key math areas • Arcade format • Supports NCTM standards
Clock Faces	2-6	Mac/PC	Micrograms Software http://www.micrograms.com/ • Students practice telling and setting time and using a calendar • Individual record keeping and tracking • English and Spanish

Name	Grade Level	Platform	Company and Product Description
Key Skills for Math	K-6	Mac/PC	Sunburst Software http://store.sunburst.com/ • Students practice key math concepts • Multiple titles by grade levels • Provides assessment reports

Many drill and practice activities reside on the Web. For example, Aplusmath (http://www. aplusmath.com/) is designed to help students improve their math skills. FunBrain (http://www. funbrain.com/), Education 4 Kids (http://drill.edu4kids.com/), Prongo (http://www.prongo.com/), and Jefferson Lab (http://education.jlab.org/) offer a variety of drill and practice games in math, science, reading, and other topics.

Simulations

Simulations provide students with the opportunity to interact in different environments. Students' decisions and actions affect the outcome of the simulation. For example, in Tom Snyder Production's Choices, Choices (grades K-5) and Decision, Decision (grades 5-10) series, students are placed in situations where they must make choices regarding what to do next. In Choices, Choices: Taking Responsibility, students must decide if they will tell on their friend who broke the teacher's vase or keep quiet and hope no one finds out. The simulation presents new events based on the students' choices. Different choices will lead to different outcomes wherein additional decisions need to be made.

Other simulations allow students to manipulate variables or instruments. For example, in Wildlife Tycoon: Venture Africa by PocketWatch Games, students create and maintain diverse habitats. Students must learn to balance food, water, and the animal population. Operation Frog by Scholastic enables students to dissect a simulated frog.

Simulations challenge students to use critical thinking and problem-solving skills. They encourage cooperative learning, reflection, and process learning. These skills and processes help define twenty-first-century learning. Many simulations support one-computer classrooms. They allow students to interact in environments that may otherwise be too dangerous, expensive, time restrictive, or unavailable. Table 5.4 lists several simulation programs.

Table 5.4. Simulation Programs

Name	Grade Level	Platform	Company and Product Description
Choices, Choices or Decisions, Decisions	K-5/5-10	Mac/PC	Tom Snyder Productions http://www.tomsnyder.com/ • Students engage in role-playing activities • Multiple titles available • Support one-computer classrooms
The Hot Dog Stand	5-12	Mac/PC	Sunburst http://sunburst.com/ • Students manage a concession stand • Practice math, problem-solving, and communication skills

The Oregon Trail	4-6	Mac/PC	The Learning Company http://www.learningcompany.com/ • Students cross the West on a wagon train • Social studies, history, and geography are emphasized
Operation Frog	4-10	Mac/PC	Scholastic/Tom Snyder Productions http://www.tomsnyder.com/ • Introduces the concepts of physiology and anatomy • Students can dissect frog
Wildlife Tycoon: Venture Africa	1-7	Mac/PC	PocketWatch Games http://www.pocketwatchgames.com/ • Students build ecosystems • Multiple levels of difficulty • Venture Arctic also available
Virtual Labs: Light and Electricity	6-12	Mac/PC	Riverdeep http://www.riverdeep.net/edmark/ • Students conduct experiments to investigate the nature of light, reflection, refraction, and more • Correlated to state standards • Has Universal Access features
BBC Science Simulations	K-6	Mac/PC	Sherston http://www.sherston.com/ • Titles available for ages five to seven, seven to nine, and nine to twelve • Titles include a variety of science topics • Perfect for interactive whiteboards

Variations of some of these simulations can be found online:

• SimCity
http://simcity.ea.com/play/simcity_classic.php

• Cyber Nations
http://www.cybernations.net/

• Lemonade Stand
http://www.coolmath-games.com/lemonade/index.html

• Coffee Shop
http://www.coolmath-games.com/0-coffee-shop/index.html

• Frogguts.com Virtual Frog Dissection
http://www.transbuddha.com/davion/media/flash/frog.swf

• The Jamestown Online Adventure
http://www.historyglobe.com/jamestown/

Several sites offer a variety of simulations and other activities, including Learn 4 Good (http://www.learn4good.com/games/simulation.htm), Energames (http://www.energames.com/games/online/simulation/), and Hypergurl (http://www.hypergurl.com/freeonlinesimgames.shtml).

Instructional Games

There are several categories of instructional games, including adventure, role-playing, board, TV quiz, word, and logic games. Instructional games are sometimes competitive, posing students against students, the computer, or time. While drill and practice programs may be competitive and include game formats, instructional games teach or reinforce instructional content without drilling or providing repetitive skills practice to students.

There are two levels of instructional games: those that engage students in higher-order thinking skills—requiring them to conduct research, problem solve, or synthesize and evaluate information—and those that focus on application, comprehension, or memory skills. For example, some instructional games like Africa Inspirer (part of the Inspirer Geography Series), The Great Solar System Rescue, and Science Court by Tom Snyder Productions require students to conduct research, analyze information, and use problem-solving skills. Other programs present information in a game format, testing students' ability to recall information previously taught. Teachers can download templates to create such games at Classroom Game Templates and More (http://www.murray.k12.ga.us/teacher/ kara%20leonard/Mini%20T's/Games/Games.htm) and PowerPoint Games (http://jc-schools.net/tutorials/ PPT-games/). These games are designed in PowerPoint and are based upon classic and popular television game shows such as *Jeopardy, Who Wants to be a Millionaire, Wheel of Fortune, Are You Smarter than a Fifth Grader?, Family Feud*, and more. Teachers can create their own content for each program. Instructional games, depending on the format, support twenty-first-century learning skills in different ways. In some cases, emphasis is on problem solving and critical thinking; in other cases, emphasis is on reinforcing core subject areas.

Some instructional games provide students with role-playing opportunities like simulations, but there are right and wrong answers versus multiple outcomes. For example, in Where in the USA is Carmen Sandiego? by The Learning Company, students assume the role of a detective and travel through the United States, picking up clues in order to track down a suspect. Location clues are provided to help students travel to the next state, and criminal clues help them narrow down the list of suspects. If students travel to the wrong state, they receive feedback indicating they are in the wrong place. There is only one correct path to find the criminal. Several instructional games are presented in Table 5.5.

In addition to templates, teachers can find other instructional games on the Web. One example is Ace Detectives (http://www.planetozkids.com/Ace_Detectives/index.html). Ace Detectives provides mini-mysteries involving four teenagers who travel the world. Users make decisions to help guide the detectives through the mysteries. Another is Create Your Own Interactive Games

Table 5.5. Instructional Games

Name	Grade Level	Platform	Company and Product Description
Where in the USA is Carmen Sandiego?	3-6	Mac/PC	The Learning Company http://www.learningcompany.com/ • Students learn U.S. geography and trivia • Where in the World is Carmen Sandiego? is available, also.
Science Court Series	4-6	Mac/PC	Tom Snyder Productions http://www.tomsnyder.com/ • Challenges misconceptions in earth, life, and physical science topics in an animated courtroom environment • Supports one-computer classrooms • Several titles available

How the West Was 1+3×4	4-8	Mac/PC	Sunburst http://store.sunburst.com/ • Students construct and solve arithmetic equations as they race toward a finish line
Africa Inspirer	4-12	Mac/PC	Tom Snyder Productions http://www.tomsnyder.com/ • Students learn African geography • Supports one-computer classrooms • Part of the Inspirer series
Timez Attack	2-5	Mac/PC	Big Brainz http://www.bigbrainz.com/ • Students solve math and other problems to escape capture • 3-D video game • Free basic version is free
The Great Solar System Rescue	5-8	Mac/PC	Tom Snyder Productions http://www.tomsnyder.com/ • Students investigate features of the solar system • Supports one-computer classrooms • Role-play scientific experts • Great Ocean Rescue also available
Word Way 2	K-2	Mac/PC	Ingenuity Works http://ingenuityworks.com/ • Reinforces grammar, spelling, and vocabulary skills • Ten interactive activities • Online subscription also available

(http://www.oswego.org/staff/cchamber/techno/games.htm). In addition to premade games, users can create their own games. Dole (http://www.dole5aday.com/) provides a variety of activities and games to help kids learn more about good nutrition. Teacher and parent resources are also available.

Problem Solving

Problem-solving software engages students in critical thinking, reasoning, and other higher-order thinking skills. Students must be flexible and adaptable in their thinking. These are all key components of twenty-first-century learning. What differentiates problem-solving software from other categories is that problem-solving software is not content dependent. For example, simulations and instructional games engage students in higher-level thinking skills, but the focus is on the content or lessons being learned. Problem-solving software emphasizes critical-thinking skills rather than content.

Some problem-solving programs provide a menu of multiple games or challenges for students to solve. Most provide many levels of difficulty. Other problem-solving programs embed puzzles and challenges into adventure stories, requiring students to solve a puzzle or complete a task before moving forward in the story. For example, in ClueFinders by The Learning Company, students are introduced to a mystery and must solve puzzles, logic problems, and other activities to continue on their journey to solve the mystery. Other programs present students with an overview of a crisis and enlist their help to solve the problem. For example, in Zoombinis Logical Journey by The Learning Company, students must solve numerous puzzles with four levels of difficulty in order to save Zoombini Isle. Other programs provide students with interactive tools to help them with strategic thinking and problem-solving skills. For example, in The Factory Deluxe by Sunburst, students choose and organize machines to produce a desired product. In Puzzle Tanks, also by Sunburst, students fill, empty, and transfer liquids between storage tanks to reach desired amounts. These and other problem-solving programs are presented in Table 5.6.

Table 5.6. Problem-Solving Programs

Name	Grade Level	Platform	Company and Product Description
ClueFinders Series	3-6	Mac/PC	The Learning Company http://www.learningcompany.com/ • Puzzles reinforce basic skills in a variety of subject areas • ClueFinder titles target specific grade levels
Zoombinis Logical Journey	3-12	Mac/PC	The Learning Company http://www.learningcompany.com/ • Puzzles are based on characters' attributes (hair, eyes, nose, and feet) • Other Zoombinis titles available
The Factory Deluxe	4-8	Mac/PC	Sunburst http://sunburst.com/ • Students choose and organize machines to produce desired products • Record-keeping options for multiplayer use
Puzzle Tanks	3-8	Mac/PC	Sunburst http://sunburst.com/ • Students fill, empty, and transfer liquids between storage tanks • Bilingual (Spanish/English)
Dr. Brain Action Reaction	5-12	PC	Knowledge Adventure http://www.knowledgeadventure.com/ • Students solve puzzles in 3-D world to escape capture • Other Dr. Brain titles available
Nancy Drew: Message in a Haunted Mansion	5-12	PC	Her Interactive http://www.herinteractive.com/ • Students encounter puzzles and other challenges as they help Nancy solve a mystery • Many titles available
Thinkin' Things Collection 1	PreK-3	Mac/PC	Riverdeep http://web.riverdeep.net/pls/portal/url/page/RVDP_PO • Features multiple activities to address different intelligences • Other titles available
Crazy Machines: The Wacky Contraptions	3-12	Mac/PC	Viva Media http://www.viva-media.com/ • Students are challenged to create different machines • Students apply principles of basic physics

Numerous problem-solving activities can be found on the Web. For example, the classic Crossing the River challenge can be found at http://www.mathcats.com/explore/river/crossing.html. Students must take a cabbage, wolf, and goat across a river, one at a time. The wolf cannot be left with the goat, and the goat cannot be left with the cabbage. PBS Kids (http://pbskids.org/) offers a variety of games, many of which include problem solving. BrainBashers (http://www.brainbashers.com/) offers a number of logic games, puzzles, and other games. Towers of Hanoi (Tower Puzzle) and many other logic and math games can be found at Math Playground (http://www.mathplayground.com/).

Discovery, Reference, and Other Learning Tools

Many software programs do not fit into the above categories. Some software programs are designed for research (for example, *Encyclopedia Britannica Deluxe* by Britannica Online) or exploration and discovery (for example, A to Zap! by Sunburst). Reference programs are generally used for research, enabling students to access material in multimedia formats (text, sound, video, and graphics). Exploration and discovery programs are open-ended, encouraging students to play, investigate, and manipulate different parts of the program. For example, in A to Zap!, various animations and options occur when students click on different alphabet blocks. An airplane flies across the screen when they click on the letter A; students can paint the blocks when they click on the letter P; and so forth. In JumpStart First Grade by Knowledge Adventure, students play games and explore different activities as they learn about various topics—reading, math, music, science, art, and more. Sometimes programs combine a variety of learning strategies: tutorial, game, discovery, drill and practice, and other learning strategies. Table 5.7 lists reference and other titles.

Table 5.7. Reference and Other Software Titles

Name	Grade Level	Platform	Company and Product Description
Encyclopedia Britannica Deluxe	K-12	Mac/PC	Britannica Online http://www.britannica.com/bps/home • Reference tool
A to Zap!	PreK-1	Mac/PC	Sunburst http://store.sunburst.com/ • Students explore the alphabet
JumpStart First Grade	K-1	Mac/PC	Knowledge Adventure http://www.knowledgeadventure.com/ • Students explore educational play areas • Correlated to NCTM and NCTE/IRA standards
Bailey's Book House	PreK-2	Mac/PC	The Learning Company http://www.learningcompany.com/ • Students explore a multisensory environment, learning math, reading, and science basics • Designed by early learning and special-needs experts • Universal Access
Merriam's Collegiate Dictionary & Thesaurus Deluxe	K-12	Mac/PC	Innovative Knowledge http://www.innovative-knowledge.com/ • Audio pronunciations • Compatible with iPod • Integrates into other programs

Name	Grade Level	Platform	Company and Product Description
3D Weather Globe and Atlas	3-12	Mac/PC	MacKiev Software http://www.mackiev.com/ • Geographical atlas • Provides real-time weather • Satellite images
3D Froggy Phonics	PreK-3	Mac/PC	Ingenuity Works, Inc. http://www.ingenuityworks.com/ • Helps students learn phonics skills • Animated environment incorporates several instructional modes • Teachers can customize

There are numerous reference tools and other materials on the Internet. There are online dictionaries, encyclopedias, newspapers, telephone books, maps, and more. Examples include Encyclopedia Britannica (http://www.britannica.com/bps/home), the Merriam-Webster Dictionary (http://www.merriam-webster.com/), the *Los Angeles Times* (http://www.latimes.com/), Yellowpages.com (http://www.yellowpages.com/), Google Maps (http://maps.google.com/), and Great Quotes (http://www.great-quotes.com/). Discovery and other learning activities include Starfall (http://www.starfall.com/), iKnowThat.com, and Google Earth. Starfall provides numerous online activities for beginning readers. iKnowThat.com (http://www.iknowthat.com/) provides an assortment of activities in math, science, language arts, social studies, and the arts. Google Earth (http://earth.google.com/) allows users to explore the world and sky in 3-D.

The Web provides the most current information. Offline resources come in handy when Internet access is restricted or unavailable. As discussed in the next chapter, users need to be cautious consumers of the Internet; anyone can post information and the information may not always be true. This is where another twenty-first-century skill—information, media, and communication literacy—is necessary.

In addition to commercial and Web-based programs, there are numerous software programs that can be downloaded from the Internet for free. Some programs (shareware) may be downloaded on a "buy it if you like it" basis or as a limited version of the program. Developers will send a password to unlock the full version for a fee. Shareware sites include Shareware.com (http://www.shareware.com/), Tucows (http://www.tucows.com/), and Shareware Connection (http://www.shareware connection.com/). Other programs are free. For example, Tux Paint (http://www.tuxpaint.org/) is a free, open-source program developed by volunteers around the world. Tux Paint is a drawing program designed for ages three to twelve. It has an easy-to-use interface, a variety of drawing tools, and sound effects. Scratch (http://scratch.mit.edu/) is a free programming language designed for children ages eight and up. It allows them to create their own interactive stories, games, animations, music, and more. In addition to design, students learn important mathematical and computational ideas supporting twenty-first-century learning skills. The KDE Education Project (http://edu.kde.org/) provides many free software titles in multiple languages.

There are countless software programs available. What matters most is why the teacher is using a program, its ease of use, and how it meets the desired learner outcomes.

Evaluation Criteria

There are a variety of things to consider when choosing educational software. These include instructional objectives and assessment, appropriateness, layout, functionality, management, and support features.

Instructional Objectives and Assessment

Before using a piece of software, educators must consider how it will be used to meet the desired learner outcomes.

• Does the program provide a list of objectives?

• Do the objectives support state or district content standards?

• If the program does not come with a list of objectives (that is, many application programs), how does the teacher's use of the program meet state or district content standards?

• Are assessment features built into the software? If not, how will assessment take place?

Appropriateness

Given the software helps teachers meet desired learner outcomes, educators must determine if it is appropriate for their students.

• What is the readability level of the program? Students should be able to read the information provided in the program.

• Is its design appealing and motivating to the educator's students? A high school student reading at a third-grade level may not appreciate a reading program designed for an eight-year-old.

• Does the program provide appropriate feedback? For example, in a drill and practice program, students should receive immediate feedback for their correct and incorrect answers. Sometimes feedback is corrective (the program provides the correct answer or additional hints) or students are informed their answer is incorrect. Pupils should not be scolded or degraded for wrong answers or encouraged to make incorrect answers. For example, if students are "rewarded" with cute animations stating they are incorrect, sometimes they will purposely choose incorrect answers to see the cute animations.

Educators must also consider if the software meets the needs of ELL and other special-needs students.

• Does the software provide help in the students' native language? If not, does it come in the students' native language?

• Does it encourage cooperative or paired learning? Peer coaching can assist special-needs students.

• Are icons or pictures available to assist ELL students? Text with representative pictures or icons can facilitate language learning.

• Does the program include both text and audio directions and feedback? In addition to assisting ELL students, both options make the software more accessible to students who are visually or hearing impaired.

• Does the program have Universal Access features, allowing touch screens, modified keyboards, or other devices to be used?

In addition, educators must determine if the software is instructionally sound and unbiased.

• Is the content, grammar, and spelling correct?

• Are the instructions easy to follow?

• Can students review material or return to a previous screen?

• Is the program culturally sensitive?

• Are females and males equally represented?

• Are stereotypes present?

Most of these criteria will be reflected in drill and practice, tutorials, simulations, and problem-solving programs. Application and reference programs typically do not include feedback, but other criteria can still be applied. For example, many application programs provide clip art libraries. These can be evaluated for cultural sensitivity, stereotypes, and equal representation of males and females. The evaluation of content, grammar, and spelling within application programs will be limited to directions and onscreen help.

Layout and Functionality

Given the software can help teachers reach desired learner outcomes and is appropriate for the educators' students, the teacher must examine the layout and functionality of the program.

- Is the program easy to use? Consider the time it takes to learn the program or the parts of the program that are necessary for the lesson.

- Is it visually appealing? Consider the colors and placement of items on the screen. Too much information or clutter can detract from learning.

- Is the layout consistent and easy to follow? Students should spend time learning the content, not trying to figure out where the text or navigation prompts will be placed next. Look for a consistent layout. For example, check to see if the text, feedback, and navigation prompts are in consistent locations, and so forth.

- Can students work at their own pace and save their work? Other than timed drills, it is important that pupils are able to work at their own pace and return to the location of instruction from their previous lesson.

- Do sound and other media elements enhance or detract from instruction? Make sure the media elements support the instructional goals. For example, verbal feedback, animal sounds connected to learning more about different animals, opportunities to hear speeches while studying famous people, and so forth enhance instruction. Bells and whistles going off each time a student presses a continue button deter instruction.

- Will the program work on the classroom computers? Not all computers are alike. If the program is being evaluated on a computer other than the one in which the software will be used, check to see if the program will run on the intended computer. Is there enough hard drive space and memory? Is it compatible with the operating system? Some older programs will not work with newer operating systems, and some newer programs may not run on older operating systems. If speakers are necessary, check to see if the intended computer has speakers or sound capabilities.

Management and Support Features

Management features include opportunities for the teacher to customize the program and track students' progress. Many programs also include support materials. Teachers will want to consider the following options:

- Does the program allow educators to enter their own information? This is helpful for personalizing instruction for groups or individual students. Some programs allow teachers to enter their own word lists, mathematics problems, and other content.

- Does the program let the teacher determine which problem sets or activities are available in the program? Several drill and practice programs allow educators to specify which types of mathematics problems (for example, addition, subtraction, multiplication, or division) or word lists (for example, long vowel, short vowel, and so forth) should be available to students. Educators can often adjust the difficulty level, number of problems, and other features, too.

• Does the program track students' progress? Some programs provide teachers with printable reports of pupils' progress, including where they are having the most difficulty. Others provide printouts of how many questions a student answered correctly or incorrectly, but no details. Some programs provide students with a printable certificate when they complete or master a section of the program.

• Are supplementary or instructional materials available to support the use of the program? Many programs are available as school or teacher editions. These typically come with various supplementary materials, lesson plans, and extension activities. Programs such as these are often referred to as courseware. Lesson plans, ideas, activities, and more are sometimes available at the company's Web site.

• Is technical support available? Check to see if there is a toll-free number to call if installation or other technical problems occur.

Other issues to consider when evaluating software are whether or not a printer, microphone, or projection device is needed, and if the software requires or makes use of Internet access, can be installed on handheld devices such as iPods, and supports one computer or interactive whiteboard, whole group, or cooperative learning environments. Educators will want to consider the cost of the software, too, reflecting on its ability and use—within a single classroom, multiple school use, and so forth. Many programs are available in lab packs (usually five copies at a reduced price), networked versions (multiple computers can access and run the program from a school's server), or as a site license (a determined or unlimited number of copies of the program may be used on a school's computers). A software evaluation form is included at the end of this chapter.

Evaluation Resources

As already mentioned, hands-on software reviews are the best way to see whether or not a program is appropriate for students. Input from colleagues and outside reviews is a good place to start, however. They can help teachers narrow their selection of software choices.

Software reviews can be found in educational journals, computer magazines, and other publications. In addition, software reviews are available on the Internet, published by education and parent organizations and others. Many are published in database format so educators can search for programs specific to their grade level, subject areas, and other needs. Table 5.8 provides a list of resources for software reviews.

To conduct hands-on evaluations, check to see if the publisher has demonstration or trial versions available. Sometimes demonstration and trial versions are available from a company's Web site. Some companies offer online tours of their products.

Educators may examine software in their colleagues' classroom if a fellow teacher is using a program of interest to the teacher. County offices of education, district offices, and local universities may have preview centers for reviewing educational software. There are many ways to determine whether or not a program meets the needs of your students.

Summary

It is important for teachers to evaluate software before using it with their students. The software should support the desired learner outcomes and be appropriate for the students. There are many categories of software from which to choose. Each has its own instructional purpose and may address twenty-first-century learning outcomes in different ways. Educators will want to select software that supports their instructional goals and philosophy of teaching. Educators need to consider the

Table 5.8. Software Reviews

Name and Source	Description
Educational Software Preview Guide http://ed.fnal.gov/espg/	An online searchable directory of favorably reviewed software, hosted by the Fermi National Accelerator Laboratory, Education Office.
EvaluTech http://www.evalutech.sreb.org/	Online reviews by trained educators. Searchable database is a collaborative effort among departments of education.
MultiMedia & Internet@Schools http://www.mmischools.com/Categories/ ProductReviews.aspx	An online educational technology magazine providing software reviews and more.
Children's Technology Review http://www.childrenssoftware.com/	Web site and periodical containing reviews of software, Internet sites, and more. Reviews by trained educators working with test families.
California Learning Resource Network http://www.clrn.org/home/	Searchable database of electronic resources that address California curriculum frameworks and standards. Sponsored by the California Department of Education.
Learning Village http://www.learningvillage.com/html/guide. html	Online educational software reviews categorized by subject area.
Discovery Education http://school.discoveryeducation.com/parents/ reviewcorner/software/	Online educational software reviews categorized by interest and age.
SuperKids Educational Software Review http://www.superkids.com/	Online reviews of educational software. Teams of teachers, parents, and children write the reviews.
Education World http://www.education-world.com/ a_tech/archives/edurate.shtml	Online software reviews by educators for educators.

software's instructional objectives, assessment features, appropriateness, layout and functionality, and its management and support features.

Activities

1. Using the "Software Evaluation" blackline master, evaluate two drill and practice or two tutorial programs designed for the same grade level and subject matter. Summarize the programs' similarities and differences. State whether or not you would use the programs.

2. Using the "Software Evaluation" blackline master, evaluate two simulations or two instructional games designed for the same grade level and subject matter. Summarize the programs' similarities and differences. State whether or not you would use the programs.

3. Interview three teachers at your school regarding the software they have used with their students. What software titles do they recommend? Why? Which software titles do they not recommend? Why? Include the teachers' grade level and their computer background (for example, computer training or courses, the number of computers in their classroom, or their comfort level using computers) in your report. Analyze and discuss your findings.

4. Compare evaluations of the same software product among three different review sites (see Table 5.8). Summarize the differences and similarities of the reviews and why you believe the differences and similarities exist. List the reviewers' background (if available) for each site.

5. Contact your district, county of office of education, and local university to discover if they have software preview centers or offer other support for hands-on software evaluation. Report your findings.

6. Visit the Web sites of five educational software publishers and provide a summary of the available teacher resources, lesson plans, and other educational materials (if any) they supply to support their software products.

Blackline Masters

- Software Evaluation Form (1 of 2)
- Software Evaluation Form (2 of 2)

Software Evaluation Form (1 of 2)

Software program: _____ Cost: _____

Publisher: _____ Publication date: _____

Publisher's Web site: http://_____

Grade level(s): _____ Platform/OS:_____

Required hard drive space: _____ RAM: _____

Necessary equipment other than computer, monitor, keyboard, and mouse:

_____ printer _____ microphone _____ Internet access

_____ headphones _____ projection device for whole class viewing

other: _____

Type of program (for example, drill and practice):

Program's special features (for example, text-to-speech, multiple languages, universal access, designed for one-computer classroom):

Program overview:

Evaluator: _____ Evaluator's rating: _____
(1 to 4 with 4 being the highest)

From *A Teacher's Guide to Using Technology in the Classroom*, Second Edition by Karen S. Ivers. Westport, CT: Libraries Unlimited. Copyright © 2009.

Instructional Objectives and Assessment	Yes	No	N/A	
Does the program provide a list of objectives?				
Do the objectives support state or district content standards?				
If the program does not come with a list of objectives (e.g., many application programs), how does the teacher's use of the program meet state or district content standards?				
Are assessment features built into the software?				
If assessment features are not built-in, how can assessment take place?				
Appropriateness	Yes	No	N/A	
Is its design appealing and motivating to students?				
Does the program provide appropriate feedback?				
Does it provide help in the students' native language?				
Does the software come in other languages?				
Does it encourage cooperative or paired learning?				
Are icons or pictures available to assist students?				
Does it include both text and audio directions and feedback?				
Does the program have Universal Access features?				
Is the content, grammar, and spelling correct?				
Are the instructions easy to follow?				
Can students review material or return to a previous screen?				
Is the program culturally sensitive?				
Are females and males equally represented?				
Are stereotypes present?				
What is the readability level of the program?				
Layout and Functionality	Yes	No	N/A	
Is the program easy to use?				
Is it visually appealing?				
Is the layout consistent and easy to follow?				
Can students work at their own pace and save their work?				
Do sound and other media elements enhance instruction?				
Will the program work on the classroom computers?				
Management and Support Features	Yes	No	N/A	
Does it allow teachers to enter their own information?				
Does the program let the teacher determine which problem sets or activities are available in the program?				
Does the program track students' progress?				
Are supplementary or instructional materials available to support the use of the program?				
Is technical support available?				

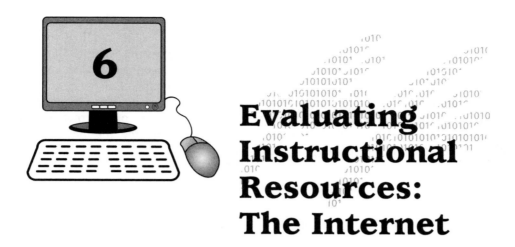

Evaluating Instructional Resources: The Internet

A Scenario

Ms. Duncan recalled the days of paper-based state reports. She was hesitant and unsure of herself when she began assigning multimedia reports using PowerPoint instead, but she soon gained confidence when she saw how quickly her students adapted and how excited they were to use the new medium. The medium was changing again. This year, she planned to use wikis, assigning students in teams of three to cover different content areas of the required state report. By using a wiki, students could easily collaborate online and Ms. Duncan could track their progress and contributions.

Ms. Duncan loved teaching fifth grade. She was amazed at how quickly technology had changed over the years, but she was even more surprised at how her students seemed to evolve with technology. Her current students were "digital natives"—born and raised in a world of digital technology. Cell phones, digital cameras, the Internet—these were common things to them. Ms. Duncan, on the other hand, was a digital immigrant. Cell phones, digital cameras, the Internet, and other technologies were not available when she was a child. She adapted, however, and continued to keep abreast of her students' world. This was important to Ms. Duncan. She knew the past was important, but she needed to help her pupils attain success in today's world and prepare them for the demands of the future. She thought back to paper-based state reports. At the time, they were appropriate and met the needs of students. "Today," Ms. Duncan thought, "students need to be prepared to work in a digital world that demands collaboration, creativity, innovation, problem solving, online communication, and much more. It's my job and responsibility to ensure they're ready."

Introduction

The Internet continues to grow and offer a wealth of resources and opportunities for instruction. Interactive programs, online experts, research activities, virtual fieldtrips, online collaborative projects—these are some of the instructional resources available on the Internet. As technology continues to improve, access, speed, and opportunities for learning and collaboration via the Internet improve.

Since the turn of the twenty-first century, a new generation of tools has emerged to support using the Web for creativity, collaboration, social networking, video and photo sharing, and other forms of information distribution. These "Web 2.0" tools include wikis, blogs, online applications, and podcasts. As mentioned in Chapter 2, teachers can use these tools to support instruction. Many Web 2.0 tools can be used for educational purposes. These, like other Internet resources and materials, need to be evaluated to determine their instructional value, purpose, accuracy, and validity.

Chapter 2 included ideas and activities for teachers' use of the Internet. This chapter focuses on how educators can use the Web with their students. Several categories of Internet activities are described. In addition, evaluation criteria and additional tips for using the Internet are discussed. Topics include:

- Resources for Students

  Web 2.0 Tools

  Interactive Programs

  Online Experts

  Web Sites for Children

- Research Activities

  Basic Research

  Advanced Research

  Original Research

- Evaluation Criteria

  Intent

  Content

- Additional Tips

  Issues to Consider

  Troubleshooting Tips for the Internet

Resources for Students

Just as there are numerous Internet resources designed to assist teachers, there are many Internet resources designed for students. These include Web 2.0 tools, interactive programs, online experts, and Web sites specifically designed for children.

Web 2.0 Tools

Web 2.0 represents a new approach to using the World Wide Web. Emphasis is on collaboration, information sharing, creativity, and interactivity. Web 2.0 tools include blogs, wikis, social networking and bookmarking sites, photo and video sharing, podcasts, virtual worlds, and more. Users are the content creators and consumers. Examples of how some of these tools may be used by teachers are presented in Chapter 2.

Web 2.0 tools can be used to support twenty-first-century learning outcomes. In addition to supporting collaboration, information sharing, creativity, and interactivity, Web 2.0 tools present opportunities to expand students' global awareness and enhance their information, media, and technology literacy skills.

Blogs

As noted in Chapter 2, a blog is an online journal or communication tool that is updated frequently and intended for a specific group or the general public. Entries are posted to a single page, usually in reverse-chronological order. Bloggers, authors of blogs, may post text, pictures, audio, video, and links to outside Web sites, as well as allow readers to post comments. Anyone can create and host a blog.

Blogs are a great way for students to share what they are learning and lead discussion topics of interest. Blogs can be used to support service learning activities, collaborative learning, literature circles, scientific investigations, and more. Ideas for using blogs in the classroom are available at TeachersFirst (http://www.teachersfirst.com/content/blog/blogideas2.cfm). Sites that provide blog service to support teachers with hosting and managing blogs for students include:

- 21classes
  http://www.21classes.com/

- ClassPress
  http://www.classpress.com/

- Gaggle.Net
  http://www.gaggle.net/

- Class Blogmeister
  http://classblogmeister.com/

Wiki

A wiki is a server program that allows users to collaboratively create and edit the content of a Web site using a regular Web browser. As noted in Chapter 2, the most commonly known wiki is Wikipedia—an online encyclopedia created by users from all over the world (see http://en.wikipedia.org/).

Wikis enable students to collaborate on writing projects by adding and editing the content of shared Web pages. Collaboration may take place within the classroom, in classrooms in a school or district, or among classrooms in the global community. Students may create study guides, group reports, community guides, and more (see http://www.teachersfirst.com/content/wiki/wikiideas1.cfm).

Teachers can create secure wikis, requiring users to enter a password for access. Tracking is possible through wikis, also, enabling teachers to assess the contributions of each student. Teachers can use the following sites to set up a classroom wiki:

- pbwiki
  http://pbwiki.com/education.wiki

- Wetpaint
  http://www.wetpaint.com/

- WikiSpaces
  http://www.wikispaces.com/

Social Networking Sites

Social networking sites provide members with the opportunity to share information about themselves and interact with others. MySpace (http://www.myspace.com/) and Facebook (http://www.facebook.com/) are popular social networking sites designed for teenagers and adults. Privacy, safety, and other issues can arise in such environments. Educators need to ensure students are prepared to use the Internet safely and ethically, as well observe etiquette and privacy rules (see Issues to Consider).

Social Bookmarking Sites

Social bookmarking sites enable users to share, organize, and access favorite Internet bookmarks. Users can "tag" these bookmarks for classification and retrieval purposes.

This creates a folksonomy—a collaborative method of creating, managing, and organizing content. Social bookmarking sites identify who posted a particular bookmark and allows users to access that person's other bookmarked resources. Tags can be searched as well, helping users identify and use key structures within the folksonomy. Social bookmarking sites include:

- del.icio.us
  http://del.icio.us/

- Furl
  http://www.furl.net/

- Backflip
  http://www.backflip.com/

- Blinklist
  http://www.blinklist.com/

Social bookmarking sites enable educators to share bookmarks with their students and colleagues, establish student-created knowledge pools (lists of bookmarked sites) for specific projects, and more. Unlike browser-based bookmarks, bookmarking sites allow users to access their bookmarks using any computer.

Photo and Video Sharing

There are numerous sites on the Web that support photo and video sharing. Photo-sharing sites include:

- Flickr
  http://www.flickr.com/

- Snapfish
  http://www.snapfish.com/

- Webshots
  http://www.webshots.com/

Students can organize and evaluate their own uploaded photos for group projects, as well as incorporate shared photos. Students can download photo-editing software from the Web to edit their photos. Programs include GIMP (http://www.gimp.org/) and Paint.NET (http://www.getpaint.net/). Picnik (http://www.picnik.com/) is an online photo-editing tool.

YouTube (http://www.youtube.com/) is a very popular video-sharing site. Users can upload their videos to "broadcast" themselves. TeacherTube (http://www.teachertube.com/), as mentioned in Chapter 2, is an online community for sharing instructional videos. Teachers may share students' work here as well. Jumpcut (http://jumpcut.com/) allows users to upload, edit, and share photos and videos.

As with other types of multimedia projects, the creation and sharing of video-based projects supports twenty-first-century learning skills. Multimedia production encourages collaborative learning, critical thinking and problem-solving skills, creativity, innovation, communication, and much more. Working in production teams, students learn flexibility, adaptability, social skills, and accountability, and have opportunities to engage in leadership roles.

Podcasts

Podcasts, as discussed in Chapters 1 and 2, are another way students can access and deliver information. Students (and teachers) may access or create audio only podcasts or audio/video podcasts. Podcast creation tools can be found on the Web. These include:

- PodOmatic
  http://www.podomatic.com/

- PodBean
  http://www.podbean.com/

- Gcast
  http://www.gcast.com/

- MyPodcast
  http://www.mypodcast.com/

As noted in Chapter 2, Macintosh computers come with software to help users create audio and video podcasts.

Podcasts for kids are available on a variety of sites. For example, Kid-Cast.com (http://www.kid-cast.com/) provides "kid-safe" podcasts and encourages kids to submit their own podcast for broadcasting. Storynory (http://storynory.com/) provides free audio stories; free audio stories also can be found on Apple's iTunes (Go to http://www.apple.com/itunes/store/podcasts.html and search for Children's Fun Storytime Podcast Several educational sites were discussed in Chapter 2, including The Education Podcast Network (http://www.epnweb.org/), National Geographic (http://www.nationalgeographic.com/podcasts/), and the Smithsonian (http://www.si.edu/podcasts/). As with any instructional media, it is important that the educator preview the podcasts before assigning them to his or her students.

Virtual Worlds

Virtual worlds can provide users with an advanced level of social networking and interaction. In general, users design their own character (or avatar) and participate in a virtual environment. As characters explore the virtual environment, they can socialize with other users, participate in group activities, create and trade items, and so forth. Second Life (http://secondlife.com/) is a 3-D virtual world created by Linden Research, Inc. Users ("Residents") can explore, interact with others, create items and services, start a business, attend events and parties, participate in contests, purchase land, and more. Schools, businesses, and other organizations can use Second Life to create their own space for virtual meetings, classes, training, collaboration, communication, and so forth.

Whyville (http://www.whyville.net/) is a virtual world targeting younger users. Users create their own character, earn "clams" by playing games, and can choose to start their own business, write for the local paper, interact with others, attend events, and more. Users are engaged in constructive educational activities and must demonstrate socially responsible behavior. As with other sites, privacy, safety, and other issues need to be addressed to ensure students are prepared to use the Internet safely and ethically.

Interactive Programs

There are a growing number of interactive programs on the Internet designed to help students with mathematics, geography, reading, science, and other subjects. Some of these are free; others require a fee. As noted in Chapter 5, program formats include drill and practice, tutorials, simulations, instructional games, and others. Users may need to download a plug-in (software used to expand the browser's capabilities) in order to view or interact with a program. The site usually indicates whether or not the user needs to download the plug-in and where to get it. In addition to the Internet resources listed in Chapter 5, Table 6.1 lists a variety of interactive programs available on the Web. Some have sites providing educational, interactive programs for personal digital assistants (PDAs) and Sony's PlayStations Portable (PSP).

Educators need to review online programs just as they would other educational programs (see Chapter 5). Just because the activities reside on the Internet does not mean they are effective programs or are the best tool for the instructional tasks. In some cases, depending on Internet access and speed, it may be more problematic to use online programs. Educators may want to investigate

Table 6.1. Resources for Interactive Programs

Name and Source	Description
LearningPlanet.com http://www.learningplanet.com/	Online subscription fee required for access to many activities and resources; designed for students and teachers.
The Quiz Hub http://quizhub.com/quiz/quizhub.cfm	Online subscription fee required to access all activities. Quizzes available for multiple subjects.
Quia Corporation http://www.quia.com/	Free activities across all subject areas, plus a subscription option.
Dositey.com http://www.dositey.com/	Free activities for mathematics and language arts. Software available for PDAs and PSP.
Educational Java Programs http://arcytech.org/java/	Free activities for mathematics and science.
Game Goo http://www.earobics.com/gamegoo/gooey.html	Interactive activities that help build early reading skills.
Learn Spanish http://www.studyspanish.com/	Free online lessons for learning Spanish. Additional charge for more lessons.
WannaLearn.com http://www.wannalearn.com/	Links to more than 350 free online tutorials, guides, and other instructional materials.
CompassLearning Odyssey http://www.childu.com/	Addresses multiple subjects and grade levels; sample activities are available. Subscription fee required. Site allows educators and parents to track students' progress.

whether or not the programs are downloadable, available on CD-ROM, and what copyright restrictions are involved.

Advertisements are another consideration. Many free, online programs have commercial sponsors, so students may be inundated with commercial banners, pop-up windows, and so forth. As with other instructional decisions, teachers need to ensure their use of technology—whether the Internet or other choice—is pedagogically sound.

Online Experts

One of the many advantages provided by the Internet is access to materials and resources that might not otherwise be available. This includes access to various experts. Many online expert sites specialize in a single subject area (for example, Dr. Math), while others address almost any topic (for example, All Experts). Online experts are available to assist teachers and students with their questions; however, educators must remember that anyone can serve as an online expert. As with other Internet resources, teachers and students need to consider the credibility of the source and may want to compare their findings with other experts or sources. Table 6.2 lists examples of online experts.

Most sites have archives of previously asked questions and ask users to review the archives before submitting their own questions.

Web Sites for Children

Web sites for children often provide monitored discussion forums and chat rooms; opportunities for children to post their artwork or stories; games; pen-pal clubs; interactive stories; or other activities of interest to students. Sponsors usually include information about their own interests (for example, protecting wildlife, stopping pollution, or selling instructional materials) on the Web site, as well. Web sites designed for children are often highly interactive and animated. Some require plug-ins to view. Table 6.3 provides examples of Web sites designed for children.

Table 6.2. Online Experts

Name and Source	Description
Refdesk.com Ask the Experts http://www.refdesk.com/expert.html	Provides links to experts covering a wide range of areas.
Ask Dr. Math http://mathforum.org/dr.math/	Answers questions related to mathematics. College mathematics students serve as experts.
All Experts http://www.allexperts.com/	Addresses almost any topic. Recruits volunteer experts.
Pitsco's Ask an Expert http://www.askanexpert.com/	Addresses almost any topic. Recruits volunteer experts.
Ask a Scientist http://newton.dep.anl.gov/	Answers questions related to science. Science educators serve as experts.
The Center for Innovation in Engineering and Science Education http://www.ciese.org/askanexpert.html	Provides links to online experts in a variety of science fields.

For a more extensive list, visit Yahoo Kids (http://kids.yahoo.com/) and click on the Games tab, then Games on the Web. Yahoo Kids provides activities and a search engine designed specifically for children (see Search Engines). In addition to games, Yahoo Kids provides links to music videos, homework help, an online expert, an online encyclopedia, e-cards, and more. All links are deemed safe and appropriate for children.

Table 6.3. Web Sites for Children

Name and Source	Description
ABC Toon Center http://www.abctooncenter.com/	Based on commercial cartoon characters. Activities include games, puzzles, and animated stories.
Crazy Bone http://www.crazybone.com/	Provides free home pages. Activities include games, jokes, magic tricks, recipes, and coloring pages.
EcoKids Online http://www.ecokidsonline.com/pub/index.cfm	Focus is on taking care of the environment. Activities include games, free downloads, printable activities, and an online discussion forum.
Funology http://www.funology.com/	Focus is on science. Activities include interesting facts, magic tricks, puzzles, and experiments.
Kids Space http://www.kids-space.org/	Focus is on international artistic collaboration. Children share their stories, artwork, and compositions.
Kidomatix http://www.kidomatix.com/	Activities include online painting, puzzles, and scheduler. Also in German.
Paw Island http://www.pawisland.com/	Based on commercial cartoon characters. Activities include games, coloring pages, and puzzles.
PBS Kids http://pbskids.org/	Sponsored by the Public Broadcasting Service. Includes activities, interactive stories, puzzles, and coloring pages based on PBS children shows.
Yuckiest Site in the Internet http://yucky.kids.discovery.com/	Sponsored by the Discovery Channel. Activities include games, science experiments, and informative facts.

Research Activities

The Internet provides ample opportunities for students to engage in research, problem solving, analysis, and evaluation. Barron and Ivers (1998) discuss three levels of Internet research: basic, advanced, and original. Basic research requires students to compare and report information from pre-selected sites. For example, students may use a Web hunt or WebQuest (see WebQuests) to learn facts about a particular topic. Advanced research requires students to be familiar with various techniques for searching the Internet. Students select sources to investigate; sites are not pre-selected. Students must evaluate their sources to determine if the information provided is accurate, unbiased, and complete. Original research may involve students collecting data from other students via the Internet. For example, pupils may survey students in other schools around the world to determine their favorite subject, food, book, and so forth. Students may also exchange information on plant growth, weather patterns, or other scientific observations.

Basic Research

When first introducing students to the Internet, educators will want to begin with pre-designed lessons and research activities that already include Internet addresses (URLs—Uniform Resource Locator). Educators will want to preview these sites before using the lesson to ensure they are correct and are still working. Teachers may construct their own lessons based on Internet resources listed in paper-based Internet directories, online directories (see KidClick at http://www.kidsclick.org/), teacher resource sites (for example, River Trails Middle School teacher resources at http://www. rtsd26.org/trails/Teacher_recommend.htm and Sites For Teachers at http://www.sitesforteachers.com/ resources_sharp/), or recommended Web sites published in educational magazines and journals. Teachers can use existing WebQuests, too.

WebQuests

WebQuests are inquiry-oriented activities in which some or all of the information learners access resides on the Internet. WebQuests list specific objectives and provide students with the necessary links to access the required information. For example, a WebQuest may list several questions about snakes and require students to access specific Web sites to locate the answers. Others may ask students to examine specific sites and come to a conclusion, make recommendations, and so on. For example, a WebQuest may ask students to access, analyze, and synthesize information from specific Web sites to make recommendations on the best place to live. Students may be swayed by the cost of living, the environment, entertainment access, low crime rates, and so forth. Some WebQuests may take a period or two, where others may take weeks or a month, depending on the activity.

Educators can find WebQuests and links to other WebQuests at the following sites:

- Ancient Egypt Webquest
  http://www.iwebquest.com/egypt/ancientegypt.htm

- Miscellaneous WebQuests
  http://www.macomb.k12.mi.us/wq/webqindx.htm

- Internet4Classrooms
  http://internet4classrooms.com/using_quest.htm

- The Holocaust Project WebQuest
  http://www.campbell.k12.ky.us/links/webquest/florimonte/holocaust_webquest.htm

- WebQuests at iwebquest.com
  http://www.iwebquest.com/

The WebQuest model was developed by Bernie Dodge and Tom March at San Diego State University. WebQuests generally include the following components: an introduction, a task, list of resources, how to conduct the WebQuest (the process), an evaluation, and a conclusion. Teachers should preview pre-made WebQuests prior to assigning them to their students to ensure links are still working, appropriate, accurate, and current. After teachers become familiar with the design and procedures associated with WebQuests, they may want to create their own WebQuest based on their own curriculum and needs of their pupils. Students are encouraged to create WebQuests, also. Information on creating WebQuests can be found at:

- The WebQuest Page
  http://webquest.org/index.php

- Kathy Schrock's Guide for Educators
  http://school.discovery.com/schrockguide/webquest/webquest.html

- Spartanburg School District 3 Webquests
  http://www.spa3.k12.sc.us/WebQuests.html

- Teachnology WebQuest Generator
  http://www.teach-nology.com/web_tools/web_quest/

- Creating a WebQuest: It's Easier than You Think!
  http://www.education-world.com/a_tech/tech011.shtml

Additional ideas and activities for using the Internet for basic research are available in many educational technology journals (for example, *Learning and Leading with Technology* published by ISTE), books (such as *The Internet and Instruction: Activities and Ideas* published by Libraries Unlimited, Inc.), and online resources (for example, The Lesson Plans Page at http://www.lessonplanspage.com/).

Advanced Research

As students become more familiar with the Internet, they may be asked to conduct advanced research. Teachers will want to ensure students have the tools and strategies for searching the Internet, as well as know how to critically evaluate Web sites. This section discusses various search engines and search strategies. Criteria for evaluating Web sites are presented later in this chapter.

Search Engines

There are a variety of search engines available to assist teachers and students. Some are specifically designed for children, returning only "child safe" sites. These include:

- KidsClick
  http://www.kidsclick.org/

- DibDabDoo
  http://www.dibdabdoo.com/

- Yahoo Kids
  http://kids.yahoo.com/

Although these search engines guide students to appropriate sites, they are not intended to prevent students from entering an URL of an inappropriate site. They simply limit the results of the search to Web sites that have already been previewed and deemed appropriate for children.

Other search engines, such as Ask Kids (http://www.askkids.com/) and Google's Onekey (http://www.onekey.com/), provide filtering options and are not limited to selected sites. These search engines allow users to search the entire Web, versus a select group of previewed sites. Educators must be aware that even though the search engines contain filters, objectionable material may still pass through the filters.

Most search engines are filtered and index thousands of pages on the Web. Searches vary by search engines, dependent upon the pages indexed and whether or not they search through the entire text of Web pages or just titles (or both). Some search engines produce results from several different indexes. These are referred to as "meta-search engines."

Popular search engines include:

- Yahoo!
  http://www.yahoo.com/

- Excite
  http://www.excite.com/

- Google
  http://www.google.com/

- AltaVista
  http://www.altavista.com/

- Dogpile
  http://www.dogpile.com/

Some search engines return results by Web page matches and sponsor matches. Sponsor matches are search results that are paid for by businesses or organizations. For example, if you search for "lesson plans," you will find sponsor matches that provide information on lesson plans or sell related products. Web page matches give the most extensive list of results. Some search engines may provide terms or phrases for related searches also. Excite, a meta-search engine, provides filtering options and an option to view results by search engine. Dogpile, another meta-search engine, provides users with filtering and other options, too. AltaVista, Google, and Yahoo! provide filtering options, as well as translation and language settings, and other custom features (see Figure 6.1).

Child-safe browsers also are available. MyKidsBrowser (http://www.mykidsafeinternet.com/) and KidZui (http://www.kidzui.com/) are examples of Web browsers specifically designed for children. MyKidsBrowser and KidZui provide simplified layouts and options that appeal to children (for example, special sound effects and animated characters), enable access to reviewed sites (that is, sites are predetermined), and allow parental control.

Search Strategies

Most search engines have advanced options available to assist users with limiting the results of their searches (see Figure 6.2).

Searches may be limited by using quotes and addition and subtraction symbols. For example, "multimedia projects in education" will return only sites with the phrase "multimedia projects in education." Without quotes, the search engine will return sites containing the given words, but the words do not necessarily have to appear together as in a phrase. In some cases, depending on the search engine, only one of the words needs to be present to return a site. Using addition symbols (for example, +multimedia +projects +education) often ensures all words appear on returned sites. Adding a word outside the quoted phrase (for example, "multimedia projects in education" +Ivers) will return sites with the phrase, but only those sites including the extra word(s). Using subtraction symbols, +multimedia +projects –education will return pages with both multimedia and projects, but eliminate pages with the word "education" on them. An activity page for learning more about searches is presented at the end of this chapter.

Google, Yahoo!, and other search engines provide additional search and other services as well. For example, Google and Yahoo! provide audio, video, and image searches, map searches, news searches, product searches, and more. Yahoo! provides an "ask a question" search; Google provides scholarly paper and patent searches. Many more search options are available.

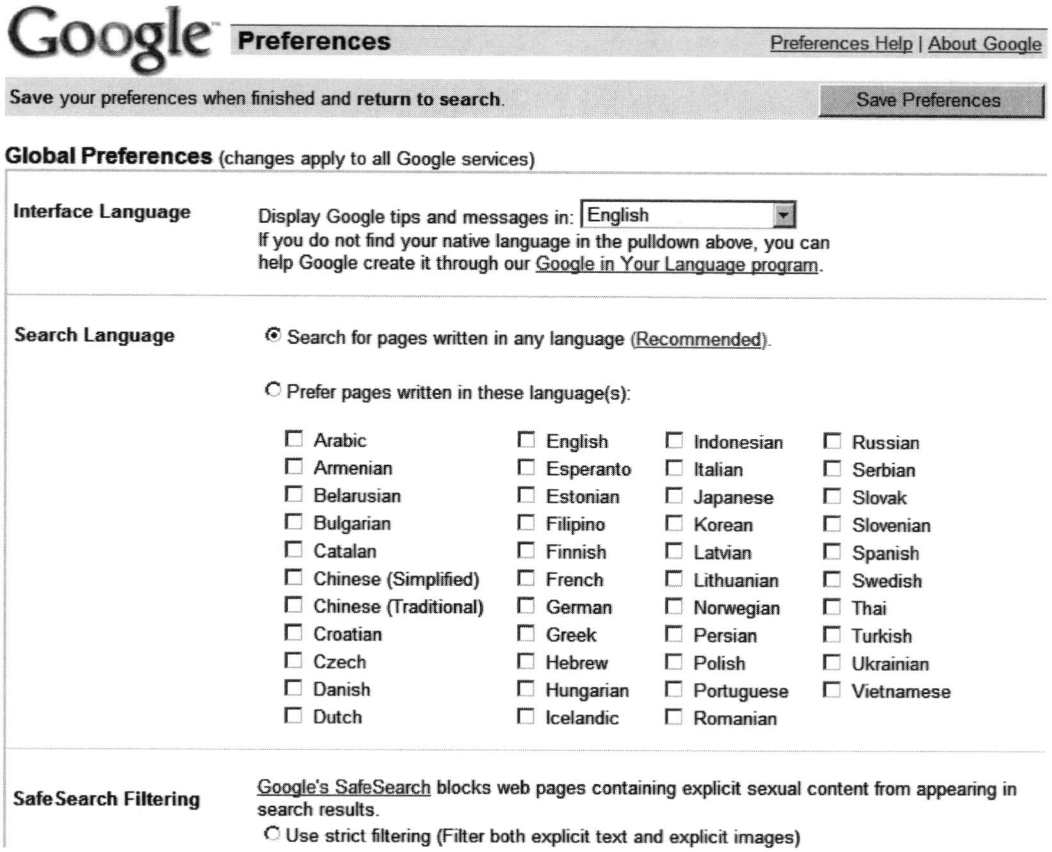

Figure 6.1. Some of the custom features in Google.

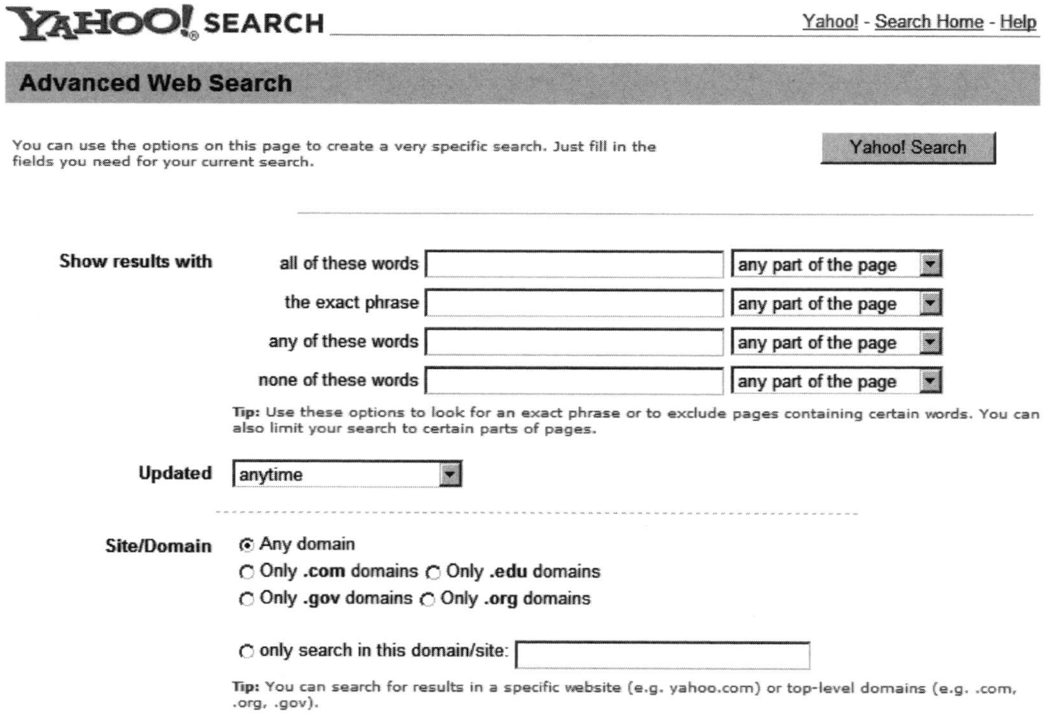

Figure 6.2. Advanced search options in Yahoo!.

Original Research

Students may conduct original research as a class or on their own, depending on their ability and familiarity with the Internet. There are many collaborative projects available to assist students conduct original research. Students can exchange information using e-mail, videoconferencing, or class Web pages, as well as obtain information through online surveys such as Survey Monkey and Zoomerang.

E-mail

E-mail provides students with opportunities to practice their communication skills, write for a specific audience, and engage in meaningful activities. Through e-mail, students can learn about students from different parts of the world, enhancing their cultural awareness, as they work on various projects together. E-mail allows students to exchange information without the cost of long-distance calls or the delay of traditional mail.

Several sites are available to assist teachers with finding and implementing e-mail projects. These include:

- Epals
  http://www.epals.com/

- Global SchoolNet's Internet Projects Registry
  http://www.globalschoolhouse.org/pr/

- Intercultural E-mail Classroom Connections
  http://www.iecc.org/

- Collaborative Projects: The Center for Innovation in Engineering and Science Education
  http://www.ciese.org/collabprojs.html

- iEARN, International Education and Resource Network
  http://www.iearn.org/

These sites specialize in matching educators with others who are interested in conducting long-distance classroom projects. Educators may work with other teachers to create their own project or join projects designed by others. Sample project ideas are presented in Figure 6.3.

Students conduct surveys about favorite pets, movies, music, books, foods, and so forth, charting and comparing results.	Students exchange poetry, stories, favorite recipes, and so forth for class books or classroom Web sites.
Round-robin or progressive stories are started and shared among participants.	Students exchange descriptions of their schools and attempt to draw each other's school.
Students compare and discuss newspaper headlines.	Students exchange local folklore and other interesting facts about their community.
Students plant the same kind of seeds on the same day, follow the same directions for care of the plants, and so forth. Plant measurements and other data are compared among participants.	Students research and exchange information about their national anthem, including author, history, date of publication, and so forth.
Students exchange, compare, and graph weather information with other students from around the world.	Students collect, chart, and compare food, gas, or clothing prices from around the world.

Figure 6.3. Sample project ideas.

Most e-mail activities can take place offline. Students can enter their messages into a word processor and copy/paste the message within an e-mail document. Before beginning an e-mail project, make sure students understand the rules of "netiquette"—the do's and don'ts of online communication. These include:

- Never type in all caps—this is difficult to read, plus it appears as "yelling."

- Remember you are communicating with a person, not a computer screen.

- Choose words carefully—text does not contain the nuances of voice or facial expressions.

- Present yourself in a professional manner—be respectful of others and forgiving of their mistakes (typos and so forth).

- Remember you are in cyberspace—nothing is private.

- Practice proper grammar, sentence structure, and punctuation.

Educators may want to remind their students that impressions are made through writing, just as they are in face-to-face meetings. Students need to present themselves in the best way possible.

Videoconferencing

Videoconferencing is another way to engage in collaborative projects. Schools may purchase videoconferencing systems or use their existing computers. With desktop videoconferencing hardware and software, teachers can use a computer to send and receive video, audio, and text in real time over the Internet. Requirements include a digital video camera (for example, Quickcam by Logitech), a microphone, a computer with sound capabilities (a sound card and speakers), and videoconferencing software.

Educators can download videoconferencing software for free. NetMeeting by Microsoft comes installed on Windows (Windows 2000 and XP); Windows Meeting Space is available on Windows Vista and can be downloaded from http://www.microsoft.com/; and Eyeball Chat by Eyeball Networks (http://www.eyeballchat.com/) provides videoconferencing for the PC. Skype by Skype Technologies (http://www.skype.com/) and iVisit by Eyematic Interface (http://www.ivisit.com/) are available for both Macintosh and PC platforms.

The Center for Interactive Learning and Collaboration (http://www.cilc.org/) provides a list of schools using videoconferencing. Educators can use this directory to locate schools in which to conduct videoconferencing projects. The Web site also includes project examples and collaborative projects opportunities. Online expeditions, where students communicate with real explorers as they travel to exotic and other interesting places, and virtual field trips can be found at Global SchoolNet (http://www.globalschoolnet.org/gsnexpeditions/), The Jason Project (http://www.jason.org/), and other Web sites.

Many institutions provide videoconferencing opportunities, too. For example, museum experts at the Albany Institute of History and Art provide guided lessons and virtual tours based on objects of study at the museum. Lessons include Colonial Life in America, Mummies and Ancient Egypt, Artists and Nature, and more. The Albany Institute of History and Art and other resources for videoconferencing opportunities are described in Table 6.4.

Educators can learn more about their school or district's videoconferencing capabilities through their technology resource teacher or media specialist.

Classroom Web Pages

Numerous district, school, and classroom Web pages exist on the Internet. Most district and school Web pages are informational and designed to assist parents with questions, teacher communication, and upcoming events. Classroom Web pages provide educators with opportunities to showcase their students' work (refer to Chapter 4 about Internet safety issues), conduct surveys, and post calls

Table 6.4. Videoconferencing Resources

Name and Source	Description
The Albany Institute of History and Art http://www.albanyinstitute.org/	Provides guided lessons and virtual tours based on objects of study in the museum.
The Center for Puppetry Arts http://www.puppet.org/	Offers K-5 hands-on puppet building workshops tailored to specific classroom topics and curriculum.
The Ocean Institute http://www.ocean-institute.org/	Provides virtual field trips and lessons on ocean life.
Wildlife Conservation Society http://wcs.org/	Offers several lessons, featuring live animals, aligned to the National Science Education Standards.
Glenn Learning Technology Project http://www.nasa.gov/centers/glenn/ home/index.html	Provides a variety of workshops connecting teachers and students with NASA scientists, engineers, and researchers.

for collaboration. A list of K-12 district and school Web pages is available on the Yahoo! K-12 Directory (http://dir.yahoo.com/Education/K_12/Schools/).

Many programs make it easy to create Web pages, offering "Save as Web Page" options. Programs include Microsoft Word, PowerPoint, and others. Specific tools are available to assist educators and students with creating Web pages, as well. These include:

- Web Easy Professional by Avanquest Software
  http://www.avanquest.com/

- WebPlus by Serif
  http://www.serif.com/

- Web Studio by Back to the Beach Software
  http://www.webstudio.com/

- Print Shop Web Designer by Broderbund
  http://www.broderbund.com/

Shareware options are available, too. Web creation programs make it easy to create Web pages; no programming is required. Most have WYSIWYG features—what you see is what you get. Users type information on the screen and add tables, pictures, etc.—just as they would in a word processor—and have it appear the same on a Web page.

There are many Web sites that provide teachers with the ability to create and customize their own classroom Web sites and learning activities or post class information for parents. These include:

- TeacherWeb
  http://www.teacherweb.com/

- Filamentality
  http://www.filamentality.com/wired/fil/

- SchoolNotes
  http://www.schoolnotes.com/

When using Web pages or specific Web tools like Zoomerang (http://www.zoomerang.com/) or Survey Monkey (http://www.surveymonkey.com/) to solicit information (for example, a survey), it is important for educators to filter the information. In some cases, responses may be inappropriate. Opening the door to a wider world allows a greater range of morals and values to enter the classroom. While most users may respond in earnest, others may intentionally submit information that is inappropriate for students. Fortunately, online survey tools such as Zoomerang and Survey Monkey allow developers to target specific responders, limiting surveys to those who have been provided with a password. Teachers may want to ask their technology resource teacher or Web master about protecting an unprotected classroom Web page survey with a password, only allowing invited groups (for example, other classes) to take the survey. Even so, teachers need to preview the information before sharing it with their students.

Educators can use Web programs to create classroom Web pages that showcase student work, provide homework information, outline classroom policies and curricular goals, provide information or support for current assignments, and so forth. Students may create Web pages to showcase a community learning activity, online collaborative projects, or other work. To post information on the Web, educators should contact their technology resource teacher or media specialist. Although teachers may have their own personal Web site or access to a commercial site that allows users to post information, educators should check their school's policy regarding posting school-related information on the Web.

The Internet contains a wealth of information and opens doors to multiple learning opportunities. In addition to research and collaborative activities, it provides distance education opportunities for students who are homebound, live great distances from educational institutions, or for other reasons cannot attend a traditional classroom. Chapter 8 provides further information on managing and assessing online learning environments.

Evaluation Criteria

The media—including television, radio, newspapers, and magazines—is a platform and distributor of facts, opinions, biases, and so forth. This is true of the Internet as well. Students must realize that anyone can publish information on the Internet and that evaluating Internet resources is critical. There are several criteria to consider when examining the intent and content of Web pages.

Intent

The intent of a Web site may be analyzed by looking at the following factors: domain name, the reason the information is posted, the target audience, and the layout.

Domain Name

An Internet address (URL) contains a protocol, a domain name, and sometimes a file location. For example, the URL: http://dir.yahoo.com/Education/ contains the Hypertext Transfer Protocol (http), specifying the source is a Web page; the domain name "dir.yahoo.com," indicating it is a commercial (.com) site; and the file location "Education," specifying the user is in a directory called "Education." The "dir.yahoo" part of the URL represents the name of the computer server (yahoo) within a specific department (dir).

Educators and students can begin evaluating a Web site by noting its domain extension (or top-level domain). Common domain extensions are listed in Table 6.5.

Table 6.5. Common Domain Extensions

Extension	Type of Institution
.edu	Education
.gov	Government
.com	Commercial
.org	Nonprofit Organization
.net	Special Network Resources

The domain extension provides information about the sponsor of the site or who is posting the information. For example, government (.gov) sites are regulated by the government, so information on the sites is likely valid. When examining the domain name, students need to ask: Is there likelihood for bias and special interests?

Reason

Students need to consider why the information is being posted on the Web. Every organization has its own agenda, sometimes explicit and other times hidden. Why is the information being presented? Students should consider if the sponsors' main purpose is to inform or influence. For example, students may ask: Is the Web site designed to attract potential customers, donations, or membership to a cause or just to provide information?

Target Audience

Just like commercials, Web sites have a target audience. Questions to consider are: Is the Web site designed for children? Does it target educators? Is it geared toward a special interest group? Students should consider for whom the information is supplied.

Layout

The layout of the information on the Web page also may provide insight into the sponsor's intent. Students should determine if the information is the main focus of the Web page or if it is an obscure part, surrounded by unrelated content, contests, and giveaways. Questions to consider are: Is the layout clear and uncluttered? Is the Web site an advertisement disguised as information? Do the graphics and links support the information or are they unrelated? Are there other items on the site (for example, animations, graphics, or flashing words) designed to distract users to other information on the site? These questions will help students determine the intent of the Web page.

Content

When evaluating the content of a Web site, students need to consider the authority, currency, bias, and verification of information.

Authority

Students can critique the authority of the information by examining whether or not it is refereed or reviewed; identifying the author and his or her expertise on the subject; and noting whether or not a bibliography is provided. Students may ask the following questions: Have others verified the document? Does it contain the author's biography and e-mail address? Is it possible to find additional information about the author? Are the author's citations accurate?

Currency

Web sites generally include the dates the sites were created and last updated. Students need to look at the Web site dates, as well as dates contained in the document, to verify the information's currency. Many Web sites are not updated on a regular basis, while others keep documents in archives for unspecified lengths of time. Students should check the timeliness of Web documents based on the publication date, not necessarily the date they found the document on the Web. Questions to consider are: When was the site last updated? When was the document published? Is more current information available?

Bias

As with all media, students need to be alert to biased materials on the Internet. Some sites are designed to persuade rather than inform. Students also must consider the point of view that is being expressed. Students need to ask: Is the information written to inform or persuade me? Does the information reflect a special interest or specific point of view?

Verification of Information

Verification of information can be achieved by looking for inconsistencies in the information being presented, identifying whether or not evidence or examples are given to support statements or conclusions, noting whether or not the information is fact or opinion (or both), and recognizing what information is being withheld and why. In addition, triangulation of information—comparing findings with sources other than the Internet—can help determine the validity and reliability of the information. Students may ask themselves the following questions: Is the author consistent? How does the author support his/her claim? Does the author present the whole story or just part? Have I verified my findings with other resources?

Web pages should never be evaluated solely by their appearance. Looks can be deceiving. If the point of the sponsor is to inform, the information should be easy to find and clearly presented on the page. Though this may not always be the case, it is a good place to start when evaluating whether or not there is an additional purpose to the Web site.

Even if the content is clearly presented, it may not always be correct. In addition to incorrect and outdated information, students must be aware of fact versus opinion, biases, and the author's expertise. An evaluation form is presented at the end of this chapter.

Additional Tips

As mentioned in Chapter 4, educators will want to follow their school's AUP, as well as instruct students on issues regarding ethics, privacy, and safety. This section reviews these issues, as well as provides educators with some troubleshooting tips for assisting teachers and students with information searches.

Issues to Consider

As with using educational software, educators need to ensure that their use of the Internet supports desired learner outcomes and is the best medium for instruction. They also will want to consider school policies regarding the use of the Internet. Educators will want to ask themselves the following questions:

- Do I have permission for my students to use the Internet in class?

- Have I followed the guidelines and safety procedures outlined in my school's AUP?

- Have my students been instructed on procedures for using the Internet as outlined in my school's AUP?

- Does the use of the Internet support the desired learner outcomes for my students?

- Do my students know what to do if they accidentally access an inappropriate site?

- Do I have a backup plan in case my school's Internet access goes down or if the assigned sites are unavailable?

- If I have students who are visually or hearing impaired, are assigned Web sites 508 compliant? (See Chapter 3.)

Ethics, privacy, and safety issues, as discussed in Chapter 4, are of great importance to educators and students. Students need to understand their ethical responsibilities and the importance of their privacy and safety. They should be instructed on proper use of material from the Internet, how to cite sources (see APA Online at http://www.apastyle.org/), and what constitutes plagiarism and copyright infringement. Students also must understand the importance of maintaining their anonymity on the Internet and the dangers associated with interacting with unknown people on the Internet.

Troubleshooting Tips for the Internet

Educators and students will often come across Web sites that have been moved to a new address or URL. In most cases, the user will be redirected to the new site automatically. If not, the old site may have an address the user can input to reach the new site. Otherwise, users may receive a message from their browser that "the server could not be found" or "the page cannot be found." If the server cannot be found, chances are the site is no longer available or is down for maintenance. Double-check the address and try again. If a page cannot be found, it may have been removed or moved to a different location on site.

To locate a document that may have been moved, try navigating through links on the Web site one directory at a time. For example, an URL directing users to The Lewis Carroll Scrapbook Collection is http://memory.loc.gov/intldl/carrollhtml/lchome.html.

Note this is a government site (.gov) and the opening or home page for the collection is "lchome.html." It is contained in the directory "carrollhtml," which is in the directory "intldl."

Begin by entering just the domain name (memory.loc.gov) to ensure the Web site is working. Next, add each directory to the domain name. For example, try:

> http://memory.loc.gov/.

If the Web site is working, add the first directory:

> http://memory.loc.gov/intldl/.

If the site is able to locate the first directory, enter the next directory:

> http://memory.loc.gov/intldl/carrollhtml/.

Continue this process to see whether or not a directory has been removed or renamed.

For long URLs, it may be easier to work backward, leaving off the requested page (for example, carrollhtml.html) and checking the immediate directory (for example, http://memory.loc.gov/intldl/carrollhtml/) for a link to the desired page.

Some URLs can be very long and complicated. Note there are no spaces and some URLs may be case sensitive. If an URL cannot be located:

- Ensure that the address is entered correctly, noting dashes, periods, underlines, slashes, or other symbols that must be included.

- Make sure there are not any spaces in the address.

- Enter the address exactly as it is written, using uppercase and lowercase letters where indicated.

- Try backing up a directory or entering just the domain name. It may be possible to navigate to the desired information. Sometimes documents are removed or placed in different directories.

- Previewing URLs, as already mentioned, is a good way to ensure successful lessons. Educators can bookmark specific sites; copy the URLs into a word-processing program, such as Microsoft Word, that allows students to click on the text to access the site; or copy the link onto a class Web page or bookmarking site (for example, del.icio.us). This removes the possibility of mistyped URLs.

In many instances, information on Web sites is removed or relocated, so educators should preview sites (again) the night before their lesson. Published URLs can go out of date quickly, and search engines may index sites that no longer exist or pages that have been moved. Knowing how to troubleshoot an URL can be helpful when looking for information.

Summary

The Internet can be likened to a library that goes on forever. There are no walls to stop the aisles from ending, and resources surround us everywhere we look. It can be very overwhelming but empowering, too.

The Internet provides students with opportunities to conduct various research activities, contact online experts, pursue their own special interests, and interact with students from all over the world. It is a great tool for supporting twenty-first-century learning. The Internet supports collaboration, information sharing, creativity, and interactivity, and it provides opportunities to expand students' global awareness and enhance their information, media, and technology literacy skills.

Although there are many sites and search engines specifically designed for children, it is important for students to be wary of the information and people they may find on the Internet. Educators can help pupils by teaching them specific search strategies, how to evaluate information on the Web, and how to maintain their privacy on the Web. The Internet provides teachers and students with resources they might not otherwise have, but, like other instructional tools, it is important to evaluate and decide if the resources are pedagogically sound.

Activities

1. Use the evaluation form presented in Chapter 5 to evaluate an online program (see Table 6.1 and Chapter 5).

2. Review and compare three different activity sites specifically for children. Discuss the activities, purpose, targeted age group, whether or not the site is selling something or depends on advertising, and other features of the site. Include if you would recommend it to a parent. Summarize your findings. See Table 6.3 or Yahoo! Kids (http://kids.yahoo.com/) for Web sites.

3. Review a WebQuest and create a WebQuest of your own, designed for your students and a specific topic.

4. Locate educational technology journals, books, or online resources and share at least three different basic research activities (other than WebQuests) for using the Internet in instruction.

5. Design a project-based learning activity that incorporates the use of Web 2.0 tools.

6. Complete the "Internet Search Strategies" blackline master at the end of this chapter and compare your results with others.

7. Use the "Evaluating Internet Information" blackline master at the end of this chapter to evaluate a source of information on the Internet. For example, you may want to go back and critique information linked to a WebQuest or search for information related to a particular topic (for example, the Civil War). Share your findings.

Reference

Barron, A. E. and K. S. Ivers. 1998. *The Internet and Instruction: Activities and Ideas.* 2nd ed. Englewood, CO: Libraries Unlimited.

Blackline Masters

- Evaluating Internet Information
- Internet Search Strategies

Evaluating Internet Information

Site name: _____

URL: http:// _____

Site's sponsor: _____ Target audience: _____

Last time the site was updated: _____

Questions to consider	Yes	No	Comments
Is the information being presented to influence?			
Is the information being presented to inform?			
Is the layout clear or cluttered?			
Is the Web site an advertisement disguised as information?			
Do the graphics and links support the information or are they unrelated?			
Are there other items on the site designed to distract users to other information on the site?			
Has the information on the site been verified or reviewed by others?			
Does the information contain the author's biography and e-mail address?			
Are the author's citations accurate?			
Is it possible to find additional information about the author?			
Is the information current?			
Is more current information available?			
Does the information reflect a special interest or specific point of view?			
Are there inconsistencies in the information being presented?			
Are evidence or examples given to support statements or conclusions?			
Does the author withhold information that may counter his/her claim?			
Can the information be verified against other sources? If yes, list two sources that verify the information on the Web site below:			

Internet Search Strategies

Conduct the following searches using the assigned search engine. Report both Web page and sponsor matches if available.

Search Engine	kittens	kittens -cat	"Charlie and the Chocolate Factory"	chocolate
Yahoo! Kids http://kids.yahoo.com/				
KidsClick! http://www.kidsclick.org/				
DibDabDoo http://www.dibdabdoo.com/				
Google http://www.google.com/				
Excite http://www.excite.com				

Search Engine	Charlie Brown	+Charlie +Brown	"Charlie Brown"	Charlie -Brown
AltaVista http://www.altavista.com/				
Dogpile http://www.dogpile.com/				
OneKey http://www.onekey.com/				
Ask Kids http://www.askkids.com/				
Yahoo! http://www.yahoo.com/				

Summarize your findings and recommendations:

Managing and Assessing Computer Use in the Classroom

A Scenario

Mrs. Morgan's sixth-grade students all had their own laptops, thanks to the school district's one-to-one laptop program. Her students had access to their own computers since the third grade, so they were very comfortable using the laptops and the Internet. Their word-processing skills were adequate, so Mrs. Morgan often had her students take notes on their laptops. Even though all of her students had their own computer, Mrs. Morgan often had them work as teams, sharing their laptops or working in cooperative group settings to maximize their learning time. Mrs. Morgan used a variety of formative assessments to track her students' progress.

At the beginning of the school year, Mrs. Morgan made it very clear how students were to use their laptops in her classroom. She had her students help her establish the rules and consequences. Last year, one of the fifth-grade teachers, Mrs. Myles, complained how her students were always off task—surfing the Internet—and not seeming to care about their classwork. After one too many frustrations, she limited the students' laptop use to "free time" and expected students to use the laptop at home for specific assignments. Mrs. Myles was new to the school and was very technology competent. Even so, it was clear she lacked classroom-management skills. Mrs. Morgan knew classroom management could be very difficult for first-year teachers; experience helped. Mrs. Morgan had been teaching for thirteen years, but she could still remember her first year of teaching. She had learned a lot over the last thirteen years and offered to exchange expertise with Mrs. Myles. "Last year is not a year I'd like to remember," stated Mrs. Myles. "Here I am, a technology guru, and I couldn't manage technology use in my own classroom! The best I could do was bribe students with free computer time. I know better." Mrs. Morgan shared her first year of teaching, noting how there was only one computer in the classroom and she didn't even know where the power switch was. One of her first graders had to point it out to her. "My first graders knew more about the computer than I did," she laughed. "Teaching is not as easy as it looks," Mrs. Morgan continued. "It takes more than a sound knowledge base and the desire to teach. We need to be able to identify our weaknesses and be willing to grow. I identified my weaknesses and did something about it. I found a teacher to mentor me, plus I continued my education in educational technology. Even so, you have a lot you can teach me. Technology changes so quickly!"

"It's a deal," grinned Mrs. Myles. "You serve as my classroom management guru and I'll serve as your computer guru. We can go as the 'gu-gu' girls or the M and M team." Humor was a good thing, thought Mrs. Morgan. With Mrs. Morgan's help, Mrs. Myles began her second year with confidence and effective strategies for managing computer use in her classroom. Mrs. Morgan would surprise her students with new technology skills....

Introduction

The key component to effective computer use is the educator. The educator is responsible for *why* students are using the computer, *when* students are using the computer, and *how* students are using the computer. Planning, managing, and assessing a lesson that involves computers is similar to planning, managing, and assessing a lesson that involves other learning tools—microscopes, globes, science kits, listening centers, and so forth. Teachers specify learning objectives and plan their lessons based on students' ability levels and background, available materials and tools, and allotted time. Assessment is ongoing to ensure that students are making satisfactory progress. Ideally, teachers will have learning materials and tools for every student or pairs of students, but this is not always the case—especially with classroom computers. This chapter provides teachers with planning, management, and assessment strategies for using computers in the classroom. Topics include:

- When to Use Computers

  Objectives and Learner Outcomes

  Assessing Resources

- Planning and Managing Computer-Based Lessons

  Grouping Strategies

  One-to-One Laptop Classrooms

  Designing a Classroom Computer Schedule

  Lesson Ideas and Examples

- Monitoring and Assessing Students' Work

  Ongoing Assessment

  Rubrics

When to Use Computers

As mentioned in previous chapters, technology is a tool to assist teachers and students. Technology can help educators and students gather and learn new information, participate in collaborative projects, create projects and presentations, and engage in activities (for example, simulations) that might otherwise be too costly or time prohibitive to complete. It is a tool to assist educators with instructional and management tasks, as well as a tool to help them achieve and assess desired learner outcomes.

When deciding on whether or not to use computers for instruction, educators must consider the following:

- What are the objectives or desired learner outcomes of the lesson?

- Will the use of technology help students meet the desired learner outcomes? If so, how?

- Can the learning objectives be accomplished just as well with a different, more accessible medium?

- Are classroom computers or a computer lab available for the lesson? If so, how will computer time be scheduled?

- Do students have the prerequisite skills necessary to use the computers and software? If not, how and when will these skills be taught?

- How will students' computer work be monitored and assessed?

In addition to the above considerations, teachers should consider their own familiarity and comfort with the topic and methods with which they plan to teach. Not only must teachers be knowledgeable about the subject matter, they should be skilled in the use of the computer and assigned software. If Internet access or the use of a specific hardware device (for example, digital cameras, scanners, etc.) is required, educators need to ensure they have the skills necessary to assist their students.

Objectives and Learner Outcomes

Educators are responsible for ensuring students meet national, state, or district technology standards (see Chapter 4). As indicated by the standards, technology should not be taught in isolation, but used as a tool to help students achieve academic goals and twenty-first-century learning skills. Hence, technology can be used to help students learn subject matter content; information, media, and technology skills; learning and innovation skills; and life and career skills. Students can learn content and twenty-first-century learning skills by conducting and evaluating research via the Internet; producing multimedia projects; engaging in simulations and online collaborative learning projects; using databases, spreadsheets, and problem-solving software; and communicating through e-mail, videoconferencing, discussion boards, wikis, presentation tools, and more.

It is important that educators are aware of the technologies and software available to assist their students meet desired learner outcomes and twenty-first-century learning skills (see Chapters 5 and 6). Too often educators feel they "have to" use computers, causing them to use computers as a reward or in some other superficial way. Computers, like any instructional tool, should be used to support specific objectives and when they are the best medium for instruction. Knowing how they can help students learn (see Chapter 3) is the first step to understanding when to use computers.

Assessing Resources

If the use of technology will support desired learner outcomes, educators must assess their technology resources to determine if the available computers, software, peripherals, and so forth can help facilitate instruction (see the "Technology Resources" blackline master in Chapter 1).

Technology resources may be located in school labs or media centers, classrooms, or both. Some resources such as portable or laptop computers, digital cameras, and projection systems may be available for checkout. Shared resources (for example, computer labs and "checkout" materials) often pose limitations to when they can be used. Educators also need to consider placement and access issues when assessing available technology resources.

Computer Labs Versus Computers in the Classroom

More and more schools are placing computers in the classroom rather than in a designated lab. Computer labs have several disadvantages:

- Students may be limited to one thirty- or forty-minute time slot per week.

- Assemblies, fire drills, holidays, and other events may cause students to miss lab time.

- Computer use is more likely to be an isolated activity and unconnected to the curriculum.

- Instructional time is lost going to and from the computer lab.

• Wear and tear on the equipment is greater because the entire school uses the same computers, printers, etc.

Computer labs have several advantages as well:

• All students have access to a computer at the same time, allowing the teacher to facilitate whole class instruction.

• A technology resource teacher may be available to assist both the classroom instructor and the students.

• It costs less to secure.

Some schools maintain a computer lab and continue to place computers in the classroom. As labs are upgraded, older computers are often placed in the classroom. Ideally, teachers will have access to both—computer labs and computers in the classroom—until there are sufficient technology resources in the classroom.

Mobile laptop carts are one way to bring the lab to the classroom. Mobile laptop carts store class sets of laptops and serve as a charging station. Like computer labs, the carts can be secured in one room. Multiple carts can be stored in the same room, providing both the same level of security and more computers for classroom use.

When placed in the classroom, computers are more likely to be used as an integral part of instruction and as a tool for learning. Computers in the classroom allow teachers to use them for:

• "Teachable moments" (for example, accessing the Internet regarding a current event or topic of interest),

• Lessons directly related to daily instruction,

• Whole group (if a projection device or large monitor is available) and small group instruction, and

• Classroom materials and management tasks.

Many software programs are designed for whole class and small group instruction using a single computer (for example, software by Tom Snyder Productions). Limited numbers of computers in the classroom make it difficult to manage individual computer time and increase the time necessary to complete computer-based projects.

One-to-one laptop programs are becoming more popular as computers become more affordable. Schools may require students to purchase their own computer or provide leasing or loan options. A specific platform may or may not be required, but there is typically a minimum standard for hardware configurations.

Dependent upon the objectives and desired learner outcomes, the teacher decides if the outcomes are best achieved through the use of a computer lab, classroom computers, or both—assessing time restrictions, scheduling options, and whether or not students will be working at the computer individually, in pairs, in small groups, or as a whole class (see Planning and Managing Computer-Based Lessons).

Software and Peripherals

In addition to the computers' location, teachers must determine whether or not the desired software and peripherals exist to support the lesson. For example, if students are producing newsletters, are printers available? If whole class instruction is necessary, is it possible to obtain a projection device or large-screen monitor? Is the desired software available, and has the school purchased enough copies for the necessary number of computers? It is important that the educator has reviewed the designated software package(s) and tested the software on the intended computers. It is possible for software to operate correctly on one computer, but not another based on the computers' RAM, operating system, and so forth. If the Internet is being used, do the computers have access to and the sufficient speed to connect to it? Has the teacher previewed the assigned Web sites? Have acceptable use policies been discussed? Do students have their parents' permission to use the Internet?

Prerequisite Skills

After assessing the available resources and securing any additional needs, teachers can begin organizing their lesson to include the desired technologies. In doing so, they need to consider the skills necessary to successfully use the technologies. For example, students may need to perform basic computer operations (for example, properly turning on and off the computer, saving and printing files, and opening and closing programs), as well as have sufficient background on how to use the designated software and peripherals. These skills may be taught as a whole class, in small groups, or by student experts (for example, peer teaching). Review guides or index cards may be used to help students remember certain aspects of a program or device. It is important that the use of technology does not obstruct the students' learning. Students should be made to feel comfortable with the technology prior to their use of the tool for content learning.

In addition to teaching the mechanics of a program (for example how to navigate, use certain tools, and so forth), teachers may need to model various strategies or procedures for using a particular software package. For example, when using programs like Where in the USA is Carmen Sandiego? by The Learning Company, it is important to model and discuss how to make good decisions, take notes, differentiate between criminal and location clues, and find information. Before using programs like the Oregon Trail (also by The Learning Company), teachers should preview the program with their students, demonstrating how to get started (for example, adding members to the wagon or buying supplies), advance in the program, keep a journal, and so forth. Many educational programs are available as "teacher's editions" and come with support materials, ideas, and strategies for helping teachers effectively use the software in their classrooms. Many resources can be found on the Web, too.

Monitoring and Assessing Students' Work

After ensuring students are ready to use the designated learning tools (for example, computer, software program, Internet, scanner, and so forth), educators need to consider how they will monitor and assess students' work. This will vary according to the type of activity, although a daily log or journal of the students' progress is something that may be applied across all activities. Some software programs have built-in record-keeping options, allowing the student or teacher to print daily progress reports. Other programs may come with supplementary material that includes assessment activities to be completed off of the computer. Educators may design their own assessment activities, find activity books written for specific pieces of software, or search the software publisher's Web site for additional ideas. It is important that students' time on the computer (including the Internet) is purposeful and can be assessed according to predetermined objectives set by the educator.

Planning and Managing Computer-Based Lessons

There are many ways to integrate technology throughout the curriculum. Students may be assigned to conduct research using the Internet, create a multimedia project, use a simulation or drill and practice program, set up a collaborative site on the Web to support a community-based learning project, and so forth. The computer may or may not be the only medium of instruction. The use of technology should support the goals of the lesson or unit, as should other instructional media. Figure 7.1 depicts possible support materials for a lesson or unit. Note that these and other resources may be accessible via the Internet, making it easier to support online instruction (see Chapter 8).

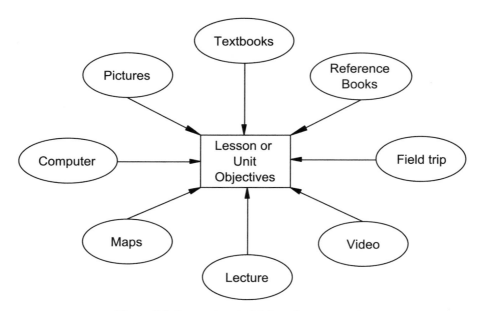

Figure 7.1. Support material for a lesson or unit.

Guest speakers, newspapers, magazines, music, and other resources also may be used to support a lesson. When planning a lesson, it is important that each resource supports the desired learner outcomes.

Each instructional resource may have its own specific purpose, yet support other activities. For example, students may take what they learn using the computer and apply it to an off-computer activity. Or, off-computer activities may support future computer activities. With a limited number of computers in the classroom, teachers need to rotate computer and off-computer activities among pupils to ensure equal access to the available technology. In many cases, teachers may want to place students into cooperative groups—even if students have their own computers.

Grouping Strategies

As mentioned in Chapter 3, there are many benefits of placing students into cooperative groups. Students may be placed into heterogeneous or homogenous cooperative groups based on their ability, learning style, gender, or other variable. Ivers and Barron (2006) note the disadvantages and advantages of placing students into cooperative groups for technology projects (see Table 7.1).

In most cases, heterogeneous groups are recommended. Johnson and Johnson (1999a) note that students in cooperative groups do just as well or better on achievement than students in competitive and individualistic learning conditions and that cooperative conditions can benefit all ability levels.

In order for a cooperative group to be successful, students need to work together to maximize their own learning, as well as their team members' learning (Johnson and Johnson 1999a). Cooperative learning groups have five defining characteristics (Johnson and Johnson 1999b):

1. Positive Interdependence (everyone succeeds or fails together)

2. Individual Accountability (everyone needs to contribute)

3. Face-to-Face Promotive Interaction (members produce joint products, providing both academic and personal support)

4. Social Skills (students practice positive interpersonal skills—communication, trust, conflict resolution)

5. Group Processing (members assess how well their team is functioning and how to improve)

Table 7.1. Advantages and Disadvantages of Various Grouping Variables

Grouping Variable	Type	Advantages	Disadvantages
Ability	Heterogeneous	Best opportunity for peer support and tutoring	Free-rider effect (less-able students may let other students do all the work)
Ability	Homogeneous	Students tend to bond and communicate more effectively	Low-ability students are often left at a significant learning disadvantage
Learning style, intelligence, or cognitive preference	Heterogeneous	Students are exposed to multiple perspectives and problem-solving methods, stimulating their learning and cognitive development	May be hard to group if students display a preference for one dominant learning style, intelligence, or cognitive preference; communication skills may be more difficult to develop because of different interests
Learning style, intelligence, or cognitive preference	Homogeneous	Students tend to bond and communicate more effectively	Students' focus and exposure to different perspectives are limited
Gender or background	Heterogeneous	Reduces stereotypes, promotes equality among perceived ability and leadership roles	Teachers may need to ensure that social skills are in place to eliminate preconceived biases
Gender or background	Homogeneous	May benefit specific special-interest groups, class topics, and girls' use of computers	May cause unnecessary tension between groups; not representative of the real world

Before placing students into cooperative groups, teachers need to make sure pupils understand these characteristics. Students may be asked to model or provide examples of each characteristic.

Cooperative Learning Techniques

There are many methods of cooperative learning techniques, including Learning Together, Jigsaw, Group Investigation, Student Teams Achievement Divisions, Teams Games Tournament, and Team Assisted Individualization (Slavin 1994; 1999; 2005; Vermette 1998):

Learning Together—heterogeneous student groups work together on a single assignment and receive the same grade for their group product. Students share tasks and responsibilities.

Jigsaw—a method of cooperative learning that assigns each of its members a particular learning task. For example, learning about pollution may involve learning about different types of pollution—air, water, and land. Each member chooses a particular form of pollution and is responsible for teaching his or her team members about their topic. Team members meet with other members from other groups to form "expert groups" to discuss and research their topic. Following research and discussion, the students return to their own teams and take turns teaching their teammates about their topic. Students take individual quizzes and earn a team score.

Group Investigation—students work in small groups toward an overall class project. Each group is assigned a different task or activity. For example, the class may be studying the solar system. Student groups are assigned different planets. Group members decide what information to gather and how to organize and present their findings.

Student Teams Achievement Divisions (STAD)—students learn about a topic as a team, contribute to the team by improving their performance, and earn bonus points based on their improvements. In general, students are heterogeneously mixed by ability and take individual weekly quizzes. For example, student teams may study ancient Egypt and take weekly quizzes on the content. Teams earn points based on each student's improvement from previous quizzes. For example, if a student scores six out of ten points on the first quiz and nine out of ten on the second quiz, she may earn nine points for her team, plus two bonus points for improving. If a student scores eight out of ten points on the first quiz and six out of ten on the second quiz, she may earn six points for her team, but no bonus points. If a student scores ten points on both quizzes, she may earn a total of twelve points (ten points for the second quiz plus two bonus points for the perfect scores) for her team.

Teams Games Tournament (TGT)— homogeneous, three-member teams are formed from the existing heterogeneous groups and compete against similar ability groups to earn points for their regular, heterogeneous group. For example, during weekly tournaments (for example, a spelling bee), low-ability groups compete against each other, average-ability groups compete against each other, and high-ability groups compete against each other. The winning homogeneous groups earn points for their heterogeneous teams.

Team-Assisted Individualization (TAI)—combines cooperative learning with individualized instruction. Student groups consist of individuals working at their own pace and level. Team members assist one another and check each other's work. Teams earn points based on the individual performance of each member in the group. Members take responsibility for each other's learning as well as their own.

Teachers need to decide on the most appropriate method of cooperative learning for the desired activity. For example, teachers may use Learning Together and have students research and create a wiki or PowerPoint presentation on a famous woman in history; Group Investigation to complete a whole class HyperStudio or Web site project; Jigsaw while students are conducting Internet research on different energy sources; or TGT during a whole class, computer-based drill activity (for example, a teacher-created Jeopardy PowerPoint game. See Chapter 5).

Group Size

Teachers also need to consider the appropriate group size. In most cases, educators will find that groups of two or three are ideal for many computer-related activities. In Table 7.2, Ivers and Barron (2006) discuss the advantages and disadvantages of group size related to creating multimedia projects.

Although Ivers and Barron (2006) discuss these advantages and disadvantages in relation to group-generated multimedia projects, most of the advantages and disadvantages are applicable to all computer-related activities. Students can help each other and rotate responsibilities (keyboarder, researcher, note taker, etc.) while at the computer.

Table 7.2. Advantages and Disadvantages of Different Group Sizes

Group Size	Advantages	Disadvantages
One	• Work at own pace • Not dependent on others	• Requires more classroom computer access time if computers are limited (every individual will need time on the computer) • Does not reflect real-world learning • Does not promote learning from different perspectives • Does not encourage cooperative problem solving • Takes a long time to complete a project • Individual may not be capable of handling all of the project's requirements

Two or three	• Learn from each other • Share project responsibilities • Supports real-world learning, learning from different perspectives, and cooperative problem solving • Classroom computer access time is cut in half, as students can work together at the computer	• Need to ensure that everyone contributes and has a chance to speak
Four	• Learn from each other • Share project responsibilities • Supports real-world learning, learning from different perspectives, and cooperative problem solving • Increases classroom computer access time • More talent and resources are available to create the project • Projects can be completed in less time	• Need to ensure that everyone contributes and has a chance to speak • May be difficult to share a computer • Requires greater interpersonal skills
Five or six	• Same as four	• Same as four • Easier for a member not to contribute • More chance of group disputes, leadership difficulties, and off-task behavior, which may delay the project • Group dynamics may be more appropriate for older, more mature students

One-to-One Laptop Classrooms

As more students have access to their own computer and wireless Internet in the classroom, teachers face new instructional and management issues. For older learners, the computer replaces paper and pencil note taking and has the potential to serve as the window and hub for all learning. For example, the wealth of educational resources available on the Internet (for example, textbooks, online experts, online applications and programs, instructional videos, and podcasts) makes it possible for classes to exist online—as many do. In face-to-face environments, teachers can capture the potential of the computer and face-to-face interactions to create a dynamic environment that supports shared learning activities on and off the computer. One-to-one computer environments should not be equated to isolated learning environments. Students should still be encouraged to work in groups. As described earlier, each pupil can take on a different responsibility and work as a team. Each student can use his or her own computer to contribute to the team's progress.

One-to-one laptop environments actually make it easier to integrate technology in the classroom if the teacher is ready to plan her instruction to take advantage of the computer's resources and potential. Challenges may arise with keeping students on task—as with other tools of instruction. The computer and the Internet bring new challenges.

Most teachers are familiar with off-task and other behavior associated with instant messaging in the classroom via cell phones and other mobile devices. Schools may ban cell phone use or have other policies written into their acceptable use plans. With a computer at every desk, educators need to ensure that students are on task. This means not using the computer when the teacher asks for the students' attention and ensuring that students are using the computer appropriately when assigned. For example, when asked, students should be taking notes rather than playing games, text messaging, surfing the Web, and so forth. Educators can alleviate off-task behavior by walking around the classroom. It is possible to monitor students' work through network systems, also, if each student is connected to the network and has the appropriate application installed. For example, SyncronEyes from SMART Technologies (http://www2.smarttech.com/) allows a teacher to monitor and communicate with individuals or groups of students from his or her own computer. The software also allows the teacher to control access to the Internet and to computer applications.

Other tips for one-to-one laptop use include:

- Never assume students already know how to use a laptop or a required program. Assign students to two or three per computer to review what they will need to know. Perhaps a first activity or assignment for the team could be a group-created "cheat sheet" to assist them in their learning.

- Be prepared. As with any lesson—on or off the computer—make sure your lesson plan is detailed and keeps students involved. Make sure all of the necessary materials are available, have been reviewed, and that laptops are charged.

- Set rules and expectations and be consistent. Let students know up front what you expect and the rules for using laptops in the classroom. Discuss consequences. You may want to have your students help to create these. Follow through and be consistent.

- Discuss cheating. Digital technology makes it much easier to cheat and plagiarize information. Ensure students understand the importance of submitting their own work, how to paraphrase, quote, cite information, and so forth. Introduce them to Turnitin.com (see Chapter 2). Make sure students' desktops and clipboards are clear before starting a test on their laptop. Students should not have additional programs open. All other devices (for example, cell phones and PDAs), books, and notes should be put away.

- Make sure students are focused on you. As noted earlier, when they are working on their laptops and you need their attention, make sure you wait until all eyes are on you and not on their computer screen. One way to accomplish this is to ask students to place the lid of their laptop down. Another way is to use software (for example, SyncronEyes) to control the students' laptops.

- Have a backup plan. Have outlets and cables available if laptops need to be recharged. Backup batteries are possible, too. Have a backup laptop or a "sharing" plan if a laptop is not working. Remember, it is not always necessary for all students to be working on their laptops at once.

- Use a timer. As with other lesson activities, use a timer to provide students with a set time to finish their work.

- Provide extension activities for early finishers. Not all students complete their work at the same time. As students finish their work, provide them with opportunities to explore and share what they have learned via their laptop. Educators may have specific Web sites for students to visit, activities related to learning more about their computer, word games involving a thesaurus, search activities, and so forth.

Designing a Classroom Computer Schedule

Until all students have access to their own classroom computer and wireless Internet, the need to develop a classroom computer schedule remains. Several variables effect how educators design their classroom computer schedule. In addition to grouping strategies, the number and condition of classroom computers will determine how computer time is allocated. Teaching schedules, allocated class periods, and the number of students in a classroom will influence computer use, too. Ivers and Barron (2006) provide several sample computer schedules based on a one-hour time period and various numbers of computers (see Figures 7.2 through 7.6).

Time	Computer Time		Project Assignments				Setting 1: Computer Classroom MW/TTH Computer Use
	MW	TTH	MW 1	TTH 2	MW 3	TTH 4	• three or four students per group • twenty-four to thirty-two students • fifteen-minute rotation schedule
9:00 A.M. to 9:15 A.M.	A	E	B F G H	B F G H	C D E	A C D	• Groups have computer time twice a week • When students are not at computers, they work on related project assignments. For example, Group A has computer time from 9:00 A.M. to 9:15 A.M. on Mondays and Wednesdays. Groups B, F, G, and H and groups C, D, and E work on related, noncomputer assignments (projects 1 and 3).
9:15 A.M. to 9:30 A.M.	B	F	F G H	B G H	A C D E	A C D E	• On Friday, students are provided with additional time to complete their related, noncomputer assignments. Groups may send one person to work with other groups to find clip art or research via the computer. For example, one person from each of groups A, B, C, and D may work together on the computer from 9:00 A.M. to 9:30 A.M., and one person from each of groups E, F, G, and H may work together on the computer from 9:30 A.M. to 10:00 A.M.
9:30 A.M. to 9:45 A.M.	C	G	A D E	A C D E	B F G H	B F H	
9:45 A.M. to 10:00 A.M.	D	H	A C E E	A C D H	B F G	B F G	

Figure 7.2. One computer rotation schedule.

Time	Computer Time	Project Assignments			Setting 2: Computer Classroom Daily Computer Use
		1	2	3	• twenty-four to thirty-two students • three or four students per group • fifteen-minute rotation schedule • When students are not at
9:00 A.M. to 9:15 A.M.	A B	C D	E F	G H	computers, they work on related project assignments. For example, Groups A and B have computer time between 9:00 A.M. and 9:15 A.M. Groups C, D, E, F, G, and H work on related, non-computer assignments (projects 1, 2, and 3).
9:15 A.M. to 9:30 A.M.	C D	E F	G H	A B	
9:30 A.M. to 9:45 A.M.	E F	G H	A B	C D	
9:45 A.M. to 10:00 A.M.	G H	A B	C D	E F	

Figure 7.3. Two computers rotation schedule.

Time	Computer Time	Project Assignments		Setting 3: Computer Classroom Daily Computer Use
		1	2	• twenty-seven to thirty-six students
9:00 A.M.	A	G	D	• three or four students per group
to	B	H	E	• twenty-minute rotation schedule
9:20 A.M.	C	I	F	• When students are not at computers, they work on related
9:20 A.M.	D	A	G	project assignments. For example, Groups A, B, and C have computer
to	E	B	H	time between 9:00 A.M. and
9:40 A.M.	F	C	I	9:20 A.M. Groups D, E, F, G, H, and I work on related, noncomputer
9:40 A.M.	G	D	A	assignments (projects 1 and 2).
to	H	E	B	
10:00 A.M.	I	F	C	

Figure 7.4. Three computers rotation schedule.

Time	Computer Time	Project Assignments	Setting 4: Computer Classroom Daily Computer Use (Version 1)
9:00 A.M.	A	E	• twenty-four to thirty-six students
to	B	F	• two to three students per group
9:30 A.M.	C	G	• thirty-minute rotation schedule
	D	H	• When students are not at computers, they work on related
9:30 A.M.	E	A	project assignments. For example, Groups A, B, C, and D have
to	F	B	computer time between 9:00 A.M.
10:00 A.M.	G	C	and 9:30 A.M. Groups E, F, G, and H, and groups I, J, K, and L work
	H	D	on related, noncomputer assignments.

Figure 7.5. Four computers rotation schedule (version 1).

Time	Computer Time	Project Assignments		Setting 4: Computer Classroom Daily Computer Use (Version 2)
		1	2	• twenty-four to thirty-two students
9:00 A.M.	A	I	E	• three or four students per group
to	B	J	F	• twenty-minute rotation schedule
9:20 A.M.	C	K	G	• When students are not at computers, they work on related,
	D	L	H	noncomputer project assignments. For example, Groups A, B, C, and
9:20 A.M.	E	A	I	D have computer time between
to	F	B	J	9:00 A.M. and 9:20 A.M. Groups E, F, G, and H work on related
9:40 A.M.	G	C	K	assignments.
	H	D	L	
9:40 A.M.	I	E	A	
to	J	F	B	
10:00 A.M.	K	G	C	
	L	H	D	

Figure 7.6. Four computers rotation schedule (version 2).

Many variations exist. For example, with only two computers in the classroom, teachers may decide to lengthen the computer time or use only pairs of students, providing pupils with computer access every other day versus every day. Blackline masters for creating a computer rotation schedule and assigning students to computer groups, times, and designated jobs (keyboarder, researcher, manager, and note taker) appear at the end of this chapter. Figures 7.7 and 7.8 provide examples for assigning students to computer groups, times, and jobs. Computers and computer time can remain constant (Figure 7.7) or they can be varied depending on the needs of the activity or students (Figure 7.8). For example, if only one classroom computer is connected to the Internet, student groups may take turns using this computer throughout the week. Numerous variations are possible.

Group number or name:		Monday	Tuesday	Wednesday	Thursday	Friday
	Computer #	1	1	1	1	1
Computer Wizards	Time	8:15 A.M. to 8:35 A.M.	8:15 A.M. to 8:35 A.M.	8:15 A.M. to 8:35 A.M.	8:15 A.M. to 8:35 A.M.	8:15 A.M. to 8:35 A.M.
Group members:						
Myra	Job	Keyboarder	Researcher	Manager	Note taker	(random pick)
Joseph	Job	Researcher	Manager	Note taker	Keyboarder	(random pick)
Tiffany	Job	Manager	Note taker	Keyboarder	Researcher	(random pick)
Abdul	Job	Note taker	Keyboarder	Researcher	Manager	(random pick)

Figure 7.7. Computer assignments and responsibilities—same time and computer.

Group number or name:		Monday	Tuesday	Wednesday	Thursday	Friday
	Computer #	1	4	1	1	1
Tech Toons	Time	9:00 A.M. to 9:20 A.M.	9:20 A.M. to 9:40 A.M.	9:00 A.M. to 9:20 A.M.	9:00 A.M. to 9:20 A.M.	
Group members:						
Hilda	Job	Keyboarder	Researcher	Manager	Note taker	
Mathew	Job	Researcher	Manager	Note taker	Keyboarder	
Ticia	Job	Manager	Note taker	Keyboarder	Researcher	
Troy	Job	Note taker	Keyboarder	Researcher	Manager	

Figure 7.8. Computer assignments and responsibilities—variation.

Planning computer time in classrooms with limited computer access is similar to organizing a rotation schedule for different activity centers. For example, student groups may access information about insects through the Internet or from a computer software program (for example, Insects by Discovery School) while they are on the computer, then illustrate and diagram different insects when they are no longer on the computer. Additional off-computer activities may involve learning more about insects from science texts or reference materials, examining insect specimens with the teacher or science specialist, or writing a research paper about an insect. If a teacher is facing limited resources (for example, one computer in the classroom), he or she may want to examine software designed for whole class instruction to determine if the software will support his or her instructional needs and objectives.

Lesson Ideas and Examples

When considering whether or not to use a particular software program, remember that most instructional software programs are not designed to be completed or mastered in one class period. For example, many simulations, instructional games, tutorials, and drill and practice programs are designed to take several class periods or weeks to complete. These programs have "bookmark" or saving features that return users to the location or position they last completed. Make sure the allocated time for the lessons or units supports the use of the software.

Some uses of technology can take more or less time dependent upon the scope of the project. For example, some multimedia projects can take considerable time to complete, depending on the size and requirements of the project. Working in cooperative groups is essential, as is off-computer planning. There are a variety of strategies and tips teachers can follow to effectively implement student-created multimedia projects.

Planning and Managing Multimedia Projects

The creation of multimedia projects supports research on how the brain learns—helping students construct knowledge and making subject matter more meaningful and motivating to learn (Metiri Group 2008; Wolfe 2001). Multimedia parallels the natural way people learn and supports inquiry-based learning (Bagui 1998; Metiri Group 2008; So and Kong 2007). The use of multimedia can be effective for teaching and learning with all levels of students, including those with special needs (Badge, Dawson, Cann, and Scott 2008; Eshet and Chajut 2007; Liao 1999; Steelman 2005; Walsh 2007). There are many benefits of implementing student-created multimedia projects in the classroom. Like other uses of technology, the effectiveness of multimedia projects is dependent upon the educators' ability to plan, manage, and assess them.

In their book, *Multimedia Projects in Education: Designing, Producing, and Assessing* (3rd ed.), Ivers and Barron (2006) present the DDD-E model for planning, managing, and assessing multimedia projects. The first phase of the model, Decide, represents the preparation and research stage:

- Instructional goals are set.

- Resources, prerequisite skills, and background knowledge are assessed.

- Project guidelines are provided.

- Students are assigned to groups.

- Students brainstorm and conduct research about their topic.

The second phase, Design, focuses on the planning steps for student projects. During the Design phase, students outline the content of the project (based on their research in the Decide phase) and create flowcharts and storyboards. A flowchart depicts how storyboards are linked or how one storyboard accesses another. For example, a five-card (page) report on raccoons may begin with a title card which links to a menu card. The menu card may provide options to link to information about raccoon sounds, eating habits, or their habitat (see Figure 7.9).

A storyboard represents a single screen, card, or page of the report and contains the text, graphics, and navigation links. For example, the menu card for the raccoon sample presented in Figure 7.9 may look like the storyboard presented in Figure 7.10.

Information about the graphics, links, and other storyboard elements can be written on the back or to the side of the storyboard. A sample storyboard blackline master appears at the end of this chapter. Students also may use index cards to design and layout their storyboards.

Educators need to assess students' work after each step of the Design phase to ensure they are meeting the requirements of the lesson. For example, before students are allowed to progress to the flowchart and storyboard stage, teachers need to review their content outlines to confirm they are

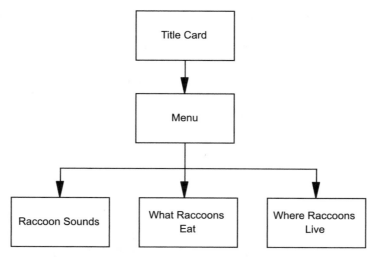

Figure 7.9. Flowchart illustrating how cards or pages of a multimedia report are linked.

Figure 7.10. Storyboard menu for a raccoon multimedia project.

meeting the lesson's objectives. Teachers also review students' flowcharts and storyboards prior to letting them start their work on the computer.

The Decide and Design phases of multimedia development are invaluable for helping students plan and organize their work. It is not until the third phase, Develop, that students actually begin constructing their project on the computer. Evaluation (representing the E in the DDD-E model) is ongoing throughout the entire process. Teachers ensure students are meeting the instructional goals by assessing their work during each phase of the DDD-E model (see Table 7.3).

Table 7.3. DDD-E Assessments

DDD-E Phase	What Is Assessed
Decide	Resources, prerequisite skills, background knowledge
	Brainstorming and research activities
Design	Content outline
	Flowchart and storyboards
Develop	First version of multimedia project (reviewed by peers)
Evaluation (final)	Final version of multimedia project

The model presented by Ivers and Barron (2006) is applicable for HyperStudio, PowerPoint, Web-based, and other types of multimedia projects.

In many cases, teachers may find that they already implement the Decide and Design phases into their instruction. For example, it is common for educators to use graphic organizers and webbing techniques to help their students see and describe the relationship among different topics. Teachers often begin lessons by providing background information (research) and organizing this into meaningful chunks. After several lessons, the class may create a graphic organizer to help students remember and discuss what they have learned. Figure 7.11 represents a graphic organizer for teaching how animals become endangered.

Causes of Endangerment

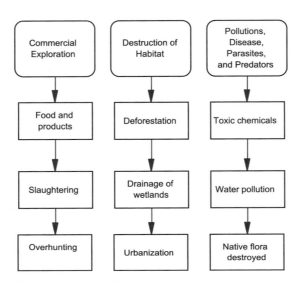

Figure 7.11. Graphic organizer for teaching how animals become endangered.

Graphic organizers are perfect springboards for developing whole class multimedia projects. Using the example presented in Figure 7.11, the teacher assigns student groups to conduct further research on a particular topic for inclusion into a whole class multimedia project. For example, Group One may conduct further research on deforestation; Group Two may gather more information on toxic chemicals, and so forth. Adding what they learn to their prior knowledge, students create a storyboard for their topic. After the teacher reviews the students' storyboards, students develop their work on the computer. Students' work is linked to submenus or a main menu created by the teacher. Each student can be presented with a copy of the whole class project for review.

Learning by creating or reconstructing knowledge through multimodalities enhances students' ability to learn new information (see Chapter 3). In many cases, teachers already engage in the planning stages for multimedia projects. Introducing and organizing content into graphics organizers aids in the natural development of multimedia projects.

Additional Tips for Integrating Computers Throughout the Curriculum

Proper planning for computer activities will help ensure students have equal access to the computers, stay on task, know what is expected of them, and are assessed on their progress. Educators can do several things to help them integrate computers throughout the curriculum. In addition to developing computer schedules, educators should:

• Be familiar with the software they plan to use with their students.

• Decide how they will evaluate students' progress while on the computer.

- Determine if there is enough time during the lesson or unit to use the desired technology.

- Model the use of the software as a whole class when possible, pointing out the mechanics of the program as well as instructional strategies.

- Provide students with review guides on how to use the software or technology device.

- Make sure students know how to take proper care of the computer and software, as well as have the necessary skills to use the desired technologies.

- Ensure students have completed the preliminary activities or research necessary for their computer use prior to their computer time.

- Place students in heterogeneous groups or pairs when possible.

- Avoid conducting whole class lessons when individuals are on the computer; educators should work with small groups or individuals who need assistance.

- Apply knowledge gained from computer activities to off-computer activities.

- Ensure cables and cords cannot be tripped over or accidentally pulled loose by anyone walking by the computers. If using battery-charged laptops, make sure batteries are fully charged.

- Place computers in a location where the teacher can see the monitors at all times (for example, against the back wall where they won't be a distraction to other students but are still visible to the teacher).

- Always consult the district or school acceptable use policies regarding the use of technology (including the Internet) in the classroom.

Many software programs provide teacher's guides that contain worksheets to assist them with pre-instructional, instructional, and post-instructional tasks. Software guides and review pages usually are included. When shopping for software, ask for the teacher or school version to obtain these additional resources. Teachers can order school versions of software directly from the publisher or from educational software Web sites such as Educational Resources (http://edresources.com/) or the Academic Superstore (http://www.academicsuperstore.com).

Monitoring and Assessing Students' Work

There are several ways to monitor and assess students' work. Assessment may take place on a daily basis using learning logs or journals, program printouts (if available), or follow-up activities. Rubrics may be used for final assessments or as tools to gauge students' progress through various steps of a project.

Ongoing Assessment

Individual and group progress can be assessed using daily learning logs or journals. Students may be directed to record their progress in a spiral journal, a classroom blog, or asked to complete a learning log designed by the teacher. Figure 7.12 provides an example of a daily log for students working in teams. A "Team Daily Log" blackline master is provided at the end of this chapter.

Students may be asked to provide printouts of their work or printouts of the assessments provided by the computer program. As mentioned, many tutorials and drill and practice programs track and record students' progress. Several programs provide options to print scores, follow-up quizzes, and additional activities. In some cases, these programs provide diagnostic information in addition to how many problems a student may have gotten correct or incorrect. Knowing what errors students are making helps educators apply the best instructional approaches.

Team Daily Log: _____
Today's Date

Team Members:

_____

_____   Recorder's
                                    Initials:
_____

_____

What did your team accomplish today?

What problems did you encounter?

What are your goals for tomorrow?

How well did your team work together today?   1   2   3
                                                  poor okay great

Additional notes or comments:

Figure 7.12. Team daily log.

Students also may be asked to provide printouts of their work in progress. For example, if students are creating a story, newsletter, picture, or presentation on the computer, teachers may ask students for copies of their work even though it is incomplete. This allows educators to see how pupils are progressing and provides opportunities to give ongoing feedback and additional instruction if necessary. If student groups are creating a wiki, the teacher can access the wiki and track team and individual student progress. Short, online surveys and quizzes also can be used to assess individual and team progress (see Chapter 2).

Students may be asked to take notes during certain computer activities. For example, if students are using Where in the USA is Carmen Sandiego? as part of a U.S. geography unit, teachers may require them to keep track of the states and cities they visit, interesting facts about these cities and states, information about historical monuments they encounter, and so forth. This data may be integrated into the students' final state report, overview of the United States, and into a class-culminating project.

Many school versions of programs come with follow-up material to assist educators with tracking students' progress and meeting national standards. These include programs by Tom Snyder Productions, Sunburst, The Learning Company, and others. For example, Timeliner by Tom Snyder includes a comprehensive teacher's guide that includes student activities, worksheets, and lessons to meet state and national standards across a variety of subject areas. There is a user resources page available on the Tom Snyder Productions Web site, also, with links to additional clip art and worksheets, information sites for students, and free time lines.

Educators can find extension ideas and activities on the Web for a variety of software programs. These can be found on the publisher's Web site and in online lesson plans and publications, blogs, and other online resources. Activities booklets for certain software titles are available at teacher supply stores.

Rubrics

A rubric is a scoring guide that provides educators with an alternative method for assessing students' work. Instead of multiple-choice, true/false, and short answer forms of assessment, rubrics can be designed to indicate how well students are meeting objectives through specific, predefined criteria. Rubrics are especially helpful for assessing computer-based projects such as presentations, WebQuests, and other multimedia assignments. They can also be used to evaluate newsletters, stories, and other creative activities.

Rubrics show students how their work will be evaluated and provide teachers with criteria to measure and document students' progress. Rubrics are usually distributed before an assignment, providing pupils with project guidelines and expectations. In most cases, educators will want students to contribute to the creation of a rubric. Student input allows them to create their own learning experiences and to work toward individual goals.

When creating a rubric, educators will want to consider:

• State or district standards they plan to address,

• Knowledge, skills, or concepts they want to assess,

• Students' performance levels, and

• Criteria to judge students' performance.

It is important that educators focus on measuring a stated objective and specify specific criteria that indicate the degree to which the objective has been met. For example, a requirement for a multimedia project about famous explorers may require students to discuss the contributions of four explorers. Students may score a 4 if they correctly identified and described the contributions of four explorers, score a 3 if they correctly identified and described the contributions of three explorers, score a 2 if they correctly identified and described the contributions of two explorers, and so forth. To maintain objectivity and consistency, criteria should be as specific as possible. Educators should avoid making general statements such as, "The student covers the topic completely and in-depth." What constitutes completely or in-depth? Educators will want to define each criterion. Vague or general statements reduce the reliability and validity of rubrics (Moskal and Leydens 2000).

When designing a rubric, categorize topic areas (for example, content, grammar, and technology) or provide separate rubrics for each area, depending on the complexity of the project. Teachers can find sample rubrics on the Internet, as well as resources to assist educators in creating rubrics. Table 7.4 lists and describes several Web sites with rubrics resources and information.

Table 7.4. Rubric Information on the Internet

Name and Source	Description
Kathy Schrock's Guide for Educators: Assessment and Rubric Information http://school.discovery.com/ schrockguide/assess.html	Lists multiple links to rubric resources, including subject specific and general rubrics, Web page rubrics, articles, and more.
MidLink Magazine Teacher Resource Room http://www.ncsu.edu/midlink/ho.html	Provides links to rubrics, evaluation resources, and downloadable rubric templates.
Rubistar http://rubistar.4teachers.org/	Provides pre-created rubrics that teachers can customize for a variety of topics, as well as an online rubric generator. Both English and Spanish versions are available.

Rubrics for Teachers http://www.rubrics4teachers.com/	Provides links to ready-made rubrics.
Teach-nology Rubrics http://teachers.teach-nology.com/ web_tools/rubrics/	Provides online rubric generators for a variety of topics.
TeacherVision: Creating Rubrics http://www.teachervision.fen.com/ teaching-methods-and-management/rubrics/4521. html	Provides step-by-step information on how to create rubrics.

Ivers and Barron (2006) provide numerous rubrics for helping teachers assess student-created multimedia projects. As mentioned, it is important that assessment is ongoing. Rubrics can be used to measure various stages of projects; for example, students' storyboards may be evaluated using a storyboard rubric (see Figure 7.13) before they are allowed to proceed to the computer to develop their project.

Storyboard Rubric

CRITERIA	0	1	2	3
Content	Content is missing or is incomplete.	Content is complete, but not correct.	Content is complete, but difficult to read and understand.	Content is complete, correct, and easy to understand.
Links	No links are indicated or described.	More than one link or description is incomplete.	One link or description is incomplete.	All links are indicated and described.
Layout	The design is inconsistent in more than one area.	The design is inconsistent in one area.	The design is consistent, but not clear.	The design is consistent and clear.
Media Elements	The required media elements are not included.	Some of the required media elements are included and desc ribed .	All of the required media elements are included, but not all are described.	All of the required media elements are included and described.
Font, background, and transition information	Font, background, and transition information is incomplete.	Two of the required elements are incomplete.	One of the required elements is incomplete.	Font, background, and transition information is complete.
Other				
Notes:				

Total Score _____ ____

Figure 7.13. Storyboard rubric adapted from Ivers and Barron (2006).

Rubrics can be used to provide students with specific feedback regarding the progress of their work, as well as a form of final evaluation. It is important that students understand the criteria in which they are being evaluated and are allowed opportunities to contribute to the making of rubrics.

Summary

Computers may be used to assist educators with many tasks. These include facilitating cooperative groups, teaching research and analytical skills, engaging students in written and verbal communication skills, addressing individual needs and learning styles, managing records, and creating instructional materials. The computer, in and of itself, does nothing. Teachers decide how, when, and why the computer will be used.

The computer's effectiveness often depends upon the teacher's ability to plan, manage, and assess computer-related activities. This involves identifying objectives and learner outcomes, available resources, students' background, assessment issues, and whether or not the computer activity enhances and supports desired learner outcomes. To be used effectively, the computer should be used to support twenty-first-century learning skills. Planning off-computer activities, grouping strategies, computer rotation schedules, and ongoing assessment can help teachers more effectively integrate the use of computers across the curriculum.

Activities

1. Create a database or list of the available software in your classroom and in the school lab (if applicable).

2. If possible, observe a one-to-one laptop classroom. Interview the teacher and ask about his or her management tips for using laptops in the classroom. Share your observation and interview findings.

3. Design a lesson that integrates students' use of computers in the classroom. List the objective(s), content standard(s), technology standard(s), materials, procedure, assessment, and so on. Include a computer rotation schedule for the lesson (see the "Computer Rotation Schedule" blackline master).

4. Use the "Computer Groups" blackline master to create student computer times and responsibilities for the above lesson.

5. Think of an activity where you currently use a graphic organizer to teach and review information. Describe and illustrate how this activity could be developed into a multimedia project.

6. Create a rubric for activity number one or another lesson using one of the online rubric generators or templates listed in Table 7.4. Attach your lesson plan.

7. Observe another instructor teaching a lesson that integrates students' use of computers in the classroom. Discuss the lesson with the teacher. Summarize your observations and discussion, including what you learned.

Resources

Discovery School
http://teacherstore.discovery.com/

Sunburst
http://sunburst.com/

The Learning Company
http://www.learningcompany.com/

Tom Snyder Productions
http://tomsnyder.com/

References

Badge, J. L., E. Dawson, A. J. Cann, and J. Scott. 2008. Assessing the accessibility of online learning. *Innovations in Education and Teaching International* 45 (2): 103–113.

Bagui, S. 1998. Reasons for increased learning using multimedia. *Journal of Educational Multimedia and Hypermedia* 7 (1): 3–18.

Eshet, Y. and E. Chajut. 2007. Living books: The incidental bonus of playing with multimedia. *Journal of Educational Multimedia and Hypermedia* 16 (4): 377–388.

Johnson, D. W. and R. T. Johnson. 1999a. *Learning Together and Alone: Cooperative, Competitive, and Individualistic Learning.* 5th ed. Needham Heights, MA: Allyn & Bacon.

Johnson, D. W. and R. T. Johnson. 1999b. Making cooperative learning work. *Theory into Practice* 38 (2): 67–73.

Liao, Y. C. 1999. Effects of hypermedia on students' achievement: A meta-analysis. *Journal of Educational Multimedia and Hypermedia* 8 (3): 255–277.

Metiri Group. 2008. *Multimodal Learning Through Media: What the Research Says.* Available at: http://www.cisco.com/web/strategy/docs/education/Multimodal-Learning-Through-Media.pdf. (Accessed April 29, 2008).

Moskal, B. M. and J. A. Leydens. 2000. Scoring rubric development: Validity and reliability. *Practical Assessment, Research & Evaluation* 7 (10). Available at http://pareonline.net/getvn.asp?v=7&n=10. (Accessed November 27, 2008).

Slavin, R. E. 1999. Comprehensive approaches to cooperative learning. *Theory into Practice* 38 (2): 74–79.

———. 1994. *Cooperative Learning: Theory, Research, and Practice.* 2nd ed. Needham Heights, MA: Allyn & Bacon.

———. 2005. *Educational Psychology Theory and Practice.* 8th ed. Boston, MA: Allyn & Bacon.

So, W.-M. W. and S.-C. Kong. 2007. Approaches of inquiry learning with multimedia resources in primary classrooms. *Journal of Computers in Mathematics and Science Teaching* 26 (4): 329–354.

Steelman, J. D. 2005. Multimedia makes its mark. *Learning and Leading with Technology* 33 (1): 16–18.

Vermette, P. J. 1998. *Making Cooperative Learning Work: Student Teams in K-12 Classrooms.* Upper Saddle River, NJ: Prentice Hall.

Walsh, C. S. 2007. Creativity as capital in the literacy classroom: youth as multimodal designers. *Literacy* 41 (2): 79–85.

Wolfe, P. 2001. *Brain Matters: Translating Research into Classroom Practice.* Alexandria, VA: Association for Supervision and Curriculum Development.

Blackline Masters

- Computer Groups
- Computer Rotation Schedule
- Storyboard Rubric
- Storyboard Template
- Team Daily Log

Computer Groups

	Monday	Tuesday	Wednesday	Thursday	Friday
Group number or name: _____ / **Computer #**					
Time					
Group members: / **Job**					
Job					
Job					
Job					

	Monday	Tuesday	Wednesday	Thursday	Friday
Group number or name: _____ / **Computer #**					
Time					
Group members: / **Job**					
Job					
Job					
Job					

Computer Rotation Schedule

Use the following template to create your own computer rotation schedule. See Figures 7.2 through 7.6 for more information.

Time	Computer Time	Project Assignments			
					Number of computers: _____
					Number of students: _____
					Number of students per group: ___
					Describe computer activity:
					Describe project assignments:

Storyboard Rubric

CRITERIA	0	1	2	3
Content	Content is missing or is incomplete.	Content is complete, but not correct.	Content is complete, but difficult to read and understand.	Content is complete, correct, and easy to understand.
Links	No links are indicated or described.	More than one link or description is incomplete.	One link or description is incomplete.	All links are indicated and described.
Layout	The design is inconsistent in more than one area.	The design is inconsistent in one area.	The design is consistent, but not clear.	The design is consistent and clear.
Media Elements	The required media elements are not included.	Some of the required media elements are included and described.	All of the required media elements are included, but not all are described.	All of the required media elements are included and described.
Font, background, and transition information	Font, background, and transition information is incomplete.	Two of the required elements are incomplete.	One of the required elements is incomplete.	Font, background, and transition information is complete.
Other				
Notes:				

Total Score _____

From *A Teacher's Guide to Using Technology in the Classroom*, Second Edition by Karen S. Ivers. Westport, CT: Libraries Unlimited. Copyright © 2009.

Storyboard Template

Storyboard title: _____   Storyboard #: _____

Font and background:	
Graphic(s):	
Sound(s):	
Video(s):	
Links and transitions:	

Team Daily Log: _____

Today's Date

Team Members:

_____

_____

_____

_____

Recorder's Initials:

What did your team accomplish today?

What problems did you encounter?

What are your goals for tomorrow?

How well did your team work together today?

1	2	3
poor	okay	great

Additional notes or comments:

Managing and Assessing Online Computing Environments

A Scenario

As a child, Mr. Nick recalled how he needed to be home-schooled while he fought a rare form of cancer. Mr. Nick was always an active child and enjoyed coming to school to be with his friends. When Mr. Nick learned of his condition and what needed to be done, he was devastated. Fortunately, his teacher and classmates were not going to let Mr. Nick feel alone and isolated. The school managed to set up a videoconferencing system so, while he was at home recovering, he could still interact with his classmates and teacher. Mr. Nick never forgot his experience. He recovered and finished school with his classmates. Because of his experience, Mr. Nick decided to become a teacher and an advocate for distance education. When his colleagues ask him why he enjoys teaching online, he explains that distance education is a way to keep students engaged and connected no matter where the students live. He shares, "With today's tools, students can interact with each other asynchronously (not at the same time) and synchronously (at the same time), creating a richer learner environment where everyone has a chance to participate."

Introduction

Distance education has been part of the American education system for many years. It has provided learning opportunities for homebound students, students in remote areas, and students with special interests. For some, the thought of distance education creates images of isolated learning and pre-packaged, self-paced instruction. Time, technology, and the needs of society have changed how distance education is designed and delivered. This chapter provides a brief history of distance education, a discussion of programs and resources that support online learning, and suggestions for managing and assessing students' work in virtual learning environments. Topics include:

• Distance Education: Then and Now

   Five Generations of Distance Learning

   Standards for Delivering Instruction over the Internet

151

- Virtual Environments for Learning

  Course Management Systems

  Additional Support for Delivering Online Instruction

  Resources for Developing Course Content

- Planning and Managing Online Learning

  Elements of Online Environments That Support Student Learning

  Requirements, Expectations, and Recommendations

- Monitoring and Assessing Students' Work in Online Learning Environments

  Rubrics for Online Participation

  Multiple Assessment Measures

  Helpful Tips and Tricks

Distance Education: Then and Now

Distance education, the concept that students and teachers are in different locations while instruction is taking place, has been around for hundreds of years. Distance education dates back to as early as 1728, to a newspaper advertisement by Caleb Philips, seeking to teach students shorthand through mailed lessons (Holmberg 2005). This was the first evidence of correspondence, distance education. As nations began developing inexpensive and reliable postal systems, correspondence schools emerged. The first correspondence school to offer higher education courses was the Chautauqua Correspondence College, later renamed the Chautauqua College of Liberal Arts in 1883 (Moore and Kearsley 2005).

Distance education has run parallel with traditional or "face-to-face" instruction for many years. While one may argue instructional delivery in face-to-face environments has not changed much over the last 100 years—even with advancements in technology—the same is not true for distance education. As technology has evolved, so has the delivery and structure of distance education. Distance education is no longer limited to an isolated, linear delivery system of information. It can be a robust, interactive, multimodality, and reflective learning experience.

Five Generations of Distance Learning

Moore and Kearsley (2005) identify five generations of distance education: correspondence, broadcast radio and television, open universities, teleconferencing, and Internet/Web. Correspondence education is based on postal delivery of information and is often referred to as independent or home study. Broadcast radio and television education, like correspondence education, makes it possible to deliver one-way instruction but to large groups of people in the same place at one time. This enables a guest speaker to be at one location and deliver information to a class of students somewhere else. Radio, limited to an audio format, did not live up to educators' expectations. Educational television, on the other hand, quickly became part of many school districts and universities, as well as public-service offerings.

Open universities, the third generation of distance education, began in Great Britain, combining television broadcasts with correspondence instruction. Many open universities are open to anyone seeking a degree and rely on large enrollments to obtain both cost effectiveness and quality. Usually, students are admitted on a first come, first serve basis. Instruction is pre-designed or "canned" and delivered via a distance (there are not any classrooms), with faculty serving as tutors or coaches.

CalStateTEACH (see http://www.calstateteach.net/) is a California State University (CSU) teacher preparation program based on the open university model. Developed by a team of CSU faculty experts, the curriculum is divided into four terms (about eighteen months) and was originally delivered via instructional binders and textbooks, with the majority of support taking place over the Internet. With the widespread availability of broadband Internet access, program materials and instruction are now accessed online. Learning support faculty (LSF) are assigned to groups of students and serve as coaches and assessors of students' work. Instruction is pre-designed. Students work at their own pace but within a given time line, submitting their work over the Internet to their LSF for assessment. The LSF typically observes the student during student teaching once a month. Each student also has an onsite mentor or master teacher. There are several regional centers throughout the state for CalStateTEACH, each responsible for specific counties. CalStateTEACH meets the needs of students who live a great distance from California State universities. Most students serve as interns in outlying schools or in schools where there is a great shortage of teachers.

Teleconferencing, the fourth generation of distance education, began as audio-conferencing designed for group use. It allowed the instructor to deliver information to students in a designated location, plus it let students respond to or ask questions of the instructor during the conference. Unlike correspondence, television, or radio methods of instruction, teleconferencing allows students to interact with their instructors in real time. Interactive videoconferencing is now available, enabling students and instructors to be in different locations but still able to see and speak with each other in real time. Advances in technology and broadband access have made interactive videoconferencing a common practice over the Internet.

The Internet/Web represents the fifth generation of distance education and, like previous generations of distance education, provides new opportunities, challenges, and ways of organizing and delivering instruction.

Standards for Delivering Instruction over the Internet

Although advancements in technologies have enabled new ways to provide distance learning, many educators still perceive distance education as an isolated activity, where students learn independently from posted lecture notes or modules—a digital correspondence system, if you will. Interaction is limited, if it exists, and is usually between the student and the instructor. The curriculum may or may not be created by the instructor, whose role has become that of a coach or tutor. Assessments may be limited to multiple-choice, true/false, or other formats of objective quizzes. Of course, this may describe existing distance education programs and courses, just as it may describe a large lecture hall format in a face-to-face learning environment. Both environments, face-to-face and distant, have the potential to make learning an isolated, rote, and passive experience. The teacher and how instruction is designed and delivered make the difference.

In September 2007, the North American Council for Online Learning (NACOL) released *National Standards of Quality for Online Courses* (NACOL 2007). In 2008, NACOL released standards for online teaching (see *Skills of the Teacher*). Both sets of standards are available on NACOL's Web site (http://www.nacol.org/nationalstandards/) and include subcategories for each standard, as well as a rating scale:

- 0 Absent—component is missing

- 1 Unsatisfactory—needs significant improvement

- 2 Somewhat satisfactory—needs targeted improvements

- 3 Satisfactory—discretionary improvement needed

- 4 Very satisfactory—no improvement needed

There are six standards for delivering instruction online: Content, Instructional Design, Student Assessment, Technology, Course Evaluation and Management, and 21st-Century Skills. As mentioned, each standard has subcategories. For example, under Instructional Design, the following categories are listed (NACOL 2008, p. 4):

- Course design reflects a clear understanding of student needs and incorporates varied ways to learn and multiple levels of mastery of the curriculum.

- The course is organized into units and lessons.

- The course unit overview describes the objectives, activities, and resources that frame the unit. It includes a description of the activities and assignments that are central to the unit.

- Each lesson includes a lesson overview, content and activities, assignments, and assessments to provide multiple learning opportunities for students to master the content.

- The course is designed to teach concepts and skills that students will retain over time.

- The course instruction includes activities that engage students in active learning.

- Instruction provides students with multiple learning paths to master the content based on student needs.

- The teacher engages students in learning activities that address a variety of learning styles and preferences.

- The course provides opportunities for students to engage in higher-order thinking, critical-reasoning activities, and thinking in increasingly complex ways.

- The course reflects multicultural education and is accurate, current, and free of bias.

- The teacher can adapt learning activities to accommodate students' needs.

The National Education Association (NEA) provides a guide to high school online courses (see http://www.nea.org/technology/onlinecourseguide.html). It provides standards for online teaching (see *Skills of the Teacher*) and it provides questions for policymakers, online teachers, managers and administrators of online courses, parents and guardians, and students. Both NACOL and the NEA highlight the importance of teaching students twenty-first-century skills; providing a rigorous curriculum that is aligned with appropriate national, state, or district standards; providing well-designed instruction; ensuring teachers are prepared to teach online; maintaining regular communication with students and engaging students in interactive activities; designing assessments that are ongoing, authentic, and provide opportunities for student reflection; ensuring ongoing course evaluation, the necessary support, and management systems; and providing an easy to use and up-to-date technology infrastructure.

Virtual Environments for Learning

Classroom and course Web pages can be used for online, interactive e-learning (electronic learning) opportunities, including distance education. Students can engage in discussion-board forums, wikis, and blogs; take online quizzes; interact with each other through chat or videoconferencing; conduct surveys; and view instructional modules and other activities built into a course Web site. Many programs have been specifically designed for e-learning and distance education. Chapters 5 and 6 provide examples of e-learning opportunities such as online programs and resources. This section discusses course management systems, other options for online learning, and resources for developing instructional material for distance education.

Course Management Systems

A course management system (CMS) is a comprehensive software package that facilitates the design, delivery, assessment, and management of online courses and professional development. In some cases, instructors may use a CMS (also called an LMS—a learning management system) as a supplement within a face-to-face class. For example, teachers may use a CMS to distribute material or share URLs to support a lesson, provide quizzes so students can check their understanding, and post grades so students can keep track of their progress. Teachers may also use the system to post homework assignments and lectures for review. Teachers may choose to use other features within the CMS, such as the discussion forum, chat, and other options to support their instruction. Teachers also may use the CMS as a substitute for a face-to-face session or class. A CMS supports hybrid (both face-to-face and distance learning approaches to instruction) and completely online courses and programs. A CMS can be password protected, prohibiting unregistered users or nonstudents access to the course. Course management systems typically provide templates and other tools to help educators design, deliver, assess, and manage course instruction.

There are many CMS options available. Blackboard by Blackboard, Inc., is a CMS designed for universities, K-12 schools, and corporations. The company offers a variety of different products and services, including the Blackboard Learning System for facilitating instruction, communication, and assessment; the Blackboard Community System for expanding communication, collaboration, and connections across and beyond the district or campus; and the Blackboard Content System for storing and managing content more effectively (see http://www.blackboard.com/ for more information). Blackboard, Inc., also provides a CMS specifically for K-12 schools, Blackboard K-12 School Central. Figure 8.1 is a sample course page, from the instructor's perspective, provided by Blackboard in their online demo of K-12 School Central (see http://www.blackboardschoolcentral.com/).

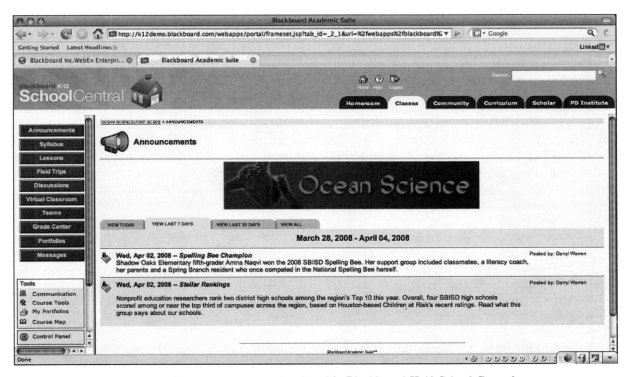

Figure 8.1. Sample course page developed in Blackboard K-12 School Central.

Moodle is another CMS designed to help educators create effective online instruction. It is an open-source program, meaning it complies with several criteria, including:

• It's free.

• The source code is available so a programmer can modify the program if desired.

• Modifications and derived works are redistributed under the same terms as the original software license.

Moodle is available in a variety of languages and includes discussion forums, quiz options, surveys, chat, online grading, peer assessment, and other activities (see http://moodle.org/).

Angel Learning (http://www.angellearning.com/) supports K-12 teaching and learning also. Communication and collaboration tools include discussion boards, chat, podcasting, wikis, blogs, and games. Angel Learning provides language packs to support non-English-speaking students and a variety of other tools (for example, attendance manager, online gradebook, monitoring options for parents, customized learning options, and more) to support online instruction. Demo accounts are available.

Additional Support for Delivering Online Instruction

Other options for delivering online instruction include MyClass.net (http://www.myclass.net/) Yahoo! Groups (http://groups.yahoo.com/), and Scholastic's Class Homepage Builder (http://teacher. scholastic.com/homepagebuilder/). MyClass.net includes class and community discussion boards, a drop box for homework, e-mail, and more. Yahoo! Groups features chat, calendar, discussion board, database, and polling options. Yahoo! Groups is free but supported through online advertising. Educators should note that advertisements appear on course Web pages and e-mail. Scholastic's Class Homepage Builder is also free but does not provide advertisements to students. Teachers can post homework assignments, class assignments and projects, and important links and resources. These and other online resources provide educators with opportunities to engage students in shared learning opportunities and discussions via the Web.

Resources for Developing Course Content

In addition to templates provided by course management systems and class Web sites, there are a variety of software programs that can be used to help teachers design and create instruction. Microsoft PowerPoint is supported by most course management systems. Files can be saved in a Web format (for example, Save as Web Page) and displayed on the Web. PowerPoint presentations can be converted to Flash files, also, by using a PowerPoint to Flash converter (see http://www.authorgen. com/). The file will retain the sound, animation, timings, and so forth that were in the original PowerPoint presentation. Advantages of Flash files include reduced size, secure content, and easy distribution on the Web.

Articulate (http://www.articulate.com/) provides a variety of software tools to support online instruction. Products include Presenter, Quizmaker, Engage, and Articulate Online. They can be purchased individually or in a suite. Presenter converts PowerPoint presentations into Flash files; Quizmaker allows users to create Flash-based quizzes, assessments, and surveys; Engage enables users to add interactive content to their courses; and Articulate Online tracks student learning. Packaged together, these products offer many of the same tools available in course management systems. Free fifteen- and thirty-day trials are available.

Camtasia Studio by TechSmith (http://www.techsmith.com/) enables users to record their computer screen and voice. For example, a teacher may demonstrate how to create a formula in Excel just as she or he would in a face-to-face classroom, with step-by-step instructions and examples. The software makes a movie (for example, a Flash file) of the events on the computer screen and records the narration simultaneously. There is also an option to add or edit narration, music, and other media to the file. Files can be produced in a variety of formats, including Flash, MP3, iPod video, RealMedia, and more. TechSmith also produces Camtasia Relay, Snag It, and other products. Camtasia Relay is a quick way to record and distribute a presentation or lecture. Snag It allows users to capture and edit anything they see on their computer screen. Most Techsmith products are available for a thirty-day trial period.

As noted in Chapter 5, podcasts can be created and shared over the Web and through mobile devices to enhance instruction. Web-based podcast creation tools include PodOmatic (http://www. podomatic.com/), PodBean (http://www.podbean.com/), Gcast (http://www.gcast.com/), and MyPodcast (http://www.mypodcast.com/). Other options include Podcast Station by Audion Laboratories (http://www.podcaststation.com/), Propaganda by MixMeister Technology, LLC. (http://www.

makepropaganda.com/), and Audacity by Source Forge (http://audacity.sourceforge.net/). Each creates audio podcasts. Audacity is a free, open-source program. Digital still and video cameras can be used to capture pictures and video for video podcasts. Apple's iMovie (http://www.apple.com/ilife/imovie/), Premiere Pro by Adobe (http://www.adobe.com/products/premiere/), and other video-editing programs can be used to make video podcasts.

There are numerous resources to help teachers develop online course content that addresses multimodality learning. The Internet also provides access to online experts, e-books, interactive programs, virtual field trips, discussion forums, collaborative projects, and more to help educators create robust and high-quality online learning experiences that reflect twenty-first-century learning skills.

Planning and Managing Online Learning

Teachers organize their classrooms to support student learning, access to materials, efficiency, and safety. The day is structured and there is a consistent schedule of events that takes place throughout the week. Good teachers set clear expectations and consistently follow through with issues involving student behavior, expectations, consequences, and so forth. The learning environment is well defined. Online settings require the same attention. Like face-to-face environments, online learning environments need to be designed to support student learning, access to materials, efficiency, and safety.

Elements of Online Environments That Support Student Learning

Online environments that support student learning are dependent upon the layout and design of the online learning environment; the organization, structure, delivery, and sharing of content; and the skills of the teacher.

Layout and Design of an Online Learning Environment

In most cases, educators will find themselves relying on layout and design templates provided by course management systems or other course Web sites. In rare occasions, educators may need to rely on instructional designers, graphic artists, Web developers, and other media specialists to design their course Web site. The educator serves as the content expert and works with his or her team of media specialists to develop the online learning environment. Basic points to consider when creating the layout and design of an online learning environment are:

- Create an environment that targets your learners. In other words, know your learners and create the environment to appeal to their age and ability levels.

- Provide clear and consistent navigation prompts.

- Make sure text and menus are readable and accessible by all students. Use at least a twelve-point font and ensure there is high contrast between the color of the text and the background. Comply with Section 508 requirements (see Chapter 3).

- Keep the layout simple and consistent.

Additional information on designing Web sites can be found at http://www.webstyleguide.com/index.html?/contents.html. If the course is one of many courses linked to the same program (for example, degree, semester or year of study, certificate, etc.), maintain the same layout, design, and navigation features so students do not have to relearn the instructional environment and can focus on the content.

Organization, Structure, Delivery, and Sharing of Content

Content by itself does not make a course. One of the many roles of educators is to organize, portion, and deliver content to make it meaningful and comprehensible to students. This isn't to say all content has to be delivered by the teacher. The teacher can provide opportunities for students to learn content in multiple ways. This may be through cooperative group learning, inquiry, project-based learning, and so forth. Students may lead or participate in online discussion forums or groups, generate wikis or blogs, develop multimedia projects, access online textbooks and articles, communicate with online experts, watch streaming videos or listen to online audio, engage in online simulations and other programs, and much more. The educator structures the learning environment to meet the learning styles and needs of his or her students. The educator organizes, structures, delivers, and shares information in ways that support student learning. This includes a multimodality approach to learning (see Chapter 3) and scaffolding instruction.

Unlike a face-to-face classroom where communication is synchronous, online learning environments are often designed to be asynchronous. Students can participate in instruction at any time of the day or night and at their own pace, usually within a given time frame. The teacher may not be there to immediately advise the student about what to do or to answer his or her questions. This highlights the importance of the need to provide clear expectations and a well-defined structure within an online program.

In addition to a well-organized program of study that includes interactivity and a multimodality approach to learning, activities must be designed to support and guide students' learning. Educators can support students in online learning environments in many ways. Educators are encouraged to:

Begin online courses with a "how to learn online" session. Review the layout and structure of the online environment, how to navigate and use tools on the site, where to find information, and who to contact for technology support. Demonstrate how to use the discussion board and other community areas and provide examples of expected levels of participation (for example, posting to a discussion forum, leading a discussion, or responding to someone else). Review rules of netiquette, copyright, and privacy issues. Demonstrate how to post or submit assignments. Share assessment tools and how students can check their grades and monitor their progress. Have students create their own schedule for success, how they plan on managing their time to ensure they can be successful online learners. Discuss your availability online, noting that their learning may take place anytime day or night, seven days a week. Provide students with specific days and times you plan to be online. Note if you will get back to them within a certain time period (for example, twenty-four hours).

Maintain ongoing communication. In addition to monitoring, participating in, and summarizing online, weekly discussions; answering independent questions; and helping to facilitate group work through online chat or other resources, it is important for online instructors to provide weekly updates (for example, reminders of when activities are due, any necessary clarifications, what the class has accomplished so far, and so forth). Research shows that the teacher's presence, response time, and social interactions with students influence their motivation, course engagement, and learning achievement (Ivers, Lee, and Carter-Wells 2005; McClure 2007).

Make learning meaningful and manageable. As mentioned earlier, it is important for educators to create instruction that accommodates the needs, interests, and learning processes of the targeted learners. Lim (2004) reminds educators that students may not have the learning strategies, knowledge, or attitude to work in an online environment. Cognitive overload can occur if too much effort is required to successfully navigate and find information on the site (see *Layout and Design of an Online Learning Environment* above), if there is too much information presented at once, or if students lack the strategies to facilitate their own learning and participation in the online learning environment. A "how to learn online" session can help students with online learning strategies; good Web design can help eliminate navigation and layout issues; and providing instruction through weekly or daily (depending on the targeted group) modules can help eliminate information overload. In situations where a student is required to take more than one course in a program, the courses should be designed to complement each other in regard to workload, exams, and due dates. For example, if a program requires students to be enrolled in two courses at the same time, the program's structure should ensure students do not have exams at the same time, major projects that overlap, and so forth.

Similar to face-to-face instructors, online educators need to be aware of their students' background knowledge. When necessary, scaffolding can be provided by the instructor, built into learning activities, or supported by peer interactions. By knowing their students, educators are more able to create meaningful learning activities—activities that appeal to their students' interests and backgrounds. Discussion board topics can be made more meaningful if, within their responses, students are asked to include how the topic or issue relates to their own experiences. By knowing and assisting each other, students can create their own "community of learners" to further engage and find meaning in their learning (Lee, Carter-Wells, Glaeser, Ivers, and Street 2006).

The roles of the student and teacher change significantly in online environments. In traditional or face-to-face classroom environments, many times it is the extroverted and engaged students who are heard and called upon. Timid or uninterested students often find it easy to sit in the back of the classroom and let others answer questions and participate. Students are told what to do and when; the teacher manages their time. This isn't necessarily the case in online learning environments. Well-designed online learning environments require students to become active participants, manage their time, and reach out to others.

Skills of the Teacher

Online programs can help students become technology competent, self-directed and flexible, develop initiative and social skills, and demonstrate leadership and responsibility—life and career skills needed for the twenty-first century (Ivers, Lee, and Carter-Wells 2005; ISTE, Partnership for 21st Century Skills, and SETDA 2007). Design and instruction are important variables; the educator plays a pivotal role.

Good online teachers share several of the same qualities as good face-to-face instructors: an interest in lifelong learning, mastery of their subjects, flexibility, and caring about kids (Armstrong 2007). The two are not the same, however. A good face-to-face teacher is not necessarily a good online instructor and vice versa. Technology savvy educators are not necessarily good online instructors, either. What defines good online teaching?

In February 2008, the North American Council for Online Learning (NACOL) released standards for quality online teaching (NACOL 2008):

- The teacher meets the professional teaching standards established by a state licensing agency or has academic credentials in the field in which he or she is teaching.

- The teacher has the prerequisite technology skills to teach online.

- The teacher plans, designs, and incorporates strategies to encourage active learning, interaction, participation, and collaboration in the online environment.

- The teacher provides online leadership in a manner that promotes student success through regular feedback, prompt response, and clear expectations.

- The teacher models, guides, and encourages legal, ethical, safe, and healthy behavior related to technology use.

- The teacher has experienced online learning from the perspective of a student.

- The teacher understands and is responsive to students with special needs in the online classroom.

- The teacher demonstrates competencies in creating and implementing assessments in online learning environments in ways that assure validity and reliability of instruments and procedures.

- The teacher develops and delivers assessments, projects, and assignments that meet standards-based learning goals and assesses learning progress by measuring student achievement of learning goals.

- The teacher demonstrates competencies in using data and findings from assessments and other data sources to modify instructional methods and content and to guide student learning.

- The teacher demonstrates frequent and effective strategies that enable both teacher and students to complete self- and pre-assessments.

- The teacher collaborates with colleagues.

- The teacher arranges media and content to help students and teachers transfer knowledge most effectively in the online environment.

Like NACOL's standards for online courses, each standard has subcategories and is rated on a scale of: 0 (Absent—component is missing) to 4 (Very satisfactory—no improvement needed).

As mentioned earlier, the NEA includes standards for online teachers in its guide to high school online courses. These can be found under Teacher Quality. Standards include:

- The online teacher has expertise in the subject matter being taught.

- The online teacher utilizes effective teaching techniques.

- The online teacher has frequent and timely interactions with students in the course.

- The online teacher models personal attributes that support a learning environment.

- The online teacher has been trained to teach online.

Similar to NACOL's online teaching standards, each standard has subcategories. For example, under "The online teacher models personal attributes that support a learning environment," the following categories are listed (NEA n.d., p. 21):

- The online teacher sets clear expectations and assumes a shared responsibility with the student to ensure that learning occurs.

- The online teacher's interactions with students, families, and communities are respectful and appropriate.

The NEA (n.d.) also includes an extensive list of questions for online teachers (pp. 11–12):

- Am I ready to teach online? What do I need to know and how can I learn this prior to teaching online?

- Do I have access to computers, Internet connections, and other resources necessary for teaching a course online? Will the school provide me with necessary access and support?

- Will this change what I teach and how I teach? Can I participate in the development of the curriculum? What is "academic freedom" in the online world? Am I required to use lessons that are designed by others for the online environment? How will the online environment affect my style of communication with students?

- How will this change my assessment of student learning? What kind of authentic performance works online? How can I ensure that the student is doing his/her own work?

- What are the students' rights and responsibilities for online classes? Are there consequences for inappropriate behavior or academic impropriety? Is there an appeal process for students who believe they have been treated unfairly? Are there criteria (such as level of participation) that may affect grading regardless of how students perform on authentic assessments? Do students have access to counseling and other support services beyond what I can offer them?

- How will this change the way I interact with parents/guardians? Will I be able to contact my students' parents/guardians when needed or on an ongoing basis?

- What kinds of support structures will be in place to assist me to:

work with the technology?

accommodate individual student needs (particularly students with special needs)?

enhance my professional skills?

collaborate with colleagues?

- How will teaching online change the way I am evaluated? Will administrators at other sites have access to my online class and interactions with my students and will they evaluate me? What standards will be used for my evaluation?

- What contractual rights and protections will I have?

- How will this affect my overall workload? Will adjustments be made in my other teaching assignments in order to accommodate the workload?

- How will I be compensated for my work? Is there recognition of advanced degrees, years of experience, special skills, or other criteria, or do all online educators receive a flat rate?

- Who owns the lesson materials and teaching ideas I use online? Will I be compensated if others use my designs and ideas or if they are marketed by the "provider"?

Both NACOL and NEA standards address content, curricular, accessibility, copyright, and multi-modality issues in regard to online learning materials. Educators need to ensure that students have equal access to online materials. This includes making sure materials are compliant with Section 508; assignments and assessment methods are clearly stated; students have the necessary software, hardware, and Internet speed to access the material; and that copyright rules are being followed. Online learning environments need to be well structured and designed so information is easy to find. In most cases, educators will want to password protect online learning environments to protect students' privacy and safety.

Requirements, Expectations, and Recommendations

Planning and managing online learning environments requires students and teachers to follow online and course policies set by their district or institution. For example, a group of California State University, Fullerton (CSUF) faculty created the following policies for the approval of online courses within the College of Education. Instructors must include:

- Rubrics and grading standards for all key assessments, including how participation in online activities will be assessed and graded.

- A statement of netiquette.

- Appropriate and varied pedagogies for online instruction.

- How the instructor will track student online activities (for example, by maintaining a copy or log of online discussions and chat sessions). This refers to participation, number of postings, frequency, and timeliness of postings.

- Weekly deadlines for postings. Due dates need to be stated (dates and times).

- Office and contact hours, including how quickly the instructor responds to e-mail questions and online assignments, how often the instructor will be online, and alternate communication options.

- Safeguards as to how student work will be authenticated.

- Technical competencies expected or required of students.

- Minimum computer hardware and software specifications, as well as Web site access requirements.

- Whom to contact in case of technical problems.

- Alternative procedures for submitting work in the event of technical problems.

- On-campus meeting requirements (if any).

These requirements are in addition to the college's standard policies for syllabi and courses, as well as the university's policy for online courses. Instructors of online courses are required to use a variety of appropriate online pedagogies and assessment strategies (paralleling expectations for the college's face-to-face courses) and include a clear explanation of the weekly pacing and expectations for students' online work. Teachers, administrators, and school boards may determine policies for online courses and programs in K-12 schools.

Requirements and expectations of well-designed and effective online learning environments go beyond the role of the teacher. Institutions must provide adequate support in the areas of technological infrastructure, troubleshooting, and the professional development and workload of teachers. The technological infrastructure needs to provide the necessary tools and bandwidth for instruction and interactivity, the technology supporting the online course should work reliably, simply, and economically, and technical assistance needs to be available 24/7. Teachers need the prerequisite technology skills for online instruction and administrator support. Administrators need to compensate teachers for developing or teaching online courses, limit online class size (for example, twelve to twenty-five students), and recognize online teaching in the tenure and promotion process.

Requirements and expectations of students need to be consistent and clear, too. NEA (n.d.) states, "Students in the online course should be actively engaged in the learning process and interact on a regular basis with the teacher and online classmates" (p. 22). Students need to:

- have the basic technology skills, required Internet access, and computer and software resources to be successful in the class;

- be active participants in a learning community based on student-to-student as well as student-to-teacher discussions;

- collaborate and work with others;

- develop time-management and organizational skills;

- submit work on time;

- follow course netiquette, privacy, safety, and other rules;

- adhere to copyright laws;

- be self-directed; and

- employ critical thinking skills.

Ivers, Lee, and Carter-Wells (2005, pp. 15–17) make the following recommendations to help educators plan and design positive online learning experiences:

Prior Experience with Computers

1. Assess the minimum computer skills (for example, saving files, logging onto and navigating the Internet, etc.) needed to be successful in the online program.

2. Determine which software products in which students will need to have basic, intermediate, or advanced skills.

3. Establish minimum computer requirements (for example, Internet speed, memory, etc.) and whether or not a specific platform and operating system are required.

4. Ensure students have the necessary computer skills and meet the requirements before accepting them into the online program.

Peer Interaction

1. Create opportunities to support social interactions among students (for example, an online social forum where students can talk about topics outside of the program.)
2. Establish a safe learning environment; review and enforce rules of netiquette and cooperation.
3. Assign group projects.
4. Establish group discussions.
5. Hold face-to-face meetings (for example, orientation and midpoint, as well as optional end-of-the-program event).

Teacher/Student Interaction

1. Establish consistency in all courses across the program.
2. Balance workloads among concurrent courses.
3. Communicate clear goals and expectations.
4. Be aware and supportive of students' personal situations and needs.
5. Be committed to the students' success.
6. Maintain a constant presence on discussion boards.
7. Provide weekly summaries of discussions—citing students by names for their contributions.
8. Provide timely responses to e-mails.
9. Give supportive and positive feedback.
10. Ensure instructors have the necessary disposition, skills, and time to teach online.
11. Teach—do not put the responsibility of instruction on the textbook.

Institutional Support

1. Ensure students have the necessary support and instruction to use required tools (software, hardware, etc.).
2. If possible, provide 24/7 technical support.
3. Provide a handbook of how to access and use support services and who to contact if students encounter difficulties.

The first impression and few weeks of an online course are very important. The layout, design, requirements, and expectations of the course need to be clear and consistent, and teachers need to be welcoming, prepared to meet students' needs, and ready to facilitate a community of learners. Before making a course active, instructors need to go through the site to ensure links and multimedia elements work, content is accessible and properly placed; spelling, grammar, and punctuation are accurate; rubrics are posted; and expectations and support services are clearly identified. Instructors also should include an introductory announcement and a discussion forum where students can get to know each other and begin building an online community.

Monitoring and Assessing Students' Work in Online Learning Environments

Monitoring and assessing students' work in online learning environments is similar to monitoring and assessing students' work in face-to-face environments. Assessment may take place on a daily or weekly basis using blogs, wikis, discussion forums, work submissions, online quizzes, and so forth. The NACOL standards for quality online teaching include several standards that address assessment:

- The teacher demonstrates competencies in creating and implementing assessments in online learning environments in ways that assure the validity and reliability of instruments and procedures.

- The teacher develops and delivers assessments, projects, and assignments that meet standards-based learning goals and assesses the learning progress by measuring student achievement of learning goals.

- The teacher demonstrates competencies in using data and findings from assessments and other data sources to modify instructional methods and content and to guide student learning.

- The teacher demonstrates frequent and effective strategies that enable both teacher and students to complete self- and pre-assessments.

In addition to ensuring the validity and reliability of the assessment instruments, teachers are asked to include authentic assessments, allowing students to demonstrate their knowledge in a form other than multiple-choice or true/false testing environments. Blogs, wikis. discussion forums, hypermedia projects, project-based learning activities, and so forth can allow students to demonstrate their understanding of acquired knowledge and skills. This also supports the development of twenty-first-century skills. Authentic assessment encourages creativity and innovation, critical thinking and problem solving, and communication and collaboration.

Rubrics for Online Participation

As noted in Chapter 7, rubrics provide educators with an alternative method for assessing students' work and should be used for authentic assessments. At the beginning of an assignment, students are presented with a rubric so they know how their performance will be evaluated. Online instructors can use observational data (for example, tracking systems in course management systems, blogs, wikis, discussion forums, and e-mail) to monitor students' progress. Rubrics can be provided for participation in online discussion forums. Rubrics can help teachers establish clear and consistent guidelines in regard to the content, grammar, spelling, length, and so forth for posting information in a discussion forum. As mentioned in Chapter 7, rubrics can be found online and modified to meet the teacher's and students' needs. Table 8.1 provides a list of online resources for assessing students' participation in online discussion forums.

Multiple Assessment Measures

NEA recommends students are assessed by several different methods over the duration of the online course. Measures include (NEA n.d., p. 23):

- Contributions and responses to online discussions

- Completion of online assignments

- Portfolio submissions

- Special projects and/or presentations

- Creation of authentic products

- Tests and quizzes

Table 8.1. Online Resources for Assessing Students in Online Discussion Forums

Name and Source	Description
PBS TeacherLine http://www.pbs.org/teacherline/courses/ common_documents/disc_assess.htm	Discussion forum participation information and rubric for PBS TeacherLine courses.
Rubistar http://rubistar.4teachers.org/	Provides pre-created rubrics that teachers can customize for a variety of topics, including rubrics for online discussion boards.
Rubric for Asynchronous Discussion Participation http://www.udel.edu/janet/MARC2006/rubric.html	A zero- to three-point scale for assessing students' online discussion participation.
If You Build It, They Will Come http://www.westga.edu/distance/ojdla/ spring51/edelstein51.html	An article about creating rubrics for online discussion forums. Sample rubric provided.
EdTech http://www.edtech.neu.edu/teach/ use_blackboard/managing_your_course/	Information and resources for managing online courses, including participation guidelines and a sample rubric.

In addition to multiple assessment measures, some programs may require students to take video or oral exams (for example, use Skype or another videoconferencing tool) or attend proctored exam locations to ensure they are doing their own work. Some online programs may require attendance on campus during specific parts of the program. For example, the Master's in Instructional Design and Technology (MSIDT) program at California State University, Fullerton begins the program with a "boot-up" camp. In addition, students are required to attend a midpoint session. For entrance into the program, students complete a telephone interview. The telephone interview, "boot-up" camp, and midpoint session have proven very successful for the program. See http://msidt.fullerton.edu/ for more information.

Helpful Tips and Tricks

As with face-to-face cooperative group projects, peer evaluations may be used for online group projects and calculated into individual grades. As noted in Chapter 6, educators are encouraged to let students contribute to the creation of rubrics. Student input allows students to create their own learning experiences and to work toward individual goals. The NEA (n.d.) suggests that students actively participate in evaluating their own work and receive continual, timely, and constructive feedback on the quality of their work and their mastery of course content.

Turnitin (see http://turnitin.com) is a digital assessment tool designed to improve students' writing skills. Turnitin allows students to post their work for peer editing and feedback, enables teachers to provide feedback on student papers and manage grades and assignments online, and identifies papers containing unoriginal work. This tool can be used to support students' writing skills in face-to-face environments as well as in online environments. Blackboard K-12 School Central includes SafeAssign to teach students proper citation skills and prevent plagiarism.

As mentioned in Chapter 6, there is a variety of videoconferencing software that educators can download for free. In addition to engaging students in collaborative projects, videoconferencing can be used as an assessment tool. Examples include NetMeeting, Windows Meeting Space, Eyeball Chat, Skype, and iVisit (see Chapter 6).

Summary

Distance education has been in existence for many years, beginning with mailed lessons. Advancements in technology have significantly changed how distance education is delivered and structured. The Internet has made online instruction a common practice. Online instruction provides educators (and students) the opportunity to embrace technology as a tool for learning, sharing, creating, problem solving, and communicating.

Several variables need to be considered when designing instruction for online learning. NACOL has established national standards for quality online teaching and courses to address these variables. The NEA provides guidelines for online high school courses and raises questions about online instruction for teachers, policy makers, and others.

Course management systems and other tools are available to help teachers design, create, deliver, assess, and manage online instruction. A well-structured learning environment requires the instructor to plan ahead, anticipate potential problems, and ensure the necessary materials are available to support student learning. PowerPoint, Presenter, Camtasia, Audacity, and iMovie are some of the tools available to help teachers create online, multimodality instructional resources. Elements of online environments that support student learning include the layout and design of the online learning environment; the organization, structure, delivery, and sharing of content; and the skills of the teacher.

In addition to ensuring the validity and reliability of the assessment instruments, teachers need to include authentic assessments, allowing students to demonstrate their knowledge in a form other than multiple-choice or true/false testing environments. Rubrics should be used for authentic assessments, and teachers should use multiple measures to assess students' work. Online learning can help students become technology competent, self-directed and flexible, develop initiative and social skills, and demonstrate leadership and responsibility—life and career skills needed for the twenty-first century.

Activities

1. Create a time line of the five generations of distance learning and note how each technology impacted the classroom. Share what you believe may be the sixth generation of distance learning and how it will affect student learning.

2. Compare three different computer management systems. How are they alike? How are they different? Which one would you choose and why?

3. Download and evaluate one of Articulate's software products: Presenter, Quizmaker, Engage, or Articulate Online (see http://www.articulate.com/). How might each product be used to assist online instruction? What are the product features, strengths, and weaknesses?

4. Download Camtasia Studio by TechSmith (http://www.techsmith.com/) and make a three- to five-minute "how-to" video using your favorite software program.

5. Download NACOL's online course and teaching standards (http://www.nacol.org/national-standards/) and compare them with the NEA's Guide for High School Online Courses (http://www.nea.org/technology/images/02onlinecourses.pdf). Is there anything you would add to or delete from the standards?

6. Based on the NEA's Guide for High School Online Courses, what guidelines would you propose for middle school or elementary school online courses?

7. Reflect on your own experience as an online learner or interview someone who has taken an online class. How was the course managed? What types of interactions took place? Describe the instructional approaches. Was multimedia a part of the instructional approach? What kinds of assignments were required? How was knowledge assessed? What were the strengths of the class? What were the weaknesses? What recommendations would you make?

References

Armstrong, S. 2007. Virtual learning 2.0: Professional development is a whole new ballgame for educators who teach online. *Technology & Learning* 28 (4): 26–29.

Holmberg, B. 2005. *The Evolution, Principles and Practices of Distance Education.* Studien und Berichte der Arbeitsstelle Fernstudienforschung der Carl von Ossietzky Universität Oldenburg, v. 11. Oldenburg: Bis, Bibliotheks-und Informationssystem der Universität Oldenburg.

International Society for Technology in Education (ISTE), Partnership for 21st Century Skills, and State Educational Technology Directors Association (SETDA). 2007. Maximizing the Impact: "The Pivotal Role of Technology in a 21st Century Education System." Available at http://www.setda.org/web/guest/maximizingimpactreport. (Accessed April 23, 2008).

Ivers, K., J. Lee, and J. Carter-Wells. 2005. Students' attitudes and perceptions of online learning. Research paper presented at the National Education Computing Conference (NECC). Available at http://www.iste.org/Content/NavigationMenu/Research/NECC_Research_Paper_Archives/NECC_2005/Ivers-Karen-NECC05.pdf. (Accessed July 21, 2008).

Lee, J., J. Carter-Wells, B. Glaeser, K. Ivers, and C. Street. 2006. Facilitating the development of a learning community in an online graduate program. *Quarterly Review of Distance Education* 7 (1): 13–33.

Lim, C. P. 2004. Engaging learners in online learning environments. *TechTrends: Linking Research & Practice to Improve Learning* 48 (4): 16–23.

McClure, A. 2007. Distant, not absent. Keeping online learners engaged can help them reach the finish line. *University Business* 10 (11): 40–44.

Moore, M. G. and G. Kearsley. 2005. *Distance Education: A Systems View.* Belmont, CA: Thomson/Wadsworth.

National Education Association (NEA). n.d. Guide to Online High School Courses. Available at http://www.nea.org/technology/images/02onlinecourses.pdf. (Accessed July 21, 2008).

North American Council for Online Learning (NACOL). 2008. National Standards for Quality Online Teaching. Available at http://www.nacol.org/nationalstandards/NACOL%20Standards%20Quality%20Online%20Teaching.pdf. (Accessed July 21, 2008).

North American Council for Online Learning (NACOL). 2007. National Standards of Quality for Online Courses. Available at http://www.nacol.org/nationalstandards/NACOL%20Standards%20Quality%20Online%20Courses%202007.pdf. (Accessed July 21, 2008).

Glossary

508 compliant: Refers to Section 508 of the Federal Rehabilitation Act that requires federal agencies to make their electronic and information technology accessible to people with disabilities. See http://www.section508.gov/ for more information.

Aggregator: Another name for a news or feed reader. An application that collects new information from designated Web sites and provides it back to the user in a simple format.

Angel Learning: A course management system (CMS).

Asynchronous: Not occurring at the same time. In online learning, discussion forums are considered asynchronous because users post and read messages at different times; users do not have to be online at the same time to communicate.

Blackboard: A course management system (CMS).

Blog: An online journal or communication tool that is updated frequently and intended for a specific group or the general public. Entries are posted to a single page, usually in reverse-chronological order.

Blogger: Author of a blog.

CD-R (compact disc-recordable): A compact disc format that allows one-time recording.

CD-ROM (compact disc-read only memory): A disc designed to store computer data, as well as hi-fi stereo, optically.

CD-RW (compact disc-rewritable): A compact disc format that allows repeated recording.

Course management system (CMS): A comprehensive software package that facilitates the design, delivery, assessment, and management of online courses. A CMS is also called an LMS—learning management system.

CPU (central processing unit): The "brain" of the computer, the CPU contains the circuitry that performs the instructions of a computer's program.

Download: Transfer of a document or file from a computer system to your own computer.

DVD (digital versatile disc): An optical disc technology that can hold twenty-eight times as much as a CD-ROM.

DVD+R (DVD-recordable): A DVD disc format that allows one-time recording.

DVD-RW (DVD-rewritable): A DVD disc format that allows repeated recording.

E-learning (electronic learning): Refers to instruction that is delivered via computer technology.

Flash drive: A storage device that uses flash memory (nonvolatile computer memory that can be electrically erased and reprogrammed) for storage. Nonvolatile computer memory can retain stored information even when it is not powered.

Hard drive: A set of stacked disks that records data electromagnetically in concentric circles or "tracks" on the disk.

HTTP (Hypertext Transfer Protocol): A set of rules for exchanging files (text, graphics, sound, and video).

Input device: A device used to enter information into the computer. Examples include keyboards, touch screens, and mice.

Input/output device: A device used to enter and access information from the computer. Examples include disk drives and modems.

Internet: A worldwide network of networks in which users can exchange information among other computers.

Markup language: A system of identifying how text is structured, laid out, or formatted in a document.

Moodle: An open-source course management system (CMS).

Netiquette: Etiquette or behavior protocol for using exchanges on the Internet.

Newsgroup (also referred to as Usenet news): A collection of posted discussions on a central Internet site that are distributed through Usenet.

Open source: A development methodology that allows users to access and modify a program's content and source code free of charge and for free distribution.

Operating system (OS): The program that manages all of the other programs in the computer. This includes managing memory, handling input from and output to hardware devices, and notifying users of application or system errors. Windows, Linux, and Macintosh's OS X are examples of different operating systems.

Output device: A device used to access information from the computer. Examples include monitors and printers.

PDA (personal digital assistant): A small mobile handheld device that provides computing, information storage, and retrieval capabilities.

Podcast: Digital files that can be distributed over the Internet and played back on computers and portable media devices (for example, cell phones, MP3 players, and Apple's iTouch). A podcast can be syndicated, subscribed to, and downloaded automatically when new content is added via RSS feeds.

Probeware: Devices that can be used with computers to collect, display, and analyze real-time data.

RAM (random-access memory). The location in the computer where data in current use is stored so they can be quickly accessed by the computer's processor. Data stored in RAM is temporary. Data in RAM is lost when the computer is turned off.

Really Simple Syndication (RSS): Standardized XML that allows content from one site to be republished (syndicated) by another.

ROM (read-only memory): A location in the computer that stores the programming that allows the operating system to load into RAM each time the computer is turned on. Data stored in ROM is permanent and not lost when the computer power is turned off.

RSS (Really Simple Syndication) feed: A method of receiving updated content from a selected Web site.

RSS Reader: See Aggregator.

Secondary storage: Storage of data outside of the computers memory (RAM). Examples include hard disks (hard drives), flash drives, CD-Rs, CD-RWs, DVD-Rs, and DVD-RWs.

Section 508: See 508 compliant.

Social bookmarking site: Sites that enable users to share, organize, and access favorite Internet bookmarks. Examples include del.icio.us (http://del.icio.us/) and Furl (http://www.furl.net/).

Social networking sites: Interactive sites that provide members with the opportunity to share information about themselves and interact with others. Examples include MySpace (http://www.myspace.com/) and Facebook (http://www.facebook.com/).

Streaming video: Digital transmission of highly compressed video over the Internet. The video plays as it arrives.

Synchronous: Occurring at the same time. In online learning, chat rooms and videoconferencing are considered synchronous because users need to be online at the same time to communicate.

Upload: Transfer of a document or file from your computer system to another computer system.

URL (Uniform Resource Locator): The address of a file on the Internet.

Usenet: A contraction of "USEr's NETwork," Usenet is a system that collects and posts messages from newsgroups to servers on a worldwide network.

Virus: A piece of programming code disguised as something else that typically causes some unexpected and/or adverse event to take place on a computer.

Web: See World Wide Web.

Web 2.0 tools: A new generation of tools that support using the Web for creativity, collaboration, social networking, video and photo sharing, and other forms of information distribution. Web 2.0 tools include wikis, blogs, and podcasts.

Wiki: A server program that allows users to collaboratively create and edit the content of a Web site using a regular Web browser.

World Wide Web: All of the resources and users on the Internet that are using hypertext transfer protocol (HTTP).

XML (extensible markup language): A markup language designed to transport and store data.

Index

AAC devices, 55–56

ABC keyboards, 52

ABC layouts, 52

Acceptable use policies (AUPs): ethics, privacy, and safety issues, 72–74; Web sites, 69

Accessing special characters, 9–11

Activboard, 54

ActivePen, 54

Albany Institute of History and Art, 113

Alternate keyboards: ABC layouts, 52; Bat Personal Keyboard, 53; BigKeys keyboard, 53; Chording keyboards, 53; Chubon layout, 52; Ergonomic keyboards, 53; one-handed Dvorak layout, left hand, 52; one-handed Dvorak layout, right hand, 52; programmable keyboards, 53; self-contained keyboards, 54; SMART board, 54; touch screens, 54; two-handed Dvorak layout, 51

American Federation of Teachers (AFT), 67

Angel learning, 156

Apple Computer, Inc., 66

Apple iTunes, 105

Apple menu, Key Caps keyboard, 10

Apple IIe computers, 24

Application programs for young children, 81–82

Association for Supervision and Curriculum and Development (ASCD), 67

Atomic Learning, 14, 84

A to Zap!, 91

Audio-conferencing, 153

Augmentative and alternative communication (AAC) devices, 55

Aurora Echo, 50

Aurora prediction, 50

Babel Fish, 48

Bailey's Book House, 91

Bat Personal Keyboard (Inforgrip), 53

Beacon, Mavis, 84

BigKeys keyboard (Greystone Digital, Inc.), 53

Bilingual and translation programs, 47

Bilingual software, 48

Binary digits, 5

Blackboard, 155

Blogs, 35, 102–3

Bodily-kinesthetic intelligence, 44

Braille: cells, 56; devices, 49; displays, 56–57; dots, 56; embossers, 56; note takers, 54

Bright Eyed Primary Teachers (Bright Eyed K-6), 32

Business-sponsored resource sites, 30

California Commission on Teacher Credentialing (CCTC), 3

California State University, Fullerton (CSUF), 161

CALL programs, 47–48

CalStateTEACH, 152, 153

Camtasia Relay, 156

CD-ROM, 5

CD-RW, 5

Center for Interactive Learning and Collaboration, 113

Character map, in Windows, 9, 10

Chat rooms, 36–37

Children's Online Privacy Protection Act (COPPA), 74

Child-safe browsers, 110

Chording keyboards, 53

Chubon layout, 52

Class Homepage Builder (Scholastic), 156

Classroom computer schedule: designing, 132–35; developing computer schedules, 138–39; rotation schedules, 133–34

Classroom Web pages, 113–15

Clyde, 65

CNET, 26

Computer assignments and responsibilities, 135

Computer assisted language learning (CALL) applications, 47

Computer-based lessons: designing a classroom computer schedule, 132–35; grouping strategies, 128–31; lesson ideas and examples, 136–39; one-to-one laptop classrooms, 131–32; planning and managing, 127–39

Computer clipboard, 12

Computer fraud and theft, antivirus programs, 73

Computer-generated simulation of human speech, 49

Computer labs, disadvantages, 125–26

Computer labs versus computers in the classroom, 125–26

Computer policies and issues: acceptable use policies, 68–69; ethics, privacy, and safety issues, 72–74; gender and equity concerns, 70–72; technology use plan, 69–70

Computer rotation schedule, 146

Computers: computer basics, 4–6; learning more, 6–7; managing and assessing, 123; printers and other peripherals, 6; secondary storage devices, 5–6; system recommendations, 4–5; when to use, 124–27

Computer screen: Print Screen key, 11; screenshots, 11; taking a picture of, 11–13

Computer support, 7–15

Constructivism, 44–46

Cooperative learning groups: advantages and disadvantages, 129; five defining characteristics, 128

Cooperative learning techniques: group investigation, 129; group size (advantages and disadvantages), 130–31; jigsaw, 129; learning together, 129; student teams achievement divisions (STAD), 130; team-assisted individualization (TAI), 130; teams games tournament (TGT), 130

Copyright and fair use, Web sites, 73

Core reading and vocabulary development, 47

Council for Exceptional Children (CEC), 67

Course management system (CMS), 154–56

Co:Writer, 50

Cruncher 2.0, 82

DDD-E assessments, 137

DDD-E model, 136

Decide phase, 136, 138

Design phase, 137

3D Froggy Phonics, 92

DibDabDoo, 109

Digital-age learning, 3

Digital assessment suite, 26

Digital citizenship and responsibility, 3

Digital discussions, 30–37; e-mail, 30–32

Digital Divide Network, 72

Discovery Education Lesson Plan Library, 29

Discovery programs, 91

Discussion forums: threaded discussion, 34; unthreaded responses, 35; Web sites, 34–35

Display or magnification software, to assist vision-impaired students, 51

Distance education: five generations, 152–53; standards for delivering instruction over the Internet, 153–54

Domain names, common extensions, 115–16

Drill and practice programs, 84–86

DVD, 5

DVD-RW, 5

Dvorak layout, 52

Duxbury Braille translator, 56

Duxbury Systems, Inc., 56

Easy Grade Pro (Orbis Software), 27

Easy Translator, 48

ECO-14 (Prentke Romich Co.), 56

Editorial Projects in Education (EPE), 3

Education of All Handicapped Children Act, 48

Educator-created templates, for pages, 25

Educators, resources, 6

E-mail, 30–32, 112–13; blank e-mail form in Microsoft Ooutlook, 31; netiquette (do's and don'ts of online communication), 113

Encyclopedia Britannica Deluxe, 91

English-language instruction: English-language learners (ELL), 46–48, 93; Internet resources, 48; students, 93

English language learning instruction system (ELLIS), 47

Equity concerns, 71–72

Ergonomic keyboards, 53

ESL ReadingSmart, 47

Ethics, 72–73

Evaluating instructional resources for students: evaluation criteria, 115–17; interactive programs, 105–6; online experts, 106; research activities, 108–15; Web sites for children, 106–7; Web 2.0 tools, 102–5

Evaluating Internet information, 121

Evaluating software for students: applications, 80–83; discovery, reference, and other learning tools, 91–92; drill and practice, 84–86; evaluation criteria, 92–95; evaluation resources, 95; instructional games, 88–89; problem solving, 89–91; simulations, 86–87; software categories, 80–92; software evaluation form, 98–99; software reviews, 96; tutorials, 83–84

Evaluation criteria for students: appropriateness, 93–94; instructional objectives and assessment, 93; layout and functionality, 94; management and support features, 94–95

Evaluation resources, 95

Eyeball Chat, 113

Eyegaze system, 55

EZ keys, 50

"Fabbers," 24
Federal Resources for Educational Excellence
    (FREE), 30
Federal Trade Commission (FTC), 74
Formative assessment, 26
Free blog creation sites, 35

Gardner's eight different intelligences, 44
Gender and equity concerns, 70–72
Gender issues, 70–71
Gifted learners, 57
Gifted student, definitions of, 58
Global SchoolNet Mailing Lists, 33
Google: custom features in, 111; Earth, 92;
    Onekey, 109
Gotham, 79
Gradebook, 26, 28
Grade-level technology standards, 68
GradeMark, 26
GradeQuick (Edline), 27
Graph club, 82
Graphic organizer, for teaching how animals
    become endangered, 138
Grouping variables, advantages and
    disadvantages, 129
Gus! Word Prediction, 50

Hal Screen Reader, 49
HeadMouse Extreme, 55
Hispanic American and Caribbean students,
    71

Individualized education program (IEP), 48
Individuals with Disabilities Education Act
    (IDEA), 48
Industrial age, 43
Information age, 43
Instructional games: Africa Inspirer, 89; How
    the West Was 1+ 3 × 4, 89; role-playing
    opportunities to students, 88; Science Court
    Series, 88; the great solar system rescue, 89;
    Timez Attack, 89; Where in the USA is Car-
    men Sandiego? 88; Word Way 2, 89
IntelliKeys, 53
Interactive programs, resources for, 106
International Society for Technology in
    Education (ISTE), 2, 3, 42, 66, 68, 109, 159;
    learning experiences, 67
Internet: search strategies, 122; troubleshooting
    tips for, 118–19
Internet resources: for teachers, 28–38, 40;
    blogs, 35–36; certificate creator, 29; chat,

36–37; digital discussions, 30–37; discussion
    forums, 34–35; Ivy's greeting cards, 29; les-
    son plans, 28–30; listservs, 32–33; my
    teacher tools, 29; productivity and manage-
    ment tasks, 28; RubiStar, 29; teaching tools,
    29; Teach-nology Web tools, 29; usenet
    newsgroups, 33–34; wiki, 36
Internet Service Provider (ISP), 30
Interpersonal intelligence, 44
I Speak English, 47

Jay Klein Productions, 27
JAWS, 49
Jigsaw, 129
Johnson and Johnson, 128
Joysticks, 54
Joystick-to-Mouse (Innovation Management
    Group, Inc.), 54
JumpStart Artist, 82
JumpStart First Grade, 91

KDE Education Project, 92
Kent School District (Washington), 68
Keyboard shortcuts, 14
KeyTime, 51
KidClick, 108, 109
Kids Media Magic, 81
Kidspiration, 82
Kid Works Deluxe, 81

Lake Software, 51
Learner Profile, 27
Learning management system (LMS), 154
Learning support faculty (LSF), 153
Lesson Bank, 30
Lesson Plan Search, 30
Lesson Plans Page.com (Hot Chalk), 29
Linguistic intelligence, 44
Listservs, for educators, 32
Local technology standards, 68
Logical-mathematical intelligence, 44
Longman English interactive, 47

Macintosh: Key Caps, 9; mouse, 14; Option
    key, 11; screenshot on, 12; troubleshooting
    tips, 9
Math, 106
Math Blaster, 84
MaxData, 82
Merriam's Collegiate Dictionary and Thesaurus
    Deluxe, 91
Meta-search engines, 110

Milken Exchange on Education Technology, 67

MixMeister Technology, 156

Multimedia production tools, 44, 81

Multimedia projects: in education, 44, 136; planning and managing, 136–38; student-created, 136

Multimedia software, 46

Multiple assessment measures, 165

Multiple intelligences: in the creation of multimedia projects, 44; Gardner's eight different intelligences, 44; roles of, 44

Musical intelligence, 44

MyClass.net, 156

MySpace, 103

My-T-Soft, 51

National Aeronautics and Space Administration (NASA), 66

National Educational Technology Standards (NETS): for students, 66–67; for teachers, 3

National Council for Social Studies, 33

National Education Association (NEA), 66, 154

Naturalist intelligence, 44

NaturalReader, 49

Neighborhood MapMachine, 82

Neo 2 keyboard (AlphaSmart), 54

Net Frog, 84

Newsgroup window, 34

Nick, 151

North American Council for Online Learning (NACOL), 153, 159, 160

One-handed Dvorak layout: left hand, 52; right hand, 52

One-to-one laptop programs, 126, 131–32; face-to-face environments, 131

Online computing environments: additional support for delivering online instruction, 156; managing and assessing, 151; resources for developing course content, 156–57; virtual environments for learning, 154–57

Online discussion forums, online resources for assessing students in, 165

Online experts, 106–7

Online learning: elements of, 157–63; planning and managing, 157–63; requirements, expectations, and recommendations, 161–63

Online learning environment: for student learning, 157; layout and design of, 157; monitoring and assessing students' work in, 164–65; organization, structure, delivery, and sharing of content, 157–59; skills of the teacher, 159–61

Option key, to access different character options, 10

Origin Instruments and Eyegaze Communication System (LC Technologies, Inc.), 55

Output devices, 55–57

PageMaker (Adobe), 24

Paint program, 12

Partnership for 21st Century Skills, 2

PDF (portable document format), 31

Peer Review, 26

Penfriend XL, 50

Performance-based standards for teachers, 3

Personal digital assistants (PDA), 26, 105

Philips, Caleb, 152

Photo and video sharing, 104

Pink, Daniel, 43

Plagiarism Protection, 26

Play-Stations Portable (PSP), 105

Podcasts, 15, 104–5; Web-based, 156

Pointing devices, 55

Printers and other peripherals, 6

Print Shop (Broderbund), 24

Privacy and safety issues, 73–74

Probeware, 6

Problem-solving programs, 45, 90–91

Productivity programs, 24–25

Productivity tools, for instructional and creative tasks, 24–25

Professional development opportunities, 14

Professional-looking products, 24

Programmable keyboards, 53

Promethean, 6

Promoting twenty-first century learning environments, 42–46

Quality online teaching, NACOL standards, 159–60, 165; NEA standards, 160

Raccoon multimedia project, 136, 137

RAM, how it is used, 4–5

Read and Write, 50

Reading teacher listserv (RTEACHER), 32

ReadPlease, 49

Recordable and rewriteable compact discs (CD-RW), 5

Recordable and rewriteable digital versatile discs (DVD-RW), 5

Recordable compact discs (CD-R), 5
Recordable digital versatile discs (DVD-R), 5
Record keeping, 26, 27
Refreshable Braille displays, 56
Rehabilitation Act, 48
Research activities: advanced research, 109–11; basic research, 108–9; original research, 112–15
Rosetta Stone, 47
Rubrics: for online participation, 165; information on the Internet, 141–42; storyboard, 142, 147–48
Rubric Software (New Measure, Inc.), 25

Scholastic Keys, 81
Screen magnifiers and specialized monitors, 56
Screen readers, 49
Screenshots, 11
Search engines: child-safe sites, 109, 110; search strategies, 110
Secondary storage devices, 5–6
Second Life, 105
Self-contained keyboards, 54
Shareware.com, 26, 92
Shareware Connection, 92
Simulation programs, 45, 86–87
Smart Cat Touchpad, 54
SmartDraw, 25
SMART Technologies, Inc., 6, 132
Social bookmarking sites, 103–4
Social networking sites, 103
Software and peripherals, 126–27
Spatial intelligence, 44
Special characters, accessing, 9–11
Speech recognition software, 49
Spreadsheet programs, 26
SpringBoard Lite (Prentke Romich Co.), 55
State technology standards: for students, 67–68; for teachers, 3–4
Storynory, 105
Students' Internet use, monitoring software, 74
Students' work: monitoring and assessing, 127, 138–42; ongoing assessment, 139–41; rubrics, 141–42
Student teams achievement divisions (STAD), 130
SyncronEyes, 132
System recommendations, 4–5
Systran Language Translator, 48
Switches, 54

Teacher communities, supporting Web sites, 35
Teacher Font Bundle (Visions Technology in Education), 25
Teacher interaction, collaboration, and reflection, supporting Web sites, 35
Teacher Information Manager Deluxe (Visions Technology in Education), 27
Teachers and technology, 1–15; Internet resources, 28–38
TeachersFirst, 103
Teachers' Podcast, 15
Teachers' Power Pack (Centron Software, Inc.), 24
Teachers' Tool Kit, 25
Team-assisted individualization (TAI), 130
Teams games tournament (TGT), 130
TechLEARNING, 15
Teaching Multimedia (TeachMedia), 32
Teaching Mathematics in the Middle School (math-teach), 32
Teachnet.com, 30
Technology and special-needs students: assistive technologies, English-language learners, 46–48; gifted learners, 58–59
Technology resource teacher: blackline masters, 18–21; professional development opportunities, 14–15; resource assistance, 8; roles and responsibilities, 7–8; technology tips and tricks, 8–14; troubleshooting tips and tricks, 8–9
Technology standards: for students, 66–68; for teachers, 2–4
Technology use plan (TUP), Web sites for guidelines, 69–70
Teleconferencing, 153
Tell Me More, 47
TextAloud, 49
Text-to-speech products, 49–50
Text-to-speech synthesizers, 49
ThinkWave Educator, 27
Threaded discussion, 34
3D Weather Globe and Atlas, 92
Timeliner, 82
Tool factory workshop, 81
Touch pads, 54
Touch screens, 54
Touch-sensitive surface, 54
Trackballs, 54
Traxsys, 54
Tucows, 92
Tutorial programs, 83–84
TurningPoint Technologies, 26

Tux Paint, 92
Twenty-first century learning environment, 2, 3; constructivism, 44–46; cooperative learning, 46; multiple intelligences, 44; promoting, 42
Twenty-first century skills, 2
Two-handed Dvorak layout, 51

Usenet newsgroups, accessing in Internet Explorer, 33

Videoconferencing, resources, 113–14
Virtual worlds, 105

Webinars, 15
WebQuests, for educators, 108–9
Web sites, for children, 107
Web 2.0 tools: blogs, 102–3; photo and video sharing, 104; podcasts, 104–5; social bookmarking sites, 103–4; social networking sites, 103; virtual worlds, 105; Wiki, 103

WebWhacker, 74
West Bloomfield School District (Michigan), 68
When to use computers: assessing resources, 125–27; instruction for educators, 124; objectives and learner outcomes, 125
Whyville, 105
Wildlife Tycoon: Venture Africa (PocketWatch Games), 86
Wiki (Wikipedia), Web sites, 35, 103
Window-Eyes, 50
Windows Meeting Space, 113
Word-prediction programs, 50
Word-processing programs, 31
WordQ, 50
Worksheet Magic Plus (Gameco Educational Software), 25
World Wide Web, 102

Yahoo!, advanced search options in, 111
Yahoo! Kids, 107, 109
YouTube, 104

ABOUT THE AUTHOR

KAREN S. IVERS is a Professor in the Department of Elementary and Bilingual Education at California State University Fullerton (CSUF) where she has been honored numerous times for her outstanding scholarship, teaching, service, and work with technology. She was awarded CSUF's first *Outstanding Teaching Innovations with Electronic Technology* award and was the 2006 Distinguished Faculty Marshall for the College of Education. Currently serving as chair of the Department, Dr. Ivers has taught courses in educational technology at the Master's level and contributed to the creation of CSUF's first online Master's degree program—Instructional Design and Technology—serving on the development committee, constructing several of the courses, and teaching in the program. Dr. Ivers was also selected to contribute to the development of the statewide CalStateTEACH program where she co-chaired the Educational Technology Team, developed the technology handbook, and served as the Regional Center Academic Director for Fullerton. As Acting Associate Director of the Educational Technology Professional Development Project, she oversaw CSU-wide grant projects geared toward helping K-12 teachers use technology in their classrooms. Before coming to CSUF, Dr. Ivers taught elementary school and served as her school's computer coordinator. She earned her Ph.D. in Instructional Technology and Elementary Education from the University of South Florida.